Henry Fanshawe Tozer

The Islands of the Aegean

Henry Fanshawe Tozer

The Islands of the Aegean

ISBN/EAN: 9783743321366

Manufactured in Europe, USA, Canada, Australia, Japa

Cover: Foto ©ninafisch / pixelio.de

Manufactured and distributed by brebook publishing software (www.brebook.com)

Henry Fanshawe Tozer

The Islands of the Aegean

THE
ISLANDS OF THE AEGEAN

BY THE

REV. HENRY FANSHAWE TOZER, M.A., F.R.G.S.

FELLOW AND TUTOR OF EXETER COLLEGE, OXFORD

AUTHOR OF

'THE HIGHLANDS OF TURKEY,' 'THE GEOGRAPHY OF GREECE,' ETC.

WITH MAPS

Oxford

AT THE CLARENDON PRESS

1890

[*All rights reserved*]

PREFACE.

THE present work does not profess to be more than a sketch of the subject with which it deals. For fuller information the reader is referred to such comprehensive works as Ross's *Reisen auf den griechischen Inseln*, Pashley's *Travels in Crete*, Conze's *Reise auf den Inseln des Thrakischen Meeres*, and Mr. Bent's *The Cyclades*. These (with the exception of the last-named, which was not published when I visited the central islands) were the constant companions of my journeys, and I take this opportunity of acknowledging the service which they have rendered me, both as a source of information in travelling, and as an aid in compiling this book.

The three journeys which are here described were undertaken at considerable intervals, but no great changes have taken place in those regions since the first was made. It is true that most of the ancient buildings in Delos have been excavated, and the great inscription of Gortyna has been discovered, subsequently to my visits to those places; but as the object which I have in view in writing is rather to give general impressions and to indicate the objects of greatest interest than to enter into archaeological details, I trust that my narrative will not suffer from this cause. My accounts of the two former journeys have already appeared in the *Academy* for 1875 and 1886, and these are now republished by the permission of the Editor of that journal with considerable modifications and additions. The description of my last journey, which embraced the northern islands of the Aegean, Lemnos, Thasos, and Samothrace, is now printed for the first time; and as those islands have been less frequently visited than the others, I have treated them at somewhat greater length.

From a geographical point of view the islands of the Aegean have a peculiar interest, because the group which they form is so typical, that the name of Archipelago has become a descriptive term. Their changeful history comprises many romantic events in ancient, mediaeval, and modern times. In Delos and Samothrace traces still remain of the important seats of heathen worship which they once contained; and Patmos is indelibly associated with the exile of the Apostle St. John. The marble quarries of Paros and Thasos, the Grotto of Antiparos, and the volcano of Santorin, are all remarkable for their natural features. The tunnel of Eupalinus in Samos is one of the most remarkable works which have lately been discovered by antiquarian research. The scenery

Preface. vii

also of the islands and the neighbouring seas is varied and beautiful. Thus there is no lack of attractiveness in the region which I have attempted to describe, and I shall be glad if by what I have written I succeed in persuading others to visit it.

The map has been constructed so as to mark the position of the chief places that are mentioned in the narrative, and the ancient and modern names have been distinguished as far as possible by differences of type.

H. F. T.

OXFORD,
December, 1889.

CONTENTS.

CHAP.	PAGE
I.—DELOS, RHENEIA, AND TENOS	1-24

Approach to Greece — Syra — First impressions of the islands — Delos — Mount Cynthus — Night in Delos — The Circular Lake — Temple of Apollo — Necropolis of Rheneia — Delos to Tenos — The great monastery — The old Venetian town — Panorama of the Cyclades — Italian influences — A Greek nunnery.

II.—CRETE 25-51

The Cretan sea — Khanea — Travelling prospects — The Cretan ibex — Its characteristics — General features of Crete — Cursor Gaetulus — Treachery of Murnies — Hagios Eleutherios — Site of Cydonia — Chrysopegi — Suda Bay — Ruins of Aptera — Customs and superstitions — The northern coast — Retimo — The Cretan dittany — Route southward — Disastrous condition of the country.

III.—CRETE (*continued*) 52-77

Monastery of Arkadi — Description of the siege — The central ridge — Convent of Asomatos — Apodulo — A native family — A strange history — The Demogerontia — The southern coast — Plain of Messara — Captain George — Ruins of Gortyna — Church of St. Titus — A labyrinth — A refuge in war-time — Not the original labyrinth — Eastern side of Ida — Rock-hewn tombs — Mount Iuktas — Megalo-castron or Candia — Lepers — Return to Syra — General remarks — Appearance of the Cretans.

IV.—NAXOS, IOS, AND SIKINOS 78-93

Naxos — Island of Palati — Associations of Dionysus — Duchy of the Archipelago — The city of Sanudo — Historic family names — Channel between Naxos and Paros — Greek sailors — The southern islands — Ios — Pasch van Krienen — His inscription — View of Santorin — Sikinos — Temple of Apollo.

Contents.

CHAP.
V.—SANTORIN, ANTIPAROS, AND PAROS 94–118
Approach to Santorin — Town of Thera — The volcanic group — Chief eruptions — Collections of antiquities — The Kaumene Islands — Therasia — Prehistoric dwellings — Primitive art — Southern parts of Santorin — Ancient heroum — Names and myths — A weird story — Antiparos — Descent into the Grotto — Visit of King George — Paros — The marble quarries — Traces of working — Return to Syra.

VI.—LESBOS 119–138
Storms in the Aegean — Snowy mountains — Lesbos — Bay of Iero — Its narrow entrance — Agiasso — Ascent of Mount Olympus — Names Olympus and Elias — View from the summit — A British subject — Bay of Kallone — Meeting a poet — Ruins of Pyrrha — Modern town of Mytilene — The ancient city — Descriptions by classical writers.

VII.—CHIOS 139–156
Pilgrims bound for Tenos — Earthquake in Scio — The massacre of 1822 — Finlay's narrative — Depopulation of the island — The town and harbour — Maona of the Giustiniani — Its history — Interior of the island — Monastery of Nea Mone — Story of its foundation — The church — Its mosaics — The channel of Scio — Canaris and his fire-ship — Wilhelm Müller's poem — Aytoun's translation — School of Homer.

VIII.—SAMOS 157–177
Port of Scala Nova — The Lenten Fast — Passage to Samos — Town of Vathy — Constitution of the island — Samian wine — The southern coast — Strait of Mycale — Village of Tigani — The ancient city — The theatre — Tunnel of Eupalinus — M. Guérin's exploration — The discovery — Description of it — Its course underground — Other features — The northern entrance — The fountain — Questions connected with it — The temple of Hera — Rivers Imbrasos and Chesios.

IX.—PATMOS 178–198
Voyage to Patmos — Description of the island — Volcanic soil — Monastery of the Apocalypse — The cave — Pictures in the Chapel — The 'Acts of St. John' — Story of Kynops the magician — John dictating his Gospel — Treatment in art — Ruined school buildings — Monastery of St. John — Panorama seen from it — Suited to the Apocalypse — The Library — Codex N — Other MSS. — Bull of Alexius Comnenus — The great

CHAP.		PAGE

church — Relics of the founder — Refectory and kitchen —'The Garden of the Saint'—The acropolis —Island of Leros — Connexion with Egypt— Satires on Leros —Voyage to Rhodes.

X.—RHODES 199-213
Arrival at Rhodes — Its mixed population — Position of the city — Its ancient grandeur — The fortress of the Knights — Objects recently destroyed — Church of St. John —. The deposit of gunpowder — The harbours — Gate of St. Catharine — The Jewish quarter — Moat and walls — Street of the Knights — The Priories — Difficulties in the way of sight-seeing — Antiquities in the neighbourhood — 'Tomb of the Ptolemies'— Ancient bridge.

XI.—RHODES (*continued*) 214-230
The western coast — Site of Ialysos — Kalavarda — A Rhodian peasant's house — Site of Cameiros — Monastery of Artamiti — Ascent of Mount Atabyron — View from the summit — The church — Beehives cased in stone — Woodland regions — Lindos —The Rhodian ware — Rhodian embroidery — Remains of the ancient city — Castle of Lindos — The eastern district — Return to Rhodes.

XII.—LEMNOS 231-250
The northern islands — Means of communication — The Dardanelles — Imbros and Lemnos — Their conquest by Miltiades — Connexion with Athens — Northern coast of Lemnos — View of Mount Athos — Kastro, the ancient Myrina — A Lemnian family — Connexion with Egypt — Lemnos a place of banishment — Site of Myrina — The modern fortress — View from it — Shadow of Athos.

XIII.—LEMNOS (*continued*) 251-274
The warm baths — Interior of the island — The central plain — Village of Atziki — Bay of Purnia — Kotchino — The 'Lemnian earth' — Galen's account — Its use in pharmacy — Belon's account — Modern customs and beliefs — An antidote to poison — An expiring superstition — The eastern district — Site of Hephaestia — Horned cocks — A volcano in Lemnos — Its supposed disappearance — Mount Hermacum.

XIV.—THASOS 275-293
The Thracian Sea — Salonica — Transport of petroleum — Peninsulas of Chalcidice — The Holy Mountain — Cavalla — Thasos — Its beautiful scenery —

CHAP.		PAGE
	The ancient city — Its sea-face — The theatre — The acropolis — Shrine of Pan — The view — Staircase in the rock — The city wall — Sepulchral monuments — The necropolis.	
XV.—	THASOS (*continued*)	294-309
	Thasos under the Khedive — Peculiar local currency — Interior of the Island — High pass — Theologo — An Albanian guard — The southern mountains — Remains at Alke — The marble quarries — Forest rights — The eastern coast — Kinira, the ancient Coenyra — Exquisite woodlands — Return to Limena.	
XVI.—	SAMOTHRACE	310-332
	Wild weather — Voyage to Lagos — A raid on guide-books — Dede-agatch — Difficulty of reaching Samothrace — The voyage thither — Finding a landing-place — First impressions — Ancient harbour of Demetrium — Village of Chora — Ruins at Palaeopoli — The ancient city — Extraordinary walls — Genoese towers — The mole — Sanctuary of the Cabeiri — Its importance — History of the excavations — The sacred area — Temples of the Cabeiri — The Arsinoëum — The Stoa and Ptolemaeum — Hellenic arch.	
XVII.—	SAMOTHRACE (*continued*)	333-354
	Depopulation of Samothrace — Condition of the inhabitants — Paper money — Ibexes — A learned physician — Castle of the Gatilusi — The northern coast — The Therma Loutra — Mineral springs — Position of Zerynthos — Stormy character of Samothrace — Ascent of Mount Phengari — Crest of the island — Its ruggedness — View from the summit — Western portion — Eastern portion — Mythological associations — The Homeric deities — The descent — Famous fountain — Return to Dede-agatch.	
INDEX	. . . . . .	. 355-362

LIST OF MAPS, ETC.

Map of the Aegean Sea	*Frontispiece.*
Map of Delos	*Page* 7
Crucifix of Chrysopegi	,, 37
Map of Santorin	,, 97
Map of Patmos	,, 180
The Sanctuary of Samothrace	,, 327

THE ISLANDS OF THE AEGEAN.

CHAPTER I.

Delos, Rheneia, and Tenos.

In the forenoon of March 18, 1874, I was rounding *Approach to Greece.* Cape Matapan in the French packet, having left Marseilles three days and a half before, the two first of which had been passed in clear and calm weather before we reached the Straits of Messina, but after that time we had been tossing in 'Adria,' as the sea between Sicily and Greece was regularly called by the Greek geographers: this, owing to the meeting of the Adriatic and Mediterranean currents, is usually a disturbed piece of water. The lofty range of Taygetus, which runs northward from Taenarum, and attains its greatest elevation on the western side of the valley of Sparta, formed a conspicuous object from the masses of snow with which its peaks and sides were deeply covered. As we passed between Cythera and the curious promontory of Onugnathos, or the Ass's Jaw, on the mainland opposite, the famous island looked grey and repulsive, and anything but a fitting home for the Goddess of Love. Here we were in comparatively calm water, but from former experience I knew what to expect on the other side of Malea, that headland so justly dreaded by the ancient sailors, as the epitaphs in the Greek Anthology can testify. Nor was I disappointed; for as soon as we had passed the chapel of the hermit of Malea, which lies at the foot of the promontory, we were met by a furious north-east wind—the rude Kaikias of classical writers, and the Euroclydon or Euraquilo of St. Paul's voyage—which considerably delayed our progress. Away to the south a small island (now called Cerigotto) came in sight, which forms the connecting link between Crete and Cythera; and later in the day we passed Melos, Anti-Melos, and other islands, which wore a harsh and uninviting appearance. It was midnight before we reached Syra, the great mercantile station in the middle of the Cyclades, and the best starting-point for a tour in the Greek Islands. Here I disembarked, and joined my travelling companion, Mr. Crowder, who had arrived from Athens a day or two before, bringing with him, as our dragoman, Alexandros Anemoyannes, who on various occasions had accompanied well-known travellers in Greece, as G. F. Bowen, W. G. Clark of Cambridge, John Stuart Mill, Dean Stanley, Sir T. Wyse, and others. The weather report from Athens told of bitter cold. The steamer which conveyed my friend from the Piraeus to Syra had been obliged frequently to stop, owing to the danger to navigation from the thickness of the falling snow, and snow was lying in the streets at Syra. We received similar accounts from other quarters. An Armenian gentleman, who was one of my fellow passengers on the steamer, had heard before leaving England that there was deep snow at Constantinople, and that owing to the same cause the communications between that city and the interior of Asia Minor had been broken for some time. Subsequently we learnt that the weather was equally severe at Jerusalem. The prospects of our journey looked most unfavourable, for the islands cannot properly be visited except in a boat of moderate size, which admits of being rowed in a calm; and this mode of locomotion would have been impracticable in such an inclement season.

The next morning, however, as if by magic, all this was changed. The wind was from the south, soft and warm, the sky cloudless, and the sea only moved by a gentle ripple. It was a perfect Aegean spring day, the only sign of the previous bad weather being the snow which covered the tops of the loftier islands. Accordingly, we hired a boat with three men, intending to make a trial trip to Delos, Rheneia, and Tenos, and started from the mole of Syra shortly after midday. As we left the harbour, we obtained a fine view of the town, which lies on the eastern side of the island, about half-way between its northern and southern extremities. It is now called Hermupolis, and contains 30,000 inhabitants, the most conspicuous portion being the Roman

Syra.

Catholic quarter, which rises steeply up the sides of a conical hill; this was the old town of Syra, whereas the new town, which spreads from the foot of this to the sea, and is the busiest of Oriental stations, has sprung up along with the commercial activity of the place. This is in the most literal sense a creation of the Greek War of Independence, for until 1821 Syra was an insignificant spot; but when the great massacres of the Greeks in Chios in 1822, and in Psara in 1824, took place at the hands of the Turks, it was resorted to by the refugees from those islands. These settlers became traders, and by their shrewdness in business, aided by the central position of this station, they gradually raised it to its present importance. No trees were to be seen, except a few cypresses, the greater part of the ground being uncultivated, though vineyards appeared here and there, and a great quantity of tomatos are grown. Still the stony mountain-sides have a certain beauty, owing to the extreme clearness of the air, and the contrast afforded by the wonderful blue of the sky.

First impressions of the islands. Passing the island of Gaidaro, one of two rocky islets which lie off the harbour, and in ancient times were called Didymae, or 'The Twins,' we gradually saw the Cyclades open out before us. Rheneia lay due east of us, concealing Delos entirely, while Myconos rose above and beyond its northern end; these, together with Tenos, are visible from Syra itself. Then, as we proceeded, there appeared on the left hand, first Andros, which seems a continuation of Tenos, the narrow strait that separates them being indistinguishable; then the promontory of Geraestus in Euboea; and at last Gyaros, the Botany Bay of the Romans, nearer at hand, and half hidden by a corner of Syra: on the right hand, lying along the southern horizon, were seen Naxos, Paros, Antiparos, Siphnos and Seriphos. This was an admirable island view to commence with, and it was easy to distinguish the highest points by the amount of snow which they bore: far the greatest quantity lay on the south of Euboea, next after which came Andros, and then Naxos, while on the rest none was visible. The forms were broken and yet graceful, and the afternoon sun brought out the beautiful shadows on the mountain sides which are so familiar to the traveller in Greece. The general effect of the islands, especially the more distant ones, is that of long lines on the surface of the sea. The length of Naxos is very conspicuous, notwithstanding its lofty mountains, while Paros forms a single low pyramid, bearing a striking resemblance to the other great source of white marble, Pentelicus. Tenos is distinguished by the numerous white villages which stud its sides, while behind the town of Tenos itself, on the summit of the ridge, there rises a remarkable knob of rock, faced with red: with this we were destined to make further acquaintance. The picturesqueness of the whole scene was enhanced by numerous white sails dotting the blue sea, and by an atmospheric illusion, which lifted the islands out of the water.

We had steered a little south of east, and in *Delos.*

about four hours found ourselves rounding the southernmost point of Rhencia; from hence the long soft line of Ios was visible between Naxos and Paros on the horizon. The cape is formed of fine masses of granite, curiously honeycombed, and we subsequently discovered that both this island and the sister isle of Delos are entirely composed of this kind of stone, which is not the case with most of the other Aegean islands; consequently, while the houses of the town of Delos were of granite, as we see from their remains, the materials for most of the public buildings were imported. The two islands are now called the Greater and the Lesser Deli, and run due north and south, divided by a strait about half a mile in breadth, which forms an excellent harbour, with deep water, and sheltered from every wind. There can be little doubt that it was to this feature that Delos originally owed its greatness, for it was the first place where voyagers could anchor in coming from the east, and thus became a natural resort for traders. Rowing up this channel, at the narrowest point we came to an island in mid-stream, now called Rheumatiari or Stream-island, which in ancient times was named the Island of Hecate. It is highly probable that it was here that Polycrates threw across the chain, by which he attached Rheneia to Delos, in token of its being dedicated to Apollo; and that Nicias when sent from Athens as the leader of a festival procession, having brought a bridge from Athens to Rheneia, and laid it in the night-time, proceeded to the temple on the morrow with triumphal pomp. Directly to the east of this rises Mount Cynthus, the highest point in Delos, and in a valley which descends almost from its summit towards the strait in a south-westerly direction is the bed of a stream, the ancient Inopus, which had a legendary connexion with the Nile, for Callimachus says that it was fullest when that river is flooded¹. Possibly the link of association which suggested this notion may be found in a temple on the mountain side, in which the gods of Egypt were worshipped. Passing the

---

¹ "Ἔζετο δ' Ἰνώποιο παρὰ ῥόον, ὅντε βάθιστον
γαῖα τότ' ἐξανίησιν ὅτε πλήθοντι ῥεέθρῳ
Νεῖλος ἀπὸ κρημνοῖο κατέρχεται Αἰθιοπῆος.
Callim. *Del.* 206-8 : cf. Pausan. 2. 5. 3.

island of Hecate, we landed on Delos, near where another small island, the lesser Rheumatiari, lies off the coast; here there were traces of quays, but the sea has retired and left a sandy beach.

Mount Cynthus. Within a gunshot of this point the ruins of the great temple of Apollo were plainly visible, forming a vast heap of fallen blocks of white marble; but we refrained for the moment from visiting these, our object being to ascend Cynthus before nightfall. Making our way through aromatic brushwood of lentisk and cistus, we directed our steps towards a white wall, conspicuous from below, which proved to belong to a theatre, the *cavea* of which faces west, and is clearly traceable, the back part being excavated in the hillside, while the ends are composed of masonry of Parian marble. The courses of stones, of which in one place thirteen remain, are skilfully put together, though somewhat narrow. The line of the *scena* also is well marked. Behind this, and further up the hillside, stood the small temple already referred to, which has been proved by excavation to have been dedicated to the Foreign Divinities, i.e. to the gods of Syria and Egypt. Here among other objects a hieroglyphic inscription was found. The foundations of this show that the superstructure was of white marble; the *pronaos, naos,* and an altar are visible, together with a mosaic pavement composed of pebbles. In the neighbourhood of this temple there is a curious gateway, leading into a chamber, which, when seen from a distance, resembles a cavern, but in reality is artificial, the roof being composed of

granite blocks resting against one another at an
obtuse angle; the sides are the natural granite rock,
which originally formed a narrow ravine. This
chamber is believed to have been a primitive sanctuary of Apollo[1]. We then mounted by a very
steep ascent to the summit of Cynthus, where are the
foundations and fragments of another temple, the
pillars being in the Ionic style. Numerous inscriptions which have been discovered on the site show
that it was dedicated to Zeus Cynthius and Athena
Cynthia. As this mountain is not more than 350
feet above the sea, I had often wondered how classical
writers could speak of it as lofty, especially as it is surrounded by so much higher peaks on other islands;
Aristophanes, for instance, describes it as 'the Cyn-
thian rock with lofty horn[2]:' but from its steepness
and rocky character it deserves that epithet, and
certainly it is very conspicuous from every point in
the neighbouring seas. This circumstance, especially
if it served as a landmark to vessels coming from the
open sea, may also, perhaps, explain the origin of
the name of the island, Delos, or the 'Conspicuous,'
which can hardly be otherwise than of Greek origin.
The view from this point is very fine, comprehending
all the islands we have already noticed—the Cyclades,
or 'Circling islands,' of which Callimachus says:
'Fragrant Asterie (Delos), on every side the islands
have encircled thee, and formed as 'twere a band

---

[1] See Lebègue's *Recherches sur Delos*, in which views and plans
of the chamber are given.

[2] Κυνθίαν ὑψικέρατα πέτραν. *Nub.* 596.

of dancers round thee[1]:' while Myconos is full in view to the north-east, separated by a strait about two miles wide. It was natural, therefore, that Virgil should represent Apollo as fastening his island to Myconos, when it ceased to wander on the sea :—

> Encircled by a billowy ring
>   A land there lies, the loved resort
> Of Neptune, the Aegean king,
>   And the grey queen of Nereus' court :
> Long time the sport of ev'ry blast,
>   O'er ocean it was wont to toss,
> Till grateful Phoebus moored it fast
>   To Gyaros and high Myconos,
> And bade it lie unmoved, and brave
>   The violence of wind and wave [2].

But what, except Roman ignorance of geography, or perhaps the preference for a familiar name, should make Virgil attach Delos to Gyaros instead of the nearer Rheneia or Syros, I do not understand. Here, too, the character of the island is well seen, for it is a narrow rocky ridge, between two and three miles in length, with granite knolls and barren slopes; thus justifying the story related in the Homeric Hymn to the Delian Apollo, that Latona visited all the richest spots in the Aegean before giving birth to her children ; but all were afraid to receive her, so that she betook herself to the small and rugged island.

Night in Delos.

As we were descending the hill on the opposite side from that by which we had approached, we met

[1] Ἀστερίη θυόεσσα, σὲ μὲν περί τ' ἀμφί τε νῆσοι
κύκλον ἐποιήσαντο καὶ ὡς χορὸν ἀμφεβάλοντο.
  Callim. *Del.* 300, 301.

[2] Virg. *Aen.* 3. 73-7 (Conington's trans.').

the single inhabitant of Delos, an old shepherd, who spoke a most extraordinary dialect of Greek. He did not offer to accompany us, and this our servant, who was not then with us, attributed to his regarding our sudden appearance as uncanny; the old man, however, did not seem to be superstitious, for the next day when I questioned him as to the existence of 'Vrykolakas' or Vampires in the island, he replied in the negative. At this I was surprised, for the Cyclades are the homes of innumerable strange beliefs, and it is about the neighbouring island of Myconos that Tournefort relates a marvellous story of the whole population being *bouleversé* for weeks together by such an apparition. We passed the night in some deserted shepherds huts, lying in a depression to the north of Cynthus, where the ground slopes gradually to the two seas, and has been sown with corn by the people of Myconos: these dwellings were constructed of stones put together with straw instead of mortar, while the doors were of ancient blocks approaching one another towards the top. All around grew the spreading leaves and lilac flowers of the mandrake (*Atropa mandragora*), forming large flat patches on the ground. This excessively poisonous plant, which has been a favourite with witches in all ages, and is said to utter shrieks when its root is extracted from the ground, is especially common in the Greek islands. As I lay awake part of the night in the extraordinary stillness, I was able to recall, in some measure, the crowds of worshippers, the visit of the Persians, and other romantic glories of the place—things which it is difficult to realise, when the senses are in contact with the material objects.

The Circular Lake. The next morning opened with rain, but it had cleared by eight o'clock, and we descended from our night's lodging towards the landing-place where we had left our boat. As we approached the sea, the northernmost ruins that we met with were those of the ancient city, where granite columns were lying among broken fragments of walls. Beyond this was an oval basin, about 100 yards in length, forming a kind of pond, the sides of which were banked in by a casing of stonework; it is usually dry, but at this season contained a small quantity of water. In ancient times it was kept full, and was called the Circular Lake[1], and the swans that were sacred to Apollo used to float upon it. Herodotus compares it to the lake at Sais in Egypt. If, as we are told by Theognis[2], it was near this lake that Latona brought forth her two children, then the famous palm-tree of Delos, which is mentioned in Homer, where Ulysses compares Nausicaa's beauty to it[3], must have stood here, for we are told in the Hymn to the Delian Apollo[4], as well as by Theognis, that the goddess clasped this tree when in the pains of childbirth. Callimachus, however, has followed another version of the story, when he places that occurrence on the banks of the Inopus[5].

Near this basin is a copious spring of water, and this circumstance probably determined the position

---
[1] τροχοειδὴς λίμνη, Herod. 2. 170.
[2] Line 7, in Bergk's *Poetae Lyrici*.
[3] *Od.* 6. 162.   [4] Line 117.   [5] *Del.* 206.

of the temple of Apollo. The *temenos* of this is *Temple of Apollo.* hard by to the south, and within it the ruins of the temple form a confused heap of white marble fragments, columns, bases, and entablatures lying indiscriminately together[1]. They are of the Doric order, and as many of the shafts are only partly fluted, it would seem that the details of the building were never completely finished. The wreck of so fine a specimen of architecture is a sad sight; but when we consider that the place has served for a quarry for the neighbouring islanders, and a place of pillage for foreigners from the times of the Venetian occupation to our own days, perhaps the wonder is rather that so much remains. In the south-west part of the area is a large square marble basis, hollowed out in the middle, with the remains of an inscription on one side stating that it was a gift from the Naxians to Apollo (ΝΑΞΙΟΙ ΑΠΟΛΛΩΝΙ): this pedestal supported a colossus, which was overthrown in ancient times by the falling of a palm-tree of bronze gilt, erected by Nicias in its immediate neighbourhood[2]. When Spon and Wheler visited this island in 1675, the statue remained with the exception of its head, and part of the torso, from the neck to the waist, has

---

[1] Since the time of my visit the temple of Apollo has been thoroughly examined by French *savants*. The results of this and the other excavations on Delos will be found in M. Lebègue's work already mentioned, and in the articles by MM. Homolle and Hauvette-Besnault in the *Bulletin de Correspondance hellénique*, vols. i-viii. An interesting summary of these is contained in Prof. Jebb's paper on Delos, in vol. i. of the *Journal of Hellenic Studies*.

[2] Plutarch, *Nic.* 3.

been seen within the present half century, but we could find no traces of it. A portion of the ruins in the temple area towards the coast, which are in the Corinthian style, seem to have belonged to an entrance colonnade to the *temenos*; and not far off, on the other side of a wall constructed by the shepherds, are the prostrate columns of another portico, built by Philip V of Macedon. In Spon's time eleven of these were standing, but without capitals. In the midst of the ruins, anemones of various colours— white, pink, and lilac—were growing, and I dug up some fine narcissus roots to transplant to England. For this proceeding I had good authority. Our servant informed me that J. S. Mill, when he travelled with him in the Peloponnese, besides drying flowers, had an extra baggage mule in his train for carrying plants and roots.

Necropolis of Rheneia. Embarking once more, we crossed the strait, and landed on Rheneia, at a point somewhat south of the island of Hecate. Both Rheneia and its sister island are absolutely bare of trees. At a little distance from this point, on the slopes which rise above the strait, is an ancient necropolis, containing the graves of those whose bodies were removed from Delos at the time of the Peloponnesian war. It extends over half a mile, and is a scene of wild desolation, worthy of the circle of the *Inferno* in which Farinata's spirit emerged from its fiery tomb. Broken stones lay strewn about in all directions, mixed here and there with sides and lids of sarcophagi. Usually the graves are only distinguishable by depressions in the ground, but in some places the areas and walls are traceable. About them were growing the coarse branching stems of the asphodel, a most disenchanting plant, and so rough, that if the lotus-eaters enjoyed lying among them they did not indulge in Sybarite tastes. When we returned to our boat we found the sailors eating raw limpets, which they picked from the rocks. It was now the Greek Lent, which is observed with great strictness by all the sailors in the Aegean, but bloodless fish, such as mussels and limpets, are allowed to be eaten at that season.

We now coasted along the eastern shore of Rheneia, which stretches for a long distance beyond the northernmost part of Delos. At one point the island is almost divided in two, the northern and southern portions being connected by an extremely narrow isthmus; in the neighbourhood of this is the cholera quarantine station for Syra. Greece is the strictest of all countries in enforcing quarantine, as I know to my cost, having once had to pass eleven days on a barren island in the Gulf of Volo, which is a frontier station between Greece and Turkey; but the result of these preventive measures is remarkably successful. When we reached the extremity of the island, we were caught by a fresh westerly breeze, and danced across over a tossing sea towards the southernmost cape of Tenos. The town of Myconos was here visible from the sea, its white buildings being clustered together in the recesses of a bay, and many other houses appeared scattered over the hill sides; Delos too was seen

Delos to Tenos.

well in profile, with the straits on both sides which separate it from the neighbouring islands, and the conspicuous summit of Cynthus. At the end of Tenos rises a lofty mountain, which in ancient times was called Cycnias, and still retains that name in the form of Tzikniais. Such peaks are nests of storms, and the navigation of the straits which intervene between them and neighbouring islands— as in the similar instance of the passage between Geraestus and Andros — is extremely perilous. Hence Aeolus was supposed to hold his court in the caves of Cycnias; and our dragoman described how he had seen a steamer, when on her way from Syra to Constantinople, forced in an instant to put about at this point and run before the storm. The wind prevented us from steering direct for the town of Tenos, which lies on the western side of the island; so when we reached the point, we worked our way along with oars, and rounded a promontory called Gaidaro, or 'Donkey,' from the resemblance of its ridge to the back of that animal, the shape of which has suggested many names both in ancient and modern times, as we see from the 'Oneian' mountains near Corinth. From this and every other side Tenos presents a wonderful aspect, from the way in which the mountain slopes, from top to bottom, have been formed into terraces, mainly for the cultivation of the vine. The wine, which is held in repute in the Levant, is light and somewhat sweet, and agreeable to the taste. The grape which produces the best is considered to be a lineal descendant of the vines of Monemvasia on the east coast of the Morea, the original Malmsey, and the wine is called by that name at the present day.

The town of Tenos, which is better known as Hagios Nicolas, was in former times hardly more than a landing-place, since the Venetian occupants had established themselves on the ridge above; but now its white houses and campaniles have an imposing effect as seen from the sea; while the monastery of the Evangelistria, which is the most important structure, with the great church in the centre of it, towers over the whole place. We should notice one feature in these islands, which causes them to present innumerable contrasts to other parts of Greece. This is the absence of traces of Byzantine influence. In describing the architecture of the continent of Greece and of European Turkey, it is superfluous to say that it is Byzantine; every monastery, church, or other building connected with the Greek rite is, as a matter of course, built in that style. Here, on the contrary, it hardly ever appears, and the Italian mode of building and corresponding architectural features are everywhere predominant. So, too, while in Turkey and Greece proper the material of which dwelling-houses are constructed is principally wood, in these islands we find them universally built of stone. When we had established ourselves in a house at the back of the town, we went up to the monastery, the extensive buildings of which, occupying three sides of a quadrangle, contain a school and accommodation

The great monastery.

for numerous pilgrims. We were shown the sacred picture to which the place owes its foundation, the elaborately ornamented church containing numerous votive offerings, and the place beneath it where the picture was found in the year 1824. The story is one that recurs in many countries, viz. that a nun dreamed that an icon of the Virgin was buried there, and one was discovered on the spot accordingly. The great days of pilgrimage are March 25 and August 15 (Old Style), and on these the crowds of visitors are very great; on the eve of March 25, the steamer, in which we were going from Syra to the Piraeus, was sent out of its way to Tenos for their accommodation. There are no Hellenic remains in this neighbourhood except pieces of columns, though the old town was on the site of the present one, and the monastery probably occupies the position of the temple of Poseidon, who was the patron of the island. Here, as often, the place of that deity has been taken by St. Nicolas, the guardian of sailors, from whom the town is now named. In the court of the monastery several fine palm-trees were growing, and others were to be seen in different parts of the town. Tenos is considered a very healthy island, so that many people come there from all quarters for the air and water.

The old Venetian town.

On the morrow (March 21) we started on foot, under the guidance of a young man, one of the family at whose house we were staying, to visit the old Venetian town and fort of Exoburgo, which occupies the conspicuous peak above the ridge of the island, that had before attracted our attention by its reddish hue. The path by which we ascended the steep mountain side was in part a paved way, in part a watercourse; but at one time it must have been an important road, when the Venetian authorities occupied the heights above, and even now it must be a considerable artery of communication, to judge from the numerous people whom we met coming on mules from the upper villages, and from the east coast of the island. On the way our guide had a story to tell—one of those myths of observation which we meet with so frequently—about a cave near the summit which had underground communication with one near the sea, so that two Englishmen had explored the way from one to the other As we approached the foot of the peak, we discovered that the red appearance which it assumed from a distance was caused by an ochre-coloured lichen, which thickly covered its face, with a picturesque effect. To reach the summit we had to make our way to the back of the cliffs, where lies the ruined town of Exoburgo: the buildings of this are roofless, only one or two half-dismantled churches being still used. Its name (Ἐξώβουργο) is, apparently, a mixture of Greek and Italian, meaning the suburb (*borgo*) which lay outside the citadel. Hence we clambered up the steep slopes in the midst of *débris*, passing at intervals the massive walls, composed of large blocks, by which the accessible portions of the ground were defended. Until lately a Venetian cannon remained here, but it has now been removed. The height must be about 2,000 feet above the sea, for it is somewhat lower than Cycnias, which is 2,340 feet.

<small>Panorama of the Cyclades.</small> As the view from the summit is the most comprehensive panorama in the centre of the Aegean, comprising both Europe and Asia, it may be worth while to describe it in detail. To commence from the east: Icaros (Nicaria), which forms a bridge between the Cyclades and the Asiatic islands, appeared comparatively near; then came Samos, more distant, and the coast of Asia Minor between Ephesus and Smyrna; next Chios (Scio), and Psyra (Psara), between which and Tenos, in the middle of the Aegean, lay a conspicuous rock called Kaloyero or 'The Monk,' while far away to the north, beyond the east coast of Andros, was seen the faint outline of Achilles' island, Scyros. To the west of Andros appeared the coast of Attica, near Laureium, with Hymettus behind, but the promontory of Sunium was hidden by Ceos; more in front were Gyaros, and Syra with its white town. Distant again lay the varied forms of Cythnos, Seriphos, Siphnos, Antiparos, Paros, and Naxos. We thus see the two lines of islands which form the continuations of the mountain chains of Eastern Greece; the one starting from Mount Pelion, passing through Euboea, Andros, and Tenos, and terminating in Myconos; the other starting from Attica and ending in Siphnos. Between these lie Gyaros and Syra, while Paros and Naxos may be regarded as the meeting-point of the two lines. Away to the south, and not visible from

this point, are the volcanic Melos and Thera (Santorin). Perhaps the most picturesque point in the view was the group formed by Rhencia and Delos, with the two islets between them, and Myconos: these lay as on a map below us, all separate from one another, with their numerous headlands cut out upon the surface of the sea. After being accustomed to look at these objects on a chart, where the islands resemble a handful of pebbles, lying at random close to one another, it was impossible not to be struck by their size and by the spaces of sea that lay between them—an impression which was amply confirmed by subsequent voyages from one to the other. In tracing out these topographical features with the compass and map, we were greatly assisted by our native guide, who possessed a very accurate knowledge of the localities, and was fortunately unimbued with any classical ideas.

The scene below us, in the island of Tenos itself, was most curious, and I was more than ever struck by the sight of a whole island, almost to the mountain-tops, carved into terraces, which gave evidence of vast labour employed in their construction. At our feet, both to north and south, were irregular uplands, draining some into the eastern, some into the western sea, and dotted with numerous flourishing villages, the white-washed houses of which were surrounded by olives, oranges, and fig-trees. The appearance of these dwellings, with their flat roofs, trim gardens, and battlemented *Italian influences.*

enclosures, is completely that of North Italy; and this is not to be wondered at, since the Italians held Tenos between 400 and 500 years, and it was not until 1718 that it passed out of the hands of the Venetians. This circumstance also explains the large number of Roman Catholics in the island, comprising more than half the population. Of the villages that we saw from this point, those towards the north belonged to the Latin Church, as do most of those on the north-east coast, while those towards the south were partly Orthodox (Greek) and partly mixed.

A Greek nunnery.

When we had descended to the foot of the peak, we struck off along the hills to the south, intending to return by a different route from that by which we had ascended, in order to visit a nunnery, the white buildings of which, closely clustered within a wall of circuit, are so conspicuous on the mountain side, lying some 1,500 feet above the sea, that they may be seen from a distance of twenty or thirty miles. As we proceeded thither by an irregular path, sometimes ascending, sometimes descending, we found in a hollow way a drift of snow not yet melted. We passed some curious pigeon-houses, situated in the middle of enclosures, and resembling cottages, with numerous holes for the pigeons to enter, and resting-places for them on the outside; large flocks of these birds were flying about them. There were also numerous windmills in this neighbourhood. Our track lay over soft mica slate, so friable that sometimes we appeared to be walking on tan; this kind of soil, and the numerous springs, are the cause of the great fertility of the island, but at this season of the year the absence of trees gives it a very bare appearance. We were told, however, that later on the country was blue in places from the sweet-scented hyacinths. A visit to a Greek nunnery was a novelty to us, for though Greek monasteries may be counted by hundreds, and we had again and again been grateful in former years for their hospitable shelter, yet a nunnery (μοναστήριον διὰ καλογρίαις) had never come in our way. We were doubtful, also, whether our visit would be acceptable, but on this score we found no difficulties, for on our arrival an old priest, who lives in a little house outside the gateway, and performs the services in the convent, at once ushered us in. The buildings are crowded together most irregularly within the enclosing wall, rising steeply up the sloping ground, one above another, and winding passages lead in all directions among them. From these emerged female figures in plain black dresses and veils, and we were struck with their cheerful, and intelligent faces, while some little girls, who were being educated there, were singularly pretty. In fact, the salutary effect of the air and water of Tenos, which I have already spoken of as causing it to be resorted to for the sake of health, is generally apparent in the good looks of the population. As Greek monasteries are usually excessively dirty, I was agreeably surprised by the cleanliness and order that prevailed here. They are *idiorrhythmic* (ἰδιόρρυθμοι)—a term which is applied to those monasteries where the superior is changed periodically, and where, in respect of meals and the general regulation of life, 'every man is a rule to himself;' consequently they have no common refectory. Idiorrhythmic ladies are, I fancy, an advance even on the ideas of Western Europe. They work at various employments, such as making stockings and silk tobacco-pouches ornamented with beads; these articles they sell to pilgrims (προσκυνηταί), for they are not allowed to go to the town. After visiting the church, which is handsomely decorated, we were conducted to the reception-room, where the lady superior, sitting in the corner of the divan, which in an Eastern room is the place of dignity, welcomed us, and entertained us with preserve of orange, arrack, and coffee. She said the date of the foundation of the monastery was not certain, but that according to tradition it was twelve hundred years old; the antiquity of everything in the East is, however, greatly overrated. We learnt also from her that there are sixteen nunneries in Greece, of which this is the largest, for it contains at the present time one hundred and three sisters. They come from all parts of Greece and Turkey.

When our visit was concluded, we descended by a steep path to the town, where we once more embarked, and having a favourable breeze reached Syra before nightfall.

CHAPTER II.

CRETE.

AT sunset on the day after our return from Tenos (March 22) we embarked on board the Austrian steamer, which runs weekly between Syra and Crete, the Lloyd's being the only line which keeps up communication with that island. The German name of our vessel, the *Schild*, and that of her sister-steamer, the *Wien*, looked strange in the midst of Greek and Italian titles, and sounded still more out of place in the mouths of our Greek boatmen. We were due at Khanea, the capital of the island, which lies on the northern coast, not far from its western extremity, at noon the following day, but the badness of the weather caused us to be five hours late, and gave us ample opportunity of justifying the truth of the old Greek proverb, 'the Cretan sea is wide¹.' Late in the afternoon we passed the promontory of Acroteri, which forms the eastern boundary of the bay of Khanea, and an hour later were lying off the port. For some time it was doubtful whether we could enter, for the narrow entrance has been so silted up, in consequence of long neglect, that the

The Cretan sea.

¹ Πολὺ τὸ Κρητικὸν πέλαγος.

passage is often dangerous in bad weather; the other alternative would have been to land at Suda, on the further side of the Acroteri peninsula; fortunately, however, we succeeded in passing the bar. No sooner had we cast anchor than we were first surrounded and then boarded by a motley crowd of noisy Cretans in picturesque dresses, interspersed with Nubians, many of which race have been settled in the island ever since the time when it was subject to the Viceroy of Egypt (A.D. 1830–1840). The appearance of the town was striking, as its irregular wooden buildings rose up the hill sides from the sea, interspersed with palm-trees, mosques, and minarets. There was no mistaking that we were in Turkey. The whole place is surrounded by a Venetian wall of great massiveness, and the harbour is enclosed by extensive moles. Over the sea-gate stands the Lion of St. Mark. Behind, at no great distance off, lay the mighty wall of the Sphakian mountains, deeply covered with snow, though the summits were veiled by masses of cloud.

Khanea.

When we landed, all our books, to our great indignation, were confiscated, and carried off for inspection to the residence of the Pasha, including Bradshaw's Railway Guide, which, no doubt, was regarded as a highly cabalistic volume. On enquiring the cause of this—for we had never been the victims of such a proceeding in Turkey before—we found that suspicion reigned supreme among the authorities, owing to the meeting of the Emperors of Russia, Germany and Austria, which had taken place shortly before this time, and which was supposed to bode no good to Turkey, and, in particular, to the rule of that power in Crete. Even our insignificant visit, as we found on our return from the interior, was interpreted as having a political meaning. It was discovered from our passports that I was a clergyman and my friend an officer of militia, and hence the remark was, 'What can a priest and a military man want in the island if they have no political object?'

The only *locanda* in the town—a place which from its filthiness was far worse than the bare walls of a Turkish khan—bore the highly Cretan but hardly encouraging title of 'The Rhadamanthys' ('O 'Ραδάμανθυς). It had, however, the advantage of nearness to the British Consulate, from the inmates of which we received very kind attention. Before coming to the island, we had often been asked whether travelling would not be dangerous there, from the wildness of the population and the general disaffection that prevailed; but our former experience of travelling in Turkey had taught us that the traveller is safest in the wildest and remotest districts, because there he is respected as a strange animal, and his value in exchange for a ransom is not known. In answer to our enquiries on this head, we were told that any stranger would be safe in every part of Crete, but that towards the English there existed such a kindly feeling that we should be especially well received: and this was fully confirmed in the course of our subsequent journey. We learnt that an earthquake

Travelling prospects.

had been felt the night before, and that such occurrences are not uncommon here, a circumstance which the inhabitants attribute to their nearness to the unquiet volcano of Santorin. But the absorbing subject of interest at this time was the extraordinary severity of the season, the like of which had not been felt for forty-three years. I have already spoken of this as being remarkable all over the south-eastern portion of the Mediterranean; but the island of Crete seemed to have been the focus of this area of cold. The distress thus caused was very great. The natives of the upland villages were escaping in great numbers over the snow, and arriving daily in Khanea; but in some cases the snow had hemmed them in too closely in their valleys to admit of their escaping, and many of them were starved in their homes.

The Cretan ibex. The same cause had lately brought down several of the large and rare Cretan goats, which are the representatives of an almost extinct species, from the mountain summits, to which they have now retired, and which they rarely leave. Before starting from England I had cherished a strong wish, though but a faint hope, of obtaining the skin and horns of one of these valuable ibexes; and when I mentioned this to the dragoman of the Consulate, Mr. Moatsos, a Greek gentleman well known for his attention to English visitors, he at once presented me with a very fine skin, taken from one which had been killed a few days before; this is now in the Museum at Oxford. I tried to obtain the skull, but in vain, for the natives, as might be supposed, set no value on anything but the flesh and the skin, and consequently the bones are at once destroyed. A living specimen of the animal, which was caught and sent over to England by Mr. Sandwith, who was then the British consul at Khanea, may be seen in the Zoological Gardens in London. The colour is brown, with a dark stripe down the back; the horns are two feet long, curving gently backwards, and slightly divergent, with pointed tips. The only other places in which it is known to exist are the island of Anti-Melos, an uninhabited rock to the west of Melos, and two of the islands which run off in a chain from the extremity of Mount Pelion, viz. that called Scopelos in ancient times, and that now called Joura. In these it is very scarce, and will probably soon be extinct; but the specimens that have been brought from these places, though varying in some slight points from the Cretan goat, bear a sufficiently close resemblance to it to be regarded as the same species. Naturalists consider that it is nearest akin to the Persian goat, but far removed from that of Sinai and from the European ibexes. It was probably dispersed over all the Greek islands in ancient times, and Ludwig Ross met with an engraved stone on Melos, on which the figure of the animal, and especially its horns, are very clearly represented[1]. From the length of the horns it seems highly probable that it was a goat of this class which, Homer tells us, furnished Pandarus with a bow. Of this we

---

[1] Ross, *Reisen auf den griechischen Inseln*, vol. iii. p. 21.

learn, that it was formed of the horns of a 'bounding wild goat[1],' which the hero had stalked and killed among the rocks; that the horns were each sixteen palms, i.e. four feet, in length; and that they were polished and fitted for a bow by a worker in horn.

Its characteristics.
The mountains of the western extremity of Crete seem to be the chief abode of these animals. It is reported that they are also found in the range of Ida, but they appear to be very rare in that region. Wild goats, indeed, are found there, but I gathered that these are a smaller kind—probably chamois, for the chamois exists in many places in Greece, and I myself have seen a herd of ten or twelve of them on the summits of the Thessalian Olympus. Sometimes the Cretan ibexes attain to a great size. About the year 1819 a party of native sportsmen are said to have killed two, which weighed nearly seventy and ninety pounds respectively. The flesh is allowed on all hands to be excellent eating. The great agility of the animal, and the consequent difficulty of obtaining it, are testified to by several authorities. Thus Pashley, who made a meal off the flesh of some that were killed in the Sphakiote mountains, says, 'The *agrimia*' (*agrimi*, like the German *Wild*, signifies any kind of game, but is specially used as the name for this goat) 'are so active that they will leap up a perpendicular rock of ten to fourteen feet high: they spring from precipice to precipice, and bound along with such speed that no dog would be able to keep up with them, even on better ground than where

[1] ἰξάλου αἰγὸς ἀγρίου, *Il.* 4. 105.

they are to be found. They often carry off a ball,
and, unless they fall immediately on being struck,
are mostly lost to the sportsman, although they may
have received a mortal wound[1].' This last remark
is interesting in connexion with the statement of
classical writers, which will subsequently be referred
to, that the wild goats made use of the Cretan dittany
to get rid of the arrows which had pierced them. On
Anti-Melos the breed is fast diminishing, only single
specimens being now visible, where herds of from
ten to fifteen were seen forty or fifty years ago.
This is not so much owing to sportsmen—for they
have mostly to be shot from boats with rifles, on
account of the steepness and dangerous character of
the cliffs—as to a contagious disease which was communicated to them by sheep that were turned out to
pasture on the island[2].

Before we start for the interior, it may be well for *General features of Crete.*
me to say a few words as to the character of the
country generally. This long and narrow island—
for it is 160 miles in length, while its breath varies
from forty to six miles across—is the principal link
between the southern extremities of Greece and of
Asia Minor, smaller stepping-stones being formed
by Cythera on the one side, and by Casos, Carpathos, and Rhodes on the other. It is mountainous
throughout, having a long backbone that runs
through it from end to end, but its highest summits

---
[1] Pashley, *Travels in Crete*, vol. ii. p. 271.
[2] The chief authority on these ibexes is Erhard, *Die Fauna der Cykladen.*

gather themselves up into three great groups—lofty enough to be clearly visible in fine weather from Santorin, which is sixty miles distant to the north. These are, the Dictaean mountains, as they were called in ancient times, towards the east; in the centre Ida, or, as it is now called, Psilorites, or the 'lofty mountain' (ὑψηλὸν ὄρος); and to the west the White Mountains[1], though in the interior of the country they are more commonly known as the mountains of Sphakia[2]; that being the district inhabited by the Sphakiotes, who are famed for being the most warlike and independent of the modern Cretan tribes. The two last-mentioned of these mountain groups rise to the height of between 7,000 and 8,000 feet above the sea. From what we had heard and read beforehand we expected to find large parts of the island well wooded, and had pictured to ourselves such glades and dells as may be seen on the peninsula of Athos, or on the slopes of Ossa and Pelion; but here we were doomed to disappointment. Cultivated trees, indeed, may be seen abundantly, especially the olive and the orange, and the fruit of the latter is so fine, that Cretan oranges are famous throughout the Archipelago, and a great quantity is exported; but of natural vegetation there is extremely little, and the mountain uplands are for the most part bare.

Cursor Gaetulus. On the morning after our arrival, having hired

[1] Λευκὰ ὄρη in antiquity, now Ἄσπρα βουνά, with the same meaning.
[2] Σφακιωτικὰ βουνά.

horses, and recovered our books through the dragoman of the Consulate, we left Khanea, passing through a gateway in the massive Venetian walls. The youths who accompanied our horses were two Mahometans, named Ali and Saideh, the former a Cretan, the latter a coal-black Nubian, with tattooed temples and cheeks. His history was a curious one. He had been carried off from his native country as a slave at seven years of age, and did not remember the process of tattooing, or rather gashing, by which his face had been marked, so that he could not tell us whether it had been done with the knife or by firing. After this he had been sold several times to different masters, until a Turkish dignitary brought him to Crete, where he obtained his liberty. He was a fairly intelligent fellow, and very superior to his companion, Ali. He spoke Turkish and Arabic, but his ordinary language was Greek, for in Crete, alone among the provinces of Turkey, that language is spoken by all the population, whether Mahometan or Christian. This arises from the Mussulmans, with the exception of a few in the towns, being renegade Greeks, who retain their native tongue. In Thessaly, where the Greek population is very numerous, the official proclamations are in Greek, but the Mahometans, who are Turkish immigrants, speak Turkish. After ascending a little distance from the town, we found ourselves on a plain of some extent, which reaches to the foot of the Rhiza, as the lower slopes of the Sphakiote mountains are called. At the sides of the road aloes of prodigious size were growing, the leaves of some of them reaching to the height of eight or ten feet. This tract, the soil of which is very rich, is covered with extensive plantations of olives, which, to judge from their size, and the broken wood of their trunks, must be of great age; among these stand *konaks* or villas of Turkish grandees, surrounded with cypresses and pine trees, and some with ruined walls.

Treachery of Murnies. In forty minutes we reached the dilapidated village of Murnies, the decay of which was somewhat softened by the fine orange trees and other cultivation in its neighbourhood. This is a place of melancholy memories, for it was the scene of one of the worst of the many acts of treachery of which the Turks have been guilty in the island. As far as the circumstances can be summed up in a few sentences they were as follows. At the conclusion of the Greek War of Independence, during which the Cretans had struggled vigorously for freedom, and seemed on the point of forcing the Mahometans to leave the country, it was decided by the Allied Powers that Crete should be annexed to the dominions of Mehemet Ali, and assurances were given to the inhabitants by the British Government of the system of order which that potentate would introduce. In the summer of 1833 the Viceroy of Egypt visited the island, and immediately after his departure a proclamation was published, which tended to make a great part of the landed estates throughout the country his property. To protest against this, several thousands of the Christian population assembled at Murnies, which from its position close to the foot of the Rhiza and in the neighbourhood of the capital, has frequently been the scene of such meetings on the part of the mountaineers. After some delay, promises of redress were given, and the assembly, which had throughout been peacefully conducted, dispersed with the exception of a few hundred men. When, however, an Egyptian squadron arrived, and the authorities felt themselves in a stronger position, they proceeded to Murnies, and arrested thirty-three of the people who had remained there, ten of whom were subsequently hanged, while at the same time, in order to strike terror into the Christians, twenty-one other persons were seized and executed in other parts of the island. Who can wonder, after this and similar atrocities, if an insurrection in Crete is almost an internecine struggle?

From Murnies we turned aside to the monastery of Hagios Eleutherios, which we found to be a small building, with a church in the Byzantine style, but without any pretension to architectural effect. The object of our search here, which had caused us to deviate from our proposed route along the north coast of the island, was a crucifix, which is mentioned by Pashley in his Travels, though he gives no description of it. Now it is well known to archaeologists that a crucifix in the Eastern Church is an object of extreme rarity, crucifixes having been traditionally proscribed just as much as statues, while icons, i.e. pictures, have been retained. Indeed, in all the parts of Greece and European Turkey that I have visited

Hagios Eleutherios.

I have only met with two others; one in the monastery of Xeropotamu on Mount Athos, which is set with diamonds, and has been spared, as being a reputed gift of the Empress Pulcheria; the other, at Ochrida, in Western Macedonia, the former capital of the Bulgarian kingdom, which is regarded by its possessors as an unauthorised object, and is preserved only as a relic of antiquity, and may very possibly have descended from the times of Cyril and Methodius, the apostles of the Slavonians. On enquiry, however, we found that this crucifix is now kept at the Metochi (μετόχιον) or dependent monastery of Chrysopegi, and to this we proceeded, after the monks had regaled us with preserve of quince. I may remark that, though there are no remains of antiquity at Khanea except vases, *lacrimatoria*, and similar objects, which are found in tombs in the neighbourhood, yet it is tolerably certain that the ancient city of Cydonia occupied the same site, or one in the immediate vicinity; and those persons who believe in the permanence of vegetation in certain localities, and are disposed to use it as an argument for the position of an ancient site (in whose number I cannot enrol myself) may adduce in this connexion the quinces (κυδωνίαι) which grow here, as that tree is believed to have taken its name from this city. In the course of conversation with the monks I enquired about the concealed Christians — that is, Mahometans by profession who, while they conform outwardly to that creed, practise Christianity secretly; and I was told in reply that some of

Site of Cydonia.

these remain in Crete, though their numbers are much smaller than they used to be, and that these baptize their children and observe other Christian rites in private. I had subsequent confirmation of this statement, and learnt that the greater number are to be found on the northern slopes of Mount Ida.

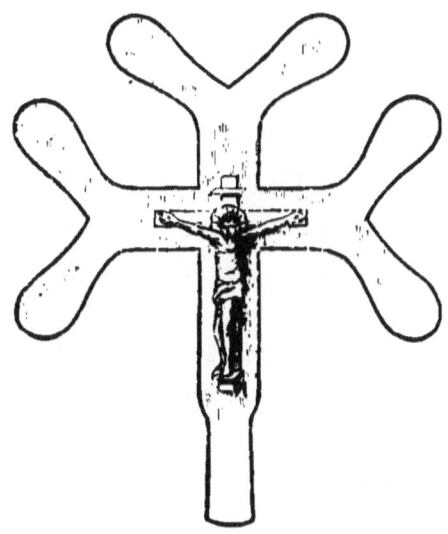

CRUCIFIX OF CHRYSOPEGI.

At Chrysopegi—which in its turn maintains that it is the original monastery, while Hagios Eleutherios is the dependency—we found in the church a handsome *iconostasis* or altar-screen of cypresswood, light in colour, which had been elaborately carved by a native artist in 1865. Behind this the crucifix was kept, and it was produced at our request. It is about eighteen inches high, of iron, flat, and hollow, in the shape of a Greek cross, with a round iron handle at the bottom to hold it by, while each of the other three limbs bifurcates at the end into two lobes. Attached to the face of this is a crucifix of silver gilt, somewhat less than half the height of the cross, with a crosspiece bearing the superscription INBI, only the upright of the B is prolonged downwards so as to form a tail. The left foot is attached by a single nail, but the other is left free: they rest on a *scabellum*, and round the loins is a waistcloth. Inside the cross there is something that rattles, and this is said to be a piece of the True Cross. One of the monks described to us the miracles it had wrought, especially at the time of the insurrection — stories like those which a predecessor of his had told to Pashley, of a monk having stood with it in his hand in the thick of a battle, when bullets were whizzing round him, while he remained unhurt. Notwithstanding this, they did not show it the profound veneration with which such relics are frequently treated in Greek monasteries, and I was allowed to make a drawing of it, which I hardly expected, for many Orientals have the greatest dislike to such a proceeding, because they consider that the possessor of the likeness retains some mysterious power over the original. The monk also said that three similar crosses exist in other parts of Crete, and that this one is supposed to have been a present from the Venetians: this however I doubt, for the history of such relics is seldom accurately known in the East, and Pashley was only informed that it was very ancient; besides which, it is singularly unlikely that members of the Greek Church should have accepted and preserved the symbol of a hostile creed. I have shown my drawing of it to my friends, Professor Westwood and Mr. St. John Tyrwhitt, who are well qualified to pronounce on its character; but they both say that it possesses so many unusual features as to make the question a very difficult one. In fact, they find it impossible to say anything confidently about its date; and yet, unless it is an early work, it cannot be genuinely Byzantine, for a Byzantine crucifix would not have been made except at an early period. The long-tailed B is probably for a minuscule Greek β and stands for βασιλεύς, which takes the place of the *Rex* of the Latin superscription: this is in favour of a Byzantine origin: but, on the other hand, the figure being unclothed is against a high antiquity. The shape is a natural one for an ancient metal cross, because it was easy to flatten and shape out the metal.

It was touching to find in the court of this monastery the graves of three English sailors who were buried here; they are covered with neat marble slabs, bearing inscriptions. The monks remarked to us that their burial-place was open to all. We had some difficulty in tearing ourselves away from the hospitality of these good Fathers, which was embarrassing to us, as we still had a long day's work before us. After passing over some rich

Suda Bay.

level ground we reached the bay of Suda, where the Turkish fleet, composed of a frigate and some smaller vessels, was lying. It is a perfect landlocked harbour, and the Turks have a project for converting it into a naval station; but the neighbourhood at present has a miserable look of desolation; the shores are marshy and unhealthy, the houses deserted, the country half-cultivated, and the people half-starved. At the mouth of the bay, towards the east, are two islands, called Leucae in ancient times, on the larger of which the town of Suda is now situated. The next point that we made for were the ruins formerly called Palaeocastro, but now better known in the neighbourhood as Aptera—a remarkable instance of antiquarian interest on the part of the natives, for Pashley was the first to identify them with that ancient city, and the point was not certainly determined until M. Wescher, of the French Government Mission, discovered an inscription which contained the name. We ascended by a rough path along the cliffs, where the pink blossoms of the wild pear tree were in great abundance, and the banks were starred with white cyclamen. As we mounted, we obtained fine views over the bay of Suda, with the Acroteri behind it, and the wide bay of Khanea stretching away to the west; on the opposite side rose the White Mountains, deeply covered with snow, all but the highest peaks of which were visible from time to time, when the heavy masses of cloud lifted. When we reached the site of Aptera, which is about 800 feet above the sea, we could also see to the south-west Mount Malaxa, the ancient Berecynthus, and to the east the commanding promontory of Drepanon, beyond which the eye ranged over a long line of coast, until at last the island of Dia, in the neighbourhood of the ancient Cnossus, appeared on the horizon. On very clear mornings, we were told, Santorin can occasionally be descried.

Independently of its elevated position, the situation of Aptera is a striking one, being a broad level, with steep sides falling away in every direction. At the highest point stands a little monastery, a dependency of the great convent of St. John the Theologos at Patmos; it is now occupied by one monk only, who lives there with his mother and one or two other persons. In the neighbourhood of this are the principal ruins, including a large Roman cistern with triple arches, and the wall of a building, probably a Prytaneium, on which are the inscriptions that Pashley and Wescher have copied. The monk recollected M. Wescher's having uncovered them, but they are now half-concealed again by a large straw-heap. One of these relates to honours conferred on Attalus, King of Pergamus, by the senate and people of Aptera: here the magistrates bear the title of *kosmoi*, and in the Doric dialect which is employed the place is called Aptara. There is also a decree in honour of Prusias, King of Bithynia, and several acts relating to their *proxenia* with various cities of Asia Minor, proving the

Ruins of Aptera.

extensive commercial relations of the city[1]. On the southern slope is an ancient theatre, very ill-preserved, and towards the west are the finest remains of the city walls; but these ruins have been much overrated, and, like all those in Crete, are disappointing to one already acquainted with the mainland of Greece. The shore below was regarded as the scene of the contest between the Muses and the Sirens, in which the latter being defeated lost the feathers of their wings, and when they had thus become white, cast themselves into the sea; whence the city was called Aptera, and the neighbouring islands Leucae. We may safely invert this last statement, and say that the whole legend is an etymological myth, originally suggested by the names.

Customs and superstitions. Descending from Aptera by a steep path on the sea side of the hill, we forded the river Khilias, and crossing an olive-clad hill, reached the town of Kalyves, the buildings of which skirt the shore, and are now in ruins. The district which reaches inland from this point is called Apocorona, and is very stony; on one of its highest ridges, nearly 1,000 feet above the sea, lies the village of Sultanieh, where we arrived after nightfall, and took up our abode in a house fragrant with the cypress wood of which it was built. Notwithstanding the animosity which prevails between the native Christians and Mahometans in Crete, our dragoman found it difficult to distinguish between them in these

[1] *Archives des Missions*, 2 Ser. vol. i. p. 441.

villages, as they use the same language, dress, and customs; the Mahometans, for instance, all drink wine. Formerly numerous intermarriages used to take place between persons of the two creeds; now, however, the people told us, these are of rare occurrence, and are discouraged by the authorities; and when a Christian becomes a Mahometan (Τοῦρκο), the Pasha sends him away to another part of Turkey. In time of war the Moslem villagers descend to the towns to join their co-religionists, and are employed as *bashi-bazouks*. I enquired about the Katakhanas, that being the peculiar name by which the Vampire is known in Crete and Rhodes, instead of the usual Vrykolakas; though the word is of some antiquity, being found in the mediaeval Greek poem of *A Lament on Constantinople* in the sense of 'a destroyer.' The answer was that such spectres were never seen there; but that after the end of the first insurrection, in Sphakia, where many persons were killed, such apparitions showed themselves, and the bodies of the dead were seen to move about over the face of the country. Another curious superstition which we found to prevail in Crete is the custom of regarding Tuesday as a *dies non*; the people have the same feeling against undertaking anything special on that day which English sailors have with regard to a Friday: this prevails also throughout the islands of the Aegean.

During this first day of our journey we had had occasional showers, but in the course of the night it set in to rain heavily, and continued to do so without

The northern coast.

intermission throughout the greater part of the following day (March 25); consequently, for many hours successively we were occupied in wading rather than riding, owing to the state of the road. We had heard the Pasha of Crete of that time spoken of as on the whole an enlightened man, but when we found that he was erecting a vast summer residence at Sultanieh, we could not help thinking that the money might be better spent in making roads and bridges, for the island suffers from nothing more than from want of proper means of communication. Descending to the valley of the Karydopotamo, we followed the banks of that river, until we reached the so-called Hellenic bridge, a high ivy-covered arch, the foundations of which may be of Roman work, but the arch itself is too steep to be of that date. We crossed this, and descended a valley filled with plane trees not yet in leaf, at the lower end of which was a sort of gorge, where the rocks at the sides were decorated with pendent fronds of polypody fern of extraordinary size. Close to this is the village of Armyro, where a large brackish fountain, which gives its name to the place[1], forms an extensive pool, the water from which turns some mills. On a neighbouring hillock stands a large square building, which may have been a Venetian fort. Shortly after this we reached the sea, and rode for several miles along a sandy beach, bright with pink shells, and intersected by numerous streams; on the land side rose the lofty mass of Mount Megaras, covered with

---

[1] Ἀρμυρό for ἁλμυρό.

newly-fallen snow. At the further end of this beach the deep rapid stream of a river called Petrais makes its exit from a gorge flanked by red limestone cliffs, and we found it so swollen by the rain as to render fording difficult; this, however, we accomplished by keeping close to the sea, though our baggage was in part submerged. Thence for some distance the path lay along the cliffs above the sea, and was as rough and bad a track as I have seen in any country. Behind us, the successive promontories of Drepanon and Acrotiri had now come into view.

At last we turn inland, and having crossed a stony upland, reach a Roman bridge with two rows of arches, in the same style as the Pont du Gard near Nismes, which spans a deep gully, and forms a picturesque object from the ochre colour of its stones, and the bushes by which it is surrounded. Immediately afterwards Retimo, the ancient Rhithymna, comes in sight. This is undoubtedly the most striking in its position of all the larger towns of Crete. It occupies a peninsula, joined to the land by a low sandy isthmus, across which runs the wall of the town, surmounted with flame-shaped battlements; within this lie the houses, which are interspersed at intervals with tall minarets, while between them and the sea rises a precipitous height, crowned by the extensive buildings of the castle. In the background of the view the lower part of Mount Ida was seen, ascending in gradual slopes, but the summits were concealed by the clouds. We arrived but just in time, for the gates are closed an hour and

Retimo.

a-half after sunset. Within, the place has all the picturesqueness of a Turkish town, being composed of irregular streets, lined with bazaars and wooden houses with projecting roofs and balconies. The port, which lies on the eastern side, is small, and inaccessible except in calm weather.

The Cretan dittany.

At Retimo we received a courteous welcome from Mr. Triphylli, a Greek gentleman to whom we had an introduction. He would hardly hear of our putting up at the khan, and entertained us at breakfast the next morning, when, among other things, he gave us some of what is considered the special Cretan dish— a mixture of cheese and honey. Both ingredients in this, as well as the combination itself, are excellent, the cheese being the soft cream cheese (*myzethra*), which is one of the best products of the island, and the honey being fragrant of herbs. When I enquired about the Cretan dittany, which was famous for its medicinal qualities in ancient times, he presented me with a parcel of the dried leaves and stems, as they are used by the people at the present day. A decoction of these is much esteemed in illness, especially in fevers. It is a low-growing herb, with a small woolly leaf, thus corresponding to the description of it given by Dioscorides[1]: by the natives it is sometimes called *erotas*, but more commonly *stamatochorton*. We hear of it in Virgil, where Venus employs it to heal Aeneas' wound:—

> Then Venus, all a mother's heart
> Touched by her son's unworthy smart,

[1] 3. 37, γναφαλώδη καί τινα ἐπίφυσιν ἔχοντα.

> Plucks dittany, a simple rare,
>   From Ida's summit brown,
> With flower of purple, bright and fair,
>   And leaf of softest down :
> Well known that plant to mountain goat,
>   Should arrow pierce its shaggy coat[1].

Theophrastus speaks of its medical efficacy, especially in childbirth, and describes it as a rare plant, owing to its growing over a small area, and to its being eaten by goats, which are very partial to it[2]. Both he and Pliny[3] mention its being peculiar to Crete, and tell the story that Virgil refers to, of the weapons falling out of the wounds when the goats eat of it. A few lines below the passage I have quoted the poet adds 'all the blood stanched in the wound;' an idea corresponding to this seems to have suggested the modern name, for *stamatochorton* signifies 'stanchplant.'

We now proposed to strike across the island towards the southern coast, and make the circuit of Mount Ida, the district in the neighbourhood of which was always in ancient times the centre of political activity. Accordingly, as the tracks in these parts were less well known than those which we had hitherto followed, we hired a guide, called Pandeli (*i.e.* Panteleēmon), who was recommended by Mr. Triphylli as well acquainted with the country, to accompany us for the remainder of our journey. During the night there had been a deluge of rain and a storm of wind, and though the weather cleared for

Route southward.

---

[1] Virg. *Aen.* 12. 412-415 (Conington's Trans.).
[2] *Hist. Plant.* 9. 18.   [3] *Hist. Nat.* 25. 8. 52.

a brief space in the course of the morning, yet when we started, a little after midday, it was raining steadily, and it continued to do so for the rest of the day. At first our route lay along the shore, on which the huge waves were plunging violently; but after a time we were forced to make a *detour* inland to reach a bridge over the river Platanios, which it was impossible to ford at the usual point. The meadows on the further side of this stream presented a spectacle of rare beauty from the anemones with which they were covered. For size, number, brilliancy, and variety of colour I have never seen such a show. Every tint was to be seen—crimson, rose pink, faint pink, purple, light mauve, and white. If, according to the ancient symbolism, these flowers represent the blood of Adonis and the tears of Aphrodite, both must have been abundantly shed here. The name for them in the country is *malakanthos*. At this point we turned southwards, and ascended gradually over one of the most fertile districts in the whole of Crete; on every side the slopes were covered with olive plantations, while the orange and the fig grew in the neighbourhood of the villages, and in the first of these that we reached—called Ardeli—we saw a fine palm-tree.

Disastrous condition of the country. It was here that we first began to realise how terrible had been the results of the last insurrection (1866-9). Every village that we passed through, and all that we could see along the hill-sides, had been plundered, gutted, and burnt; nothing but ruins met the eye; it was as if a horde of Tartars had swept over the face of the country. A few of these belonged to Mahometans, but the great majority were Christian; and on our arrival the miserable inhabitants—those, that is to say, who had not emigrated—emerged from the lower storey of their houses, which they had temporarily repaired, half-clothed and half-starved. To add to their misfortunes, for the last three years the olive crop, on which they mainly depend, had failed, and the great severity of the winter had reduced them to the last extremity. This state of things we subsequently found to prevail throughout the island; along our whole route not a single village was standing; and what distressed us most was to find that many of those who were in this lamentable condition were persons of some position and very fair education. Another thing, also, we gathered pretty plainly, viz. that they would rise in insurrection again when the next opportunity presented itself; and this was hardly to be wondered at, for they had nothing to lose, and could scarcely be in a worse plight than they were in at that time [1].

At the end of four hours of gradual ascent from Retimo, we reached the large village of Amnato, and turned round to take a last view of the town on its conspicuous peninsula, beyond which lay a wide expanse of the northern sea. All about here, and in many other places, the ground was strewn with branches of the olive-trees, which had been broken off

---

[1] Since this was written the condition of the people in Crete has improved, in consequence of more prosperous seasons and administrative changes. See below, p. 76.

by the weight of the snow that lay on them during the winter; this, however, we found to be rather a benefit than an injury to the trees, since it has in a rude way the effect of pruning, which is greatly neglected in Crete. From this point we descended towards a wide and deep gorge, along the steep side of which the path leads, and as it gradually contracts the scenery becomes fine, from the red limestone caverns, and the trees which fringe the bed of the stream. Near the head of this, where the valley is wildest, we cross it by a bridge, and mounting steeply, find ourselves on an exposed plateau where, near the edge of the ravine and fronted by a conspicuous group of stone pines, stands the monastery of Arkadi.

NOTE ON THE CRETAN DIALECT OF MODERN GREEK.

As we obtained a considerable amount of information about the modern Cretan dialect at Retimo, it may be worth while for me to introduce here a few remarks relating to it. When first we landed in the island, it seemed so different from any Greek we had heard, and the words appeared so clipped, that we almost despaired of understanding it, and our dragoman himself, who was familiar with most of the numerous Modern Greek dialects, declared with some dismay that he could not make out half of what the people said. Though in great measure these difficulties soon disappeared, yet the peculiarities of the language are very striking. As to the pronunciation, the most notable feature is the softening of κ and χ; the former being pronounced like *tch*, as προσκέφαλον, 'a pillow,' *prostchefalon*; the latter like *sh*, as βροχή, 'rain,' *vroshé*. In the vocabulary, the number of strange words which take the place of those in ordinary use is very great, as may be seen by the long list given in the late Lord Strangford's excellent essay on the subject in vol. i. of Spratt's *Travels in Crete*; some of the most important of these we verified, either through Mr. Triphylli, or by our own observation; but the most interesting are the ancient words or usages which, though lost elsewhere, have survived in this country. Thus, instead of the familiar λάσπαις, 'mud,' we always heard πηλά; for στέλνω (στέλλω), 'I send,' πέμπω, in the future form θὰ πέψω; for κρυώνω, 'I am cold,' ἐργῶ, which no doubt is by metathesis for ῥιγῶ, for the latter form is found in the dialect of Cyprus; for καταλαμβάνω, 'I understand,' κατέχω; for ἄλογον, 'a horse,' either κτῆμα (just as in classical Greek κτῆνος is used in the sense of a 'beast'), or πηγῆρι, which is the Turkish *begir*, 'horse.' Again, the lost τίθημι survives here in the future θὰ θέσω, 'I shall put,' for θὰ βάλω, and in the imperative θέσε, 'lie down,' for πλαγίαζε; πορίζω (πορεύομαι) means 'I start,' as in ἐπόρισα, 'I started,' for ἔφυγα; ἔτος, 'a year,' which in ordinary Modern Greek only survives in the salutation πολλὰ τὰ ἔτη σας, is commonly heard in place of χρόνιον. The salutation εὔβια, for 'good day' (pronounced *evvia*), was also new to us, together with the expression εὐβίβια (*evvivia*), for 'fine weather:' this is probably a corruption of the ancient εὐδία.

CHAPTER III.

CRETE (*continued*).

Monastery of Arkadi. THE convent of Arkadi, which was once regarded as the largest and richest in Crete, having an income of about £1000 a year, was at this time a mass of ruins. The siege of this place by the Turks, and the massacre that followed, from its tragic character, did more than anything else to attract the attention of Western Europe to the Cretan struggle. Only two of the survivors, a monk and a boy, were now residing within the walls; indeed, the rest of the Fathers perished at the time of the siege, and its present occupants had come from other monasteries. The Superior was a most ignorant man; his conversation consisted almost entirely in saying 'it drips, it drips' (στάζει, στάζει)—a remark that was suggested by the pitiless rain, which penetrated so constantly the patched-up roof of the room we occupied, that to avoid it we were frequently obliged to shift our position, and it even dropped on to our beds at night. At Retimo we had been told that the monastery had been rebuilt, and that we should find good accommodation; but the truth was that only two or three rooms were habitable, of which ours was the best. Throughout our tour in Crete we had to carry our provisions with us, for the natives could not supply us even with bread; wine, however, was to be had, and this was excellent. The buildings form a single quadrangle, in the middle of which stands the church; this had been repaired, as also in some measure had the western façade of the monastery; but neither of them shows any trace of Byzantine architecture, being in a debased Renaissance style, and the whole convent, at its best period, must have presented a striking contrast to the lordly structures of Mount Athos. A few tall cypresses in the court did their best to relieve the dismal desolation.

The following morning, at our request, the monk who had been present at the siege conducted us round the building and described to us the harrowing details. It took place on November 19, 1866. The Christians who defended it had assembled there some days before, and for greater safety had brought together the women, children, and old men from the neighbouring country within the walls. The Turks approached from the side of Retimo, and at first their commander offered the defenders terms of capitulation, but these were refused, because his soldiers were irregulars, and the Christians knew from experience that they would neither obey orders, nor suffer anyone to escape. A cannon, which the besiegers had dragged hither with some difficulty, was at first planted on a neighbouring height, but as it produced but little effect on the walls, and in the meantime the attacking

Description of the siege.

parties suffered greatly from the fire of the besieged, on the following day it was brought up in front of the monastery, so as to command the entrance gate, which they blew in. After a fearful struggle, they forced their way in at the point of the bayonet, and commenced an indiscriminate massacre, in which 300 souls perished. The court ran with blood, our informant said, and was so piled with bodies that it was impossible to pass from one side to the other. Simultaneously with this attack in front, another band of Turks made an assault from behind, where there was a postern; but close to it the powder magazine was situated, in a chamber over which numbers of monks and women and children were congregated together. As soon as the besiegers were close to the postern, the Christians set fire to the powder, and blew up all this part of the building, involving their friends and their enemies in common ruin. Large pieces of the shattered wall remain outside the new wall, and though most of the Turks were buried where they fell, yet the bones of others might be seen lying on the ground. In the midst of the massacre six-and-thirty Christians took refuge in the refectory, but they were pursued and all killed, and their blood still stained the walls. About sixty others collected together in a corridor, and begged for quarter, as having taken no part in the insurrection, and the lives of these were spared. The monastery was then fired, and many sick and helpless persons perished in the conflagration. The horrible narrative told by an eye-witness on the spot carried our thoughts back to the Suliotes and their destruction by Ali Pasha. It is fair, however, to remember that this same convent was the scene of a great massacre of Mahometans by Christians at the time of the first insurrection. Barbarity is the order of the day in Cretan warfare.

As we left Arkadi, all the inmates of the monastery had assembled at the gate to wish us 'God speed,' and we then pursued our journey southward over uncultivated heath-clad slopes, until in an hour's time we reached the central ridge, which forms the backbone of the island, and may be at this point about 2500 feet above the sea. At first, looking back, we obtained pretty views of the convent with the gorge by its side, between the cliffs of which the distant blue sea was seen as through a frame; and from the summit the Acroteri near Khanea unexpectedly appeared, delicately delineated on the horizon. On our left was one of the numerous forts which the Turks have constructed in commanding positions to keep the natives in check; there are said to be 290 of them in the island, but this is probably an exaggeration. The rain had now ceased, but the north wind swept over these uplands with intense bitterness. Descending on the opposite side, we struck into the best road we had seen in Crete, which leads from Retimo to the south coast, and not long after arrived at a wayside fountain, called 'The water of the stone' (τῆς πέτρας τὸ νερύ). Our guide Pandeli informed us (and his testimony was confirmed by a peasant who was passing at the time),

The central ridge.

that it is considered to have great efficacy in curing the disease of the stone, and that this is the origin of the name. Pashley says that in his time bottles of the water were exported for this purpose even as far as to Constantinople. We gradually came in sight of the south-west buttresses of Ida, which are far more precipitous than anything on the other side of the mountain; but of the summit we saw nothing more than tempting peeps of snow-peaks under the clouds. In the midst of a violent hailstorm we reached the monastery of Asomatos, or the Archangel, which is three hours distant from Arkadi, and lies in the midst of olive-groves, interspersed with numerous myrtle-bushes, in a wide rich valley deeply sunk among the mountains.

Convent of Asomatos. This convent was left uninjured during the last insurrection, though both the Turkish and Christian forces passed by this way. It is a very poor place, resembling those which we had seen on the sides of the Thessalian Olympus, and consists of a single quadrangle, surrounded by lower buildings than those of Arkadi, while stables and other irregular tenements are grouped on to it on the outside. Within are numerous fine orange-trees, on which the fruit was still hanging, and the church stands in the centre of the area. The *iconostasis* of this is finely carved and gilt, and from the roof hangs a glass chandelier, which from its appearance must have come from Venice. From a beam on one side of the court are suspended three Venetian bells, which are said to have been concealed, and only discovered in 1873; they are inscribed with the dates 1633 and 1639 respectively, and both are ornamented with figures in relief of our Lord on the cross, of the Virgin, and of St. John, while the smaller of the two has also a figure of a bishop, who the monks said was St. Spiridion. The constitution of this society is *idiorrhythmic*, or on the independent system, whereas Arkadi was a Coenobia; that is to say, it had a common table, stricter discipline, and a superior elected for life. Certainly, order was not predominant in the appearance of the monks of Asomatos, for they wore no distinctive dress, and only differed from common peasants in having their hair unshorn. The Hegumen, in particular, with his burly figure, black bushy beard, and bronzed countenance, would have made an excellent study for one of Ribera's bandits. We were entertained in a low-vaulted apartment, where a blazing fire and some of the wine of the monastery were very welcome; we found this liquor palatable, for in Crete, and in the islands generally, resin is not mixed with the wine, as it is on the mainland of Greece. We were told that no boars, or wolves, or bears, are found on Ida; according to the Cretan legend all the larger wild beasts were once for all expelled from the island by St. Paul: in ancient times the same beneficent action was attributed to Hercules. Game also is scarce; we saw nothing but a few ducks and partridges and a snipe during the whole of our journey.

We continued our route towards the south-east, *Apodulo.* until at last, in crossing one of the buttresses of Ida, we came in sight of the southern sea. Gradually the Bay of Messara opened out before us, with the headland of Matala beyond, to the eastward of which appeared a depression in the hills which border the coast, marking the site of the 'Fair Havens.' At the same time the red sunset tints, seen through a dip in the dark mountains to the west, gave cheering signs of a change in the weather. At nightfall we found ourselves at the village of Apodulo, on the mountain-side, and here we determined to pass the night. While our dragoman was enquiring for tolerable quarters for us among the ruined dwellings, we rested at the first cottage we came to, which consisted of one long ground-floor room blackened with smoke, with a clay floor and a large kitchen range, beds and a few other rude articles of furniture, while in one corner a sheep was tethered. Its occupants were three sisters, remarkably handsome girls, who were dressed as ordinary peasants, and were engaged in cooking and other domestic occupations, but from their acquaintance with a purer idiom of Greek than the native language were evidently superior to their present position. They were perfect Italian madonnas, having oval faces and oval eyes fringed with fine lashes and surmounted by arched and well-marked eyebrows, the upper lip short, and the nose well-cut and slightly aquiline. Besides an upper dress, they wore the usual dress of Cretan women, white trousers reaching nearly to the ankle, a short petticoat, and a handkerchief on the head. Shortly afterwards the mother entered, wearing a curious cape of woollen

A native family.

stuff, which hung from the head and covered the back and sides; and she again was followed by the old father, who carried a sort of crook, and looked a truly patriarchal old man. The parents only spoke the ordinary Cretan dialect. The Turks had destroyed all the property of this family during the insurrection, and this accounted for the reduced circumstances in which we found them living; but one of their relations, at all events, was on the road to fortune, and from his case we learnt how rapidly an intelligent Greek can make his way in the world. After a little conversation the old woman produced a large photograph, framed and glazed, representing a good-looking gentleman in a Frank dress; and this person we learnt was one of her sons, who had emigrated at the conclusion of the war, and now held an excellent mercantile appointment at Marseilles.

We were destined, however, to a more startling surprise. Great was our astonishment when we found that the old man's sister had married an English gentleman, and was still living in Scotland. It is a very curious history. At the time when Crete was under the dominion of Mehemet Ali, a boy and girl of the Psaraki family (for that is their name, though in Cretan it is pronounced Psaratch) were carried off with many others as slaves to Egypt. Mr. H—, who was then in that country, saw this female slave exposed for sale, and being struck with her beauty, bought her and married her. In the course of time the brother also obtained his freedom, and became a travelling servant (our dragoman was acquainted

A strange history.

with him, having met him on several occasions); and in that capacity he once accompanied his sister and her husband on a tour on the Nile. Subsequently the married couple returned to Crete, and established themselves at Apodulo. There Mr. H— built himself a house, which was made over to his wife, since he being a foreigner could not hold it in his own name, and at a later period, when they left the country and took up their residence in England, it passed into the hands of one of Mrs. H—'s brothers, the old patriarch with whom we were conversing. This dwelling was assigned to us as our abode for the night, and in its half-ruined state a most dismal habitation it was, for our room, which partook of the nature of a cellar, was fearfully damp, possessed no door, and was partly tenanted by rabbits, which seemed to have discovered the secret of perpetual motion. Of the other children of the Psaraki family, besides those whom I have mentioned, one son is the priest of the parish, while two boys live at home and attend the village school, where they get their education gratis, having only to provide their books.

The Demogerontia. These schools are regulated by the Demogerontia, an institution peculiar to the Cretan Christians, which consists of a representative council for a certain area of the country, under the presidency of the Bishop, and superintends the administration of certain properties, makes provision for widows and orphans, and directs education. It is now arranged that about a quarter of the revenues of all the monasteries shall be handed over to the Demogerontiae for the support of the schools. The Psaraki boys were quick children, and, like the girls, understood our Romaic much more readily than the parents did. The brother in Marseilles, Alexander, was anxious that one of them should come out to him to make his fortune, and the boy expressed himself ready to go, but his mother was unwilling to part with him.

The next morning (March 28) all our senses were delighted by a clear sky, a bright sun, and a fresh and gentle breeze. *The southern coast.* This weather continued during the rest of our stay in the island. The cloudless mountain summits gave us quite a new idea of the scenery, the most conspicuous being the pyramidal form of the snow-capped Kedros (6000 feet), which is the highest point that intervenes between Ida and the White Mountains. In a ploughed field in the neighbourhood of the village I found the rare and beautiful *Iris tuberosa* in flower, the greenish petals of which turn outwards with a purple lip; the gladiolus, which was growing plentifully along with it, was not yet in bud. As we continued our journey along the mountains, still towards the south-east, we obtained a distant view of the island of Gaudos, the Clauda, or rather Cauda[1], of the Acts of the Apostles, lying far away to the west. This now belongs to the Sphakiotes. Nearer to us lay an islet called Paximadi, i.e. 'Biscuit,' the name of which was evidently derived from its shape. Through a depression between Kedros and the heights that separate it from the sea,

[1] Clauda in the Authorised Version, Cauda in the Revised Version.

the White Mountains were visible, and displayed all the features of an Alpine chain; afterwards Psilorites (Ida) came in sight towards the north, presenting a vast mass of snow-fields[1]. At length, when the last range of hills was crossed, the level district of Messara, the richest in Crete, lay at our feet, reminding us of Marathon by its curving sandy shore, which fringes the soft blue water of the bay, while it is separated from the southern sea by a range of hills, beyond which lies the 'Fair Havens.'

Plain of Messara.
Descending to the low ground, where the temperature was really warm, we rode at first over irregular sloping ground, where the shepherd's horn, by which the sheep are called together, was heard in the midst of the solitudes, and thus arrived at the real plain, where orange-trees were growing in the half-ruined villages, and the plane-trees were budding near the watercourses. The range of Ida as seen from here,

[1] The relative heights of these mountains are referred to in the following little ballad, which is interesting also as a specimen of the dialect of the mountaineers of Sphakia. Observe the substitution of ρ for λ, as in ἄρρα for ἄλλα, μαρόνουσι for μαλόνουσι: ντ has the sound of the English *d*.

  Τρία βουνὰ μαρόνουσι κ' ἕνε νὰ σκοτωθοῦσι,
  τὸ Κέντρος καὶ τὸ Σφακιανὸ κι' αὐτὸν τὸ Ψηρορίτη.
  κ' ἐμπέψενε τὸ Σφακιανὸ γραφὴν τοῦ Ψηρορίτη·
  'Κάτσετ' ἐσεῖς τ' ἄρρα βουνά, 's ἐμένα μὴν παινᾶστε,
  μὰ σὰν ἐμένα τὸ βουνὸ ἄρρο βουνὸ δὲν ἕνε.'
      Jeannaraki, *Kreta's Volkslieder*, No. 101.

'Three mountains have a rivalry, they come near to slaying one another,—Kedros, and he of Sphakia, and the third, Psilorites:—and he of Sphakia to Psilorites a missive sent—"Abase yourselves, ye other mountains, plume not yourselves in comparison of me—like my mountain there is no other mountain."'

though bright with glistening snows, is not in other respects striking, as its level line is only broken by one conspicuous saddle in the ridge. The plain, which extends far inland by a gradual ascent towards the east, backed by the distant Dictaean mountains, is covered at the sides by olive-groves, while the rest was at this time a sea of green corn, since the entire expanse is unbroken by hedge-rows. On account of its great fertility this region has been appropriated by the Turks, and for the same reason in time of war it is the first object of attack to the Sphakiote mountaineers. In most parts of the island the land is in the hands of the peasants, and where the properties are large the *metayer* system prevails, and the cultivator receives half the produce. At a place called Mires, where we made our mid-day halt in great enjoyment under the shade of the olives, a Kaimakam resides, and we saw a group of Turks watching the paces of one of the spirited little horses which are bred here. It was for sale, and £60 was the price asked for it. At an hour's distance from this we reached the village of Metropoli, where we crossed a copious stream, descending from Ida to join the main river that intersects the plain, the ancient Lethaeus, and half-an-hour further we alighted at another village called Hagius Deka (Ἁγίους Δέκα), from ten saints who were martyred there in the Decian persecution. Between the two villages, at the foot of the buttresses of Ida, and on the edge of the plain, about ten miles from the sea, was situated the ancient Gortyna.

Captain George.

As both Pashley and Spratt mention in their Travels in Crete a certain Captain Elias as an important man at Hagius Deka, we enquired for his house, but we were informed that he had now been dead two years, and had been succeeded by his son, Captain George. The fine old man, of whom every one spoke in terms of praise, had gone through all the fighting of the late war, though eighty years of age, but did not long survive its close. The use of the title of Captain, which is frequently found among the Christians in Crete, is a curious concession by the rulers to the *amour propre* of the natives, for it is assumed in times of insurrection by the leaders of revolutionary bands, and is subsequently recognised officially, as a compliment, by the authorities. Captain George, a middle-aged man, with strongly-marked features, but a more careworn face even than the majority of the suffering Cretans, received us kindly into his house, which had been completely ruined, but was now roofed in at the top, though there was no floor to divide the upper storey from the ground-room. He was evidently in great poverty, but, like many others whom we met with, looked superior to his present condition. In the courtyard in front of the house were numerous fragments of white marble, and near the entrance was a piece of a column, and a sarcophagus with bulls' heads and wreaths of flowers of inferior workmanship, which was used as a trough.

Ruins of Gortyna.

The ruins of Gortyna cover a large extent of ground, but none of them are either anterior to the

Roman period, or in good preservation. The city was divided in two parts by the stream already mentioned, which takes its name, 'the Torrent of Metropolis' (τῆς Μητροπόλεως τὸ φαράγγι), from the neighbouring village: on an eminence on the further side of this was situated the acropolis, while below it, excavated in the hillside, was the theatre, which is now an almost shapeless mass of rubbish. Opposite to this, on the left bank,stood the church of St. Titus, a building of massive stone, the principal remaining part of which is a double apse; from the appearance of the arches there must originally have been three apses, and the central one has three semi-cupolas. It is certainly very ancient, and, according to some archaeologists, cannot have been built later than the fourth or fifth century. At all events, it has the interest of association, for, as Gortyna was the Roman capital of the island, and contained an old-established colony of Jews[1], there is every reason to believe that it must have been the headquarters of Titus's ministrations. He is now the patron saint of Crete. The tradition of an ancient bishopric having existed on this spot is preserved to the present day in the name Metropolis. The remaining buildings, which lie dispersed over the fields, are entirely of brick and rubble; one that we saw was circular, another rectangular; the largest is the amphitheatre, situated in the neighbourhood of Hagius Deka, of which not

Church of St. Titus.

---

[1] See 1 Macc. xv. 23.

much more than the foundations and the shape remain[1].

A labyrinth. Our object now was to recross the island on the eastern side of Mount Ida to the town of Megalocastron, or Candia, on the northern coast; but before doing so we determined to make a *détour* to visit a place which is known in all the neighbouring district by the name of 'the Labyrinth' (ὁ Λαβύρινθος). Our host, Captain George, undertook to be our guide; and accordingly the next morning (March 29) we started in his company, and fording the stream close under the acropolis of Gortyna, ascended the hills towards the north-west, and in an hour's time reached the place which bears that name. It is entered by an aperture of no great size in the mountain side, where the rocks are of clayey limestone, forming horizontal layers; and inside we found what looks almost like a flat roof, while chambers and passages run off from the entrance in various directions. The appearance at first sight is that of artificial construction, but more probably it is entirely natural, though some persons think it has served for a quarry. We were furnished each with a taper, and descended by a passage, on both sides of which the fallen stones had been piled up; the roof above us varied from four to sixteen feet in height. Winding about, we came to an upright

---

[1] For an account of the wonderful archaic inscription which was discovered on the site of Gortyna in 1884, the reader may be referred to Mr. Roberts's interesting paper in the *Classical Review*, vol. ii. pp. 9 12.

stone, the work of a modern Ariadne, set there to show the way, for at intervals other passages branched off from the main one, and any one who entered without a light would be hopelessly lost. Captain George described to us how for three years during the late war (1867-9) the Christian inhabitants of the neighbouring villages, to the number of 500, and he among them, had lived here, as their predecessors had done during the former insurrection, to escape the Turks, who had burned their homes, and carried off their flocks and herds, and all other property that they could lay their hands on. He pointed out to us the places where the stones were piled up so as to form chambers, each of which was occupied by a family. When I enquired, half in joke, where their refectory (τράπεζα) was, he replied that far, far within there was a large and lofty central hall, capable of holding 500 people together, to which they gave that name, and that there they used to meet from time to time, and dance, sing, and enjoy themselves. They had brought a provision of bread to eat and oil for light; and water they obtained from a spring in the innermost part of the cavern, which appears to be the only one, for we saw no stalactites or dripping water in other parts. The heat, he said, was often very great, owing to the confined air and the number of persons. After wandering in different directions for half an hour, during which time we had not penetrated into onetenth of its ramifications, we returned to the open air.

A refuge in war-time.

Not the original labyrinth.

Notwithstanding the modern name, and the opinion of some scholars in favour of this place, there is no reason for supposing that this was the original Cretan labyrinth. That place was in all probability a mythical conception, like the stories attached to it, though, like many other Greek legends, it may have been attached to some geographical feature, such as a cavern; but all Greek writers localise the story at Cnossus, besides which the coins of that city, of which I obtained two in the island, bear as their emblem an idealised representation of the Labyrinth. Claudian indeed speaks of 'the *Gortynian* abode of the Minotaur[1],' by which epithet perhaps he simply means 'Cretan;' but it is quite conceivable that when Gortyna became the rival of Cnossus, the inhabitants borrowed the legend, and adopted this place as their labyrinth from its singular correspondence to the traditional idea, and that hence the legend became naturalised here.

Eastern side of Ida.

Ascending the hillside, we crossed a plateau, the ground beneath which is mined by the Labyrinth, and at one point Captain George pointed out to us the position of the refectory underground. Higher up we obtained a view of all the snowy mountains of Crete together, comprising the Dictaean mountains, Ida, Kedros, and the White Mountains. I have mentioned that Ida is now called Psilorites; the original name, however, still survives in Nida (τὴν Ἴδην), as a small elevated plain is called which is deeply sunk amid the higher summits. The Captain

---

[1] 'Semiferi Gortynia tecta juvenci:' *Sext. Cons. Hon.* 634.

now parted from us, and we continued to mount over stony barren mountains and clayey valleys, in which a few oleanders were growing, until we took leave of the southern sea, and once more crossed the ridge of the island, near which is the small village of Hagia Barbara. The road which descends from hence to Hagios Thomas is excessively bad, in addition to which our guide lost his way. We observed here what had struck us also on the west side of Ida, that the tracks in the northern part of Crete are far worse than those to the south, probably owing to the greater amount of soft soil. This renders travelling a difficult matter during or after bad weather: on our journey to Arkadi our baggage-horse once sank into the mud, and was with difficulty extricated, and on this occasion nothing but extraordinary surefootedness prevented it from falling. The absence of all traffic and communication, here and everywhere, was painfully remarkable.

Hagios Thomas occupies an elevated position just below a plateau of soft limestone rock of a light grey colour, which falls to the village in precipices of 40 or 50 feet high. Here huge blocks have fallen away from the face of the cliff, and lie detached close beneath. In several of these, and also in the rock itself, very curious ancient tombs have been excavated, which reminded my companion of those of Petra, and are more akin to the Lycian sepulchres than to anything that is found in Greece Proper. One block has three of these in various parts of it, and the effect they produce is strange, from their

Rock-hewn tombs.

lying out of the perpendicular. They are all of the same shape, being entered by a small square-headed doorway, and are square within, with arched recesses surmounted by niches on three sides; the floor is also hollowed out in parts into shallow chambers. Nothing is known as to the ancient city that occupied this site, but, whatever its name, it was probably Roman, for only Roman coins were brought to me by the people of the village, one of them being a coin of the Emperor Gordian.

Mount Iuktas.

Descending again from this place by an intricate path, and passing at intervals through groves of chestnuts not yet in leaf, about nightfall we arrived at Venerato, a name which sounds as if it dated from Venetian times. On the way we obtained fine views of Mount Iuktas, which seems to have been regarded as the burial-place of Zeus, for the neighbouring villagers, hardly otherwise than through an ancient tradition, give the name of 'the Sepulchre of Zeus' (τοῦ Διὸς τὸ μνημεῖον) to a ruin on its crest, and there is ample evidence that a reputed tomb of the god was shown in Crete even later than the time of Constantine[1]. The mountain rises to the

---

[1] See Pashley's *Travels in Crete*, vol. i. p. 213, where evidence is given to show that this place has been believed in the island, at least for several centuries, to be the reputed sepulchre of Zeus. While on this subject I may draw attention to the important discovery by M. Fabricius of the Ἰδαῖον ἄντρον, or cave in Mount Ida, where Zeus was said to have been tended by the nymphs and Curetes. This cavern is situated near the upland plain of Nida, mentioned above, which is between 4000 and 5000 feet above the sea. No inscription has been discovered by which it

height of 2,700 feet, on the opposite side of a wide and deep valley towards the east, and bears on its summit a white chapel of St. John the Baptist, while the village of Kháni Castélli lies at its base. To the north the sea appeared, with the island of Dia. The village of Venerato, which is situated in a commanding position on the edge of a cliff overhanging a gorge, was in a more pitiable state of ruin than almost any we had seen. The miserable room in which we passed the night was covered with mould, and anything but rain-proof. This place was the scene of a horrible massacre at the commencement of the Greek War of Independence in 1821, when the Moslems, with the intention of intimidating the Christian population, issued from the neighbouring town of Megalo-castron, and killed all the males whom they found in this and the surrounding villages.

The next morning we descended to Megalo-castron in four hours, having timed our journey well, for not long after our arrival the smoke of the steamer by which we were to depart was in sight on the horizon. In all these parts Megalo-castron is familiarly known as The Castron, a name which in Albania we had found to be given to Argyro-castron; and similarly throughout the Aegean and

Megalo-castron or Candia.

can certainly be identified, but the position in all respects corresponds to what is said of the Ἰδαῖον ἄντρον by Diodorus, Theophrastus, and Plato, and the objects found there show that it was an important sanctuary. See *Athenische Mittheilungen*, vol. x. pp. 59-72.

in European Turkey Constantinople is spoken of as The City (ἡ πόλις). A few persons of the upper class prefer to call it Heracleion, using the name of the ancient city which occupied the site. This was the port of Cnossus, and the ruins of that ancient capital—if so they can be called, for nothing but a single wall remains—are to be seen at an hour's distance to the south, in a position remarkable neither for strength nor beauty. This last remark applies also to the two other principal Cretan cities, Cydonia and Gortyna. As to the name of Candia, by which Megalo-castron is better known in Western Europe—it is never heard now in Crete, and as a name for the island it never was used at all. Though it was commonly employed by the Venetians for the city, it is not of Italian but of Arabic origin, for it was given to the place by the Saracens, when they conquered Crete in the ninth century, and constructed a fortified camp here, surrounded by an immense moat (*khandak*). The fame of the place in history mainly depends on its gallant defence against the Turks by the Venetians under Morosini, which ended in a capitulation in 1669. It is still surrounded by the massive Venetian walls, and in approaching from the land side a deep moat has to be crossed, and a winding passage traversed, before the gateway is reached.

Outside the gateway a number of lepers were seated on the ground to beg for alms. This disease is a terrible scourge in parts of Crete, and since it is regarded as contagious, as soon as the first sign of it appears on the body, the unfortunate patient is excluded from the towns. Consequently, there is a lepers' village near Megalo-castron, and we passed a similar one not far from the gates of Retimo. The leprosy affects especially the hands and feet, the nose and eyes: one woman, who came close to me to beg, had her hand sadly disfigured, and a painful look about the eyes. Within the walls everything presented the appearance of an ordinary Turkish town. All the women were veiled, but this did not necessarily imply that they were Mahometans, for here, as in one or two other towns in Turkey, the Christian women have adopted the Moslem costume. It is a large place, containing from 15,000 to 18,000 inhabitants, but the buildings are poor and straggling. The port, which is enclosed, like that of Khanea, by Venetian moles, lies on the eastern side, and faces east, like the port of Retimo. Over a tower, which commands its entrance from the sea, the lion of St. Mark may be seen in two places, and on the land side, partly entire, and partly in ruins, stand the lofty arched roofs of the docks or sheds that were used for the Venetian galleys. During the few hours of our stay we were kindly entertained by our Vice-Consul, Mr. Lysimachus Calocherino, a man of great information about the country, and reputed to be the wealthiest man in Crete, his father having made much money in the island. Like Mr. Triphylli, of Retimo, he came originally from Cerigo. From him I learnt that parts of the poem of *Erotocritos*, the most famous work that has been written in the Cretan dialect, are still sung by the peasants, but mainly in the eastern districts, of which its author, Cornaros, was a native. He estimated the entire population of Crete as from 280,000 to 300,000 souls.

Return to Syra.

As we quitted Megalo-castron, it presented an imposing appearance from the sea, with its minarets and walls, backed by the striking ridge of Mount Iuktas, which is here seen in profile. After nightfall, as we passed along the shore, the views of Mount Ida were fine in the brilliant moonlight, and in the morning we found ourselves once more off Khanea, from which place the White Mountains were seen superbly clear, with shapes more sharply cut and bolder outlines than those of any other of the Cretan ranges. We had time to land and visit the Venetian docks, which resemble those of Megalo-castron, and have a place for drawing up the galleys; after which we walked round the eastern portion of the walls outside, where the breach was pointed out to us which had been made at the time of the siege by the Turkish cannon. After a visit to the Consul, Mr. Sandwith, and our other friends, we embarked again, and arrived the next morning at Syra.

General remarks.

A journey in Crete, such as I have described, leaves a profoundly melancholy impression on the mind. Everywhere there was poverty, which in some cases bordered on destitution. It was painful even to feel that we ourselves had enough to eat, when others had so little; and, if we had any compassion to spare from human beings, the poor starved dogs were indeed a spectacle to move it. We were assured, indeed, by Mr. Sandwith, who had done everything in his power to alleviate the distress, that we saw it at its very worst, and that there was a prospect of a good harvest, which would mitigate the suffering. The evil, however, appeared to be too deeply seated for it to be remediable by any temporary influences. We found a widespread feeling to prevail among the people, that before ten years were over they would be again in insurrection, and for this reason they did not care to repair their dwellings. Now those who know the Cretans best affirm that, when unmolested, they are a quiet, peace-loving people, and certainly all that we saw tended to confirm this. The bad reputation of their forefathers for being 'liars, evil beasts, &c.,' does not apply to the present population, and we were much struck by the few complaints we heard, and the absence of begging. The bearing of the people generally in these hard times was most manly. It must have required a large amount of misrule, neglect, and oppression to bring such a people to such a condition. All the necessaries of life, except wine, were excessively dear, and notwithstanding the fertility of the soil, the corn that was grown did not suffice for the consumption of the island. The tithe was the only regular impost, but the manner in which this was farmed greatly increased its oppressiveness. Great injury had lately been done by the introduction of a debased coinage, first by the government, and subsequently by merchants, in consequence of which the people were unwilling to receive the money. But causes such as these would have been inadequate to produce such deep-seated alienation, apart from the wholesale barbarities perpetrated by Omer Pasha's troops, which, were they not thoroughly well attested, would be quite incredible.[1]

Appearance of the Cretans.

The Cretans are usually about or a little above the middle height, though some are very tall and well-grown men. With few exceptions, they have dark hair and eyes, oval faces with rather a pointed chin, full cheeks, and noses somewhat aquiline and sometimes even hooked: the expression is generally good-humoured and intelligent. The men's dress is different from what is found elsewhere in Greece and Turkey, consisting of a long boot reaching above the calf, blue baggy trousers gathered in at the knee, a red sash, a white shirt, a blue waistcoat corresponding to the trousers, and a jacket; over this is worn a

---

[1] See M. Perrot's account in the *Revue des Deux Mondes*, vol. lxxiv. p. 896. There is no question about the facts, which called forth loud protests from the English, French, Russian, and Austrian consuls. Though the condition of Crete at the present time can hardly be called satisfactory—while these pages are passing through the press, it seems as if the old system of persecution was being renewed—yet a great improvement has taken place since the period of my visit. The fresh rising which I then anticipated took place in 1878, and after that it was arranged that the governor of the island should always be a Christian, and the constitution, which had been granted ten years before, was allowed to become a reality, and was improved and extended in various ways so as to admit a large amount of self-government. This system has, on the whole, worked well.

short capote, usually white, with a hood to cover the head, though sometimes a skull-cap is seen. Of these articles of dress, the boots and cloak seem to have come down from classical times, the former being mentioned by Galen, who thinks their use was suggested by the ruggedness of the Cretan mountains[1], the latter by Aristophanes, who calls it the *Kreticon*[2]. To classical students the interest of the island consists, not in any important historical events of which it was the scene, but in the peculiarity of its institutions, and in its having been the principal stepping-stone by which Phoenician civilisation passed into Greece.

[1] Galen, vol. xviii. Pt. 1, p. 682, ed. Kühn.
[2] Ar. *Thesm.* 730.

CHAPTER IV.

Naxos, Ios, and Sikinos.

Naxos. WE were now (April 2) about to enter on the third portion of our expedition, that is, to visit the southern Cyclades, and the neighbouring Sporades. Accordingly, having hired a tolerably large and partly decked boat, which could safely make the voyage to the outlying islands, with three sailors to manage her, we started in most lovely weather, a continuance of which our boatmen augured from the porpoises (δελφῖνες) which were playing about us. It was a dreamy, hazy day, and for some hours, during which we were becalmed and had to use our oars, the heat was great; but late in the afternoon a fresh breeze sprang up, and sped us on our way towards Naxos. As we approached the northern extremity of Paros, a long line of mountains rose in front of us from the water, while the main chain of that island lay behind; in one part the coastline retires, and forms the deep and safe harbour of Naussa, about which there is sloping ground, and a town appeared in its recesses. In ancient times this was a 'closed' harbour, the entrance having been defended by chains or other barriers. The town of Naxos, which lies on the north-western shore of the island of the same name, was visible for some time before we reached it, but the object towards which we were directed to steer was a conspicuous monastery of St. John Chrysostom on the hillside above. In the central chain of the island two peaks, both over 3000 feet, especially attracted the eye—towards the north that of Coronon, and in the centre that of Zia, both which names, like many others in this island, have an ancient sound; possibly the latter may be a corruption of Dia, one of the classical names of Naxos. A youth in the town the next day, with a touch of pedantry which is not uncommon among Greeks, called it to me 'the mountain of Zeus' (τὸ βουνὺ τοῦ Διός).

We landed first on the island of Palati, which is separated from the mainland by a channel about fifty yards wide, having been formerly joined to it by a mole, of which only parts now remain, as it has been broken by the sea. At the highest point of this little island, which rises gradually toward the open sea, where it falls in precipices, are the remains of a temple, supposed to have been dedicated to Dionysus, who was the patron god of Naxos. Some steps at the entrance of the temple have been excavated, and at the opposite end there are drums of white marble columns, the marble not being of the purest kind—not Parian, that is to say, but such as is still found in Naxos itself. But what makes the ruins remarkable is the portico, which stands erect, and is a very conspicuous object. The monolithic piers are from twenty to twenty-five feet high, and the entablature

Island of Palati.

which they support has two large bosses projecting from it; these three stones stand alone, everything else having fallen. From the idea that they formed part of a palace, the island is called Palati. The view of the town is picturesque, as seen through this stiff frame, and the white marble is beautifully contrasted with the blue of the sky.

Associations of Dionysus.
In front of the little port stands an ancient mole, corresponding to that which reaches to the island, and between this and the shore the water was so shallow that we had some difficulty in making our way through it. When at last we landed we were surrounded by an inquisitive multitude, who crowded about us with a rudeness very unusual among Greeks, and to escape them we made our way round the outside of the town, but some followed us far into the country. On our return we asked for the fountain of Ariadne, and were shown a remarkable source at the back of the town, covered in with a large erection of masonry. In the flat roof of this are two openings with marble about their mouths through which buckets can be let down, and the extensive pool formed by the water may be seen some distance below. All the antiquities here are associated with Dionysus, and even the wine is called after him; this is white, and agreeable to the taste, though slightly resined.

Duchy of the Archipelago.
The town of Naxos, though unimposing in its appearance, has an especial interest as having once been the headquarters of Italian influence in the Aegean. After the conquest of Constantinople at the time of the fourth Crusade, the Venetians found it convenient

to allow individual nobles of their own body to hold certain parts of the Eastern territory that fell to them, as fiefs of the Republic. In some such relation, though very undefined, to Venice, Mark Sanudo held the office of Duke of the Archipelago or of Naxos, having been invested with it by the Latin Emperor of Constantinople. He rebuilt the ancient town of Naxos, constructed the mole, and erected a tower in the citadel; then, having confined the city to the Latins, he obtained a bishop from the Pope, and built a cathedral. The government continued in his family, and in that of Crispo, which was related to it, until 1566, when this duchy was finally brought to an end by the Turks, after having existed 360 years. Though the Dukes were in reality independent, they were always supported by Venice for the sake of commercial influence. Their occupation was a great curse to the natives. At the time when the duchy was established, these islands were in a prosperous condition; but by the Venetian monopoly of trade, the seizure of lands by the conquerors, and other forms of oppression, they were gradually ruined. We are apt to be dazzled by the splendour of Venice, and occasionally roused to admiration by the grandeur of her policy; but her treatment of her dependencies was systematically selfish, and her influence in the East has been second only to that of the Turks in its injurious effects.

The following morning we made our way towards the upper town through steep and tortuous streets; and, passing through a gateway, entered the Venetian

The city of Sanudo.

Castro, the original city of Sanudo. This forcibly reminded me of the small Italian towns of the Riviera; in some places the projecting buildings almost met above one's head, and it would have been literally possible to shake hands across the street; in other places the way for some distance was arched over. We saw numerous pieces of Hellenic marble, and over one house a fine coat of arms was carved, which, as we were informed, was that of the Barocci family. The inhabitants of this quarter, though they speak Greek and consider themselves Greeks, are of the Latin Church, and of Italian extraction, being descendants of the original occupants. One family is that of Sommaripa, whose ancestors for a long period were the rulers of Paros. Historic names are not uncommon in these regions; two days before, in the Roman Catholic quarter of Syra, I asked a youth to lend me the rattle with which according to custom (for it was Holy Week) he was expressing his aversion to Judas Iscariot, and on it I found his name inscribed—Manuel Palaeologos. The rattle which I have mentioned is itself an instrument of Italian origin, as most persons will be aware who have passed the week before Easter on the Riviera, when the streets are filled with its detestable sound, which is supposed to represent the rattling of Judas' bones. The people whom we met looked superior to any whom we had seen elsewhere in the islands, especially the ladies, who wore black gauze veils. The boys, too, were good-looking; and their pale complexions and light hair and eyes rendered them

Historic family names.

a great contrast to the Greeks. There is a Lazarist and a Capuchin church here, and the Archbishop is not a native, but is sent from Rome. The highest point of the town is occupied by a heap of ruins, where a fort—probably that of Sanudo—seems to have stood; from this the view was fine over Myconos, Delos, Rheneia, Tenos, and Syra to the north; Paros to the west; and Sikinos and Ios to the south; while in front, the portal of the temple of Dionysus on its island formed a conspicuous object. Herodotus must have been thinking of some such panorama as this, when, with his usual keen observation of geographical features, he compared the islands of the Aegean to the Nile in inundation, at which time the cities alone are seen above the surface of the water[1].

We started again on our southward course with a favouring north wind, which carried us rapidly over the blue water through the channel which separates Naxos and Paros. This was the scene of an engagement between the Athenian fleet under Chabrias and the Lacedaemonians in B.C. 376, when for the first time after the Peloponnesian war, the Athenians won a great maritime victory, and regained the mastery of the sea. Naxos shows to greatest advantage in the morning light, for then the separate ranges of the interior are brought out distinctly, and all the rich land along the levels and hillsides is seen. It is not a mere rocky ridge, like Tenos, for we could see deep valleys running inwards, and giving evidence of fertile districts between the moun-

Channel between Naxos and Paros.

---

[1] Herod. 2. 97.

tains on the coast and the higher peaks behind. In ancient times it was regarded as the most opulent of all the islands[1], and at the present day it is very prosperous. The emery, which was already famous in Pindar's time[2], is still its principal export. Tournefort, writing nearly two centuries ago, describes its abundance by saying, 'the English often ballast their ships with it.' On the opposite side of the strait we passed the town of Marmara, near the shore of Paros, the highest point of which island, Mount Marpessa, the seat of the famous marble quarries, rose above.

Greek sailors.

Greek sailors are usually an interesting study, and our present crew were no exception to the rule. Our head man, Captain Constantine—for this title he bore in our boat's papers, which were inspected at every island—was a strange being. A Silenus in figure, for his punchy frame was nearly as broad as it was long; a Cyclops in face, for he was one-eyed and very ugly; distinguished rather for grasping and cunning than for virtue; he nevertheless was good at his oar, an excellent sailor in an emergency, and thoroughly well acquainted with the winds of the Aegean and the shores and harbours of the islands. 'Plenty of sail, plenty of way' (πολλὰ πανιὰ, πολὺς δρόμος) was his answer, when his companions remonstrated at the amount of canvas we were carrying. His views of the medical faculty were worthy of Molière—'When I go to the doctor, I get ill; as long as I keep away, I am well: when I eat much, I am well; when little, I am ill.' The second, Yanni (Jack), whom we surnamed 'the

---

[1] Herod. 5. 28.   [2] Ναξία πέτρα, *Isthm.* 5. 107.

Conspirator,' was a handsome man, with soft eyes and a thoughtful expression, but silent, and gifted with a will of his own, so that, whenever a difference arose between us and them about starting or stopping or changing our course, he was always the least disposed to yield. The third, George, who had accompanied us also on our expedition to Delos, was a capital good-humoured hard-working lad, whose complexion and hair betokened some negro blood. They strongly resembled the old Greek sailors in their vivacity, talkativeness, readiness in action, freedom in giving an opinion, and indisposition to obey any one leader[1].

When we emerge from the channel between Naxos and Paros, we see on our left Heracleia and several other small islands; to the south-east Anaphe lies like a shadow on the horizon; Nio (Ios) and Sikino are comparatively near in front; and to the right appear Pholegandro, Siphno, Antiparo, and others less important. Again, as we enter the strait that separates Nio from Sikino, the twin peaks of Melo are faintly visible in the far west, and at last Therasia and Santorin, the southernmost of all, complete the

The southern islands.

---

[1] Many of the nautical terms of the Greek sailors are from the Italian, as λάσκα 'let go' (*lascia*), τιμόνι 'rudder' (*timone*), κουβέρτα 'deck' (*coperta*), καραντί 'rolling' (*caratare* 'to balance'), φουρτοῦνα 'a storm' (*fortuna*). Others, like sailors' terms everywhere, are hard to explain. In particular, the words for 'easy' (ἔα μόλα) and 'hard' (ἔα λέσα) are very difficult of derivation: that ἔα μόλα is εἶα μάλα, as some have suggested, is impossible, and in the passage quoted from Aristophanes (*Pax*, 460), where those words are used in hauling a rope, they clearly mean 'pull hard.' Λέσα is used for 'a rope' in Constantine Porphyrogenitus.

number. We were more and more struck by the size of the islands, and their apparent distance from one another. We are now entering the Sporades, though from the vague way in which the term Cyclades was used, these outliers are sometimes included in that group. A few generations ago Heracleia was commonly called Raclia, Anaphe Naphio, and Naxos Axia, and this last form we ourselves heard used on Tenos; we observed, however, that our sailors regularly employed the correct forms. It seems almost a parallel to the prefixing and omission of the *h* in English, when we find *n* prefixed in Nio, as in many other modern Greek names, but omitted in Axia. As this word, however, signifies 'the Worthy,' it is probably an instance of the fondness of the Greeks for changing the form of a name so as to give it an intelligible meaning.

The appearance of Ios is very rugged, as seen from the sea; but when we turned into the land-locked harbour on the west coast, passing a small lighthouse at the entrance, a smiling view awaited us, for the sloping hillsides are formed into terraces, the vegetation of which was forward, owing to their western aspect. The picturesqueness of the little bay is increased by a handsome church of St. Irene, which stands on a rock above the shore, having a Byzantine cupola and an Italian bell-tower with tiers of arches —a style of building which seems to prevail in these parts: at the landing-place there a few houses, but the town is built high above, and is reached by a steep ascent of half-a-mile. We took up our quarters at the port, and then ascended to the town, where there are a few good-looking houses, while the rest are huddled together in the same way as at Naxos. The numerous small palm-trees that we saw there remind us that the island was once called Phoenice, and that the palm was inscribed on its coins; but, as a matter of fact, this tree will grow wherever it is cultivated in the Cyclades.

It is well known that in ancient times Ios claimed to be the burial-place of Homer, and in modern days the question of the discovery of his sepulchre has raised a warm controversy. The story, which is a most curious one, can only be briefly alluded to here. In the year 1771, when the Aegean islands were in the hands of the Russians, Count Pasch van Krienen, a Dutch nobleman in the employ of that power, who afterwards wrote a book entitled *Breve descrizione dell' Arcipelago*, containing much valuable information about the state of these countries at that period, professed to have found the tomb at a place called Placoto, on the north-eastern side of this island. The discovery was the result of a month spent in excavation, and the account of it is embellished with semi-mythical details of a sitting figure being seen within the tomb at the moment of opening, which immediately crumbled to dust. To this is added minute information relating to the objects found there, and copies of inscriptions which identified the spot. The professed discovery naturally aroused great interest at the moment, and its reality was much debated by Heyne and others, but the contro-

Pasch van Krienen.

versy soon died out, and was not revived until 1840. Pasch van Krienen then found a fresh advocate in the eminent traveller Ludwig Ross, while Welcker, in an elaborate essay on the subject, has endeavoured to show that the whole thing was a forgery, and this he is generally thought to have proved[1]. The facts which remain are these: that Ross found at Placoto a tolerably circumstantial tradition remaining of the place having been excavated by a stranger; and that Biörnstahl, the Swede, saw at Leghorn the packages, though as yet unpacked, in which Pasch van Krienen had brought over the inscriptions he had collected in Ios and other islands. From that time Pasch van Krienen wholly disappears from sight; and, like a character in a child's story, was 'never heard of afterwards,' neither himself nor his inscriptions, until a few years ago two of the latter, including one from Ios (unfortunately, of no great importance), were discovered in the basement storey of the British Museum, where they are still.

His inscription. Among these amusing elements of uncertainty one fact remains undisputed, viz. that on a stone slab which was used as a bench in front of a church of Hagia Caterina, in the town of Ios, Pasch van Krienen found a genuine inscription which he copied and published in his book; for this was seen by Ross in the same position, and though it had been greatly defaced by exposure, there was enough remaining to identify it with Pasch van Krienen's copy. It consists

---

[1] Welcker, *Kleine Schriften*, vol. iii.

mainly of a long list of names; and as the introductory lines seem to contain a reference to Homer, it is Welcker's opinion that there existed in Ios a Homeric school, and that a number of its members had inscribed their names on this stone. As nearly forty years had elapsed since Ross's visit, we were desirous to know whether the inscription still existed, and with this view we enquired for the church of St. Catherine. From a dirty but civil man who offered to be our guide, we discovered that there were two dedicated to that saint, a circumstance that illustrates the extraordinary number of little churches with which this town swarms; for, as our native remarked with a tone of enlightenment, 'in the Middle Ages, when persons were ignorant, the priests persuaded them that it was a pious thing to build so many churches.' Some of these were simply a tiny dome supported by four walls, almost resembling the tombs of sheikhs which are seen in Turkey. Except in some five regular places of worship, however, service is performed in the churches in Ios only three or four times a year. One of St. Catherine's shrines was in the lower, the other in the upper part of the town, but at neither of them could the stone be found; at the latter, however, a woman said that there had been an inscribed stone in the position we spoke of, but that it had been removed by the bishop to his house, probably to preserve it. The bishop unfortunately was absent, and we could not obtain admission into his precincts; thus, as far as we were concerned, this relic of Pasch van Krienen's investigations, like the rest, passed out of reach of discovery.

View of Santorin.

Above the highest part of the town rises a steep mass of granite, of which stone this portion of the island is composed. We found the summit blue with innumerable small irises (*Iris sisyrinchium*), and the view of the town below was curious from the flat roofs of the houses—a feature which is found in most of these islands and in Crete—and the numerous churches interspersed among them. But what most attracted our attention was Santorin, into the strange basin of which we now looked for the first time; and, softly delineated as it was, with the lofty peak of Hagios Elias behind, and in front the calm sea streaked with lines of currents, it looked to me a sort of Promised Land, after having been the subject of so many expectations. A gentleman of Nio, who came to visit us at the landing-place, described how he had seen it in eruption from that point (the distance to the new crater is about twenty miles), and said that the effect was very striking. The earthquake motion from the volcano is not much felt here, as we should expect it would be; and as it is more felt at Melos, it would seem that the wave of movement passes in the direction of that island.

Sikinos.

The greater part of the following day (April 4) was spent in searching for a little temple on the island of Sikinos, which was unknown to our sailors, and the position of which was incorrectly given in our maps. Before leaving the harbour of Ios, we saw one of our crew beating an octopus, which was intended for their dinner, on a stone, for this animal being bloodless is allowed by the Greek Church to be eaten in Lent, but is excessively indigestible unless well beaten. We rowed along the south coast of Sikinos in a perfect calm, until we reached a small roadstead, on the heights above which, though not visible from below, the modern town is built, having been placed at a distance from the sea, like the greater number of the towns on the coasts of the Aegean, for fear of corsairs. As we approached the shore, we found a number of old fishermen on the projecting rocks, and on asking them a question, were answered by what in a Greek play would be called a Chorus of Old Men of Sikinos, for they all spoke together, as loud and as fast as they could, and in an extraordinary dialect. When we had prevailed on them to appoint a coryphaeus, we learnt that, though the regular route to the temple would lie through the village, we should save time by making for a bight further to the west; and, accordingly. taking the spokesman, old Barb Anton, as he was called (i. e. Uncle [1] Antony) on board, we rowed away in the direction which he indicated.

Landing on the rocks, we ascended by a very rugged path in the midst of dwarf pines and other shrubs, following our barefooted guide, for in the

Temple of Apollo.

---

[1] *Barba* is an obsolete Italian word for 'uncle,' which seems to have made its way eastwards during the Middle Ages, and is now commonly used in the Aegean as a term of familiar address for old men. In the Cretan poem of *Erotocritos* (date perhaps about A.D. 1500) it occurs in the form μπάρμπας: the spelling of this is correct, for μπ in Modern Greek stands for English and Italian *b*.

hurry of embarking he had left his shoes behind him. He mounted at a splendid pace, so that in three-quarters of an hour we found ourselves on the ridge of the island, which may be about 1,500 feet above the sea. Just below this, on the southern side, stands the small rude temple, with walls of hard blue limestone, surmounted by a Byzantine cupola, which was added when it was converted into a Christian church. In consequence of the purpose which it now serves the place is known as Episcopi. It is a temple *in antis*, that is to say, a simple *cella*, with two columns in front which stand between projections of the side walls; but the intercolumniations have now been built up with masonry. The columns are in a pseudo-Doric style, with bases. The pronaos faces west—an almost unique feature in a Greek temple. Inside there is a Venetian glass chandelier, and a Russian eagle in marble, probably dating from the time of the Russian occupation of the islands in the last century, is let into the floor. A portion of the cross-pieces and slabs of the ancient roof remains. In front of the building, to the west, there is a stone platform, and an inscription in one part of this shows that the temple was dedicated to the Pythian Apollo. From the writing of this, and the style of the architecture, Ross concludes that its date is 200 B.C. The steep height which rises above is the site of the ancient city. To judge from the small size and the ruggedness of the island it was never, in all probability, a place of much importance; hence this small temple would correspond to the means of the inhabitants. We may remark that, though the ancient Greeks were fond of high places for their temples, their successors in modern times are even more so: thus here, while the ancient building was placed somewhat below the ridge, no doubt to shelter it from the force of the north wind, the moderns, not content with converting it into a church, have built another chapel on the ridge itself. The island-view from this point was fine on both sides, the broken outline of Pholegandros being the nearest and most conspicuous object. After examining this we returned once more to our vessel.

CHAPTER V.

SANTORIN, ANTIPAROS, AND PAROS.

Approach to Santorin.

IT was a lovely afternoon when we commenced our voyage to the southernmost islands. The air was so transparent that objects in Santorin were clearly visible, and the white town, perched on the rocks that flank the inside of the crater, although eighteen miles distant, was the object for which we were instructed to steer. The sky was almost cloudless, the sea oily-calm, and the islands extremely beautiful, especially the broken but tender forms of Ios and Sikinos close at hand, with shadowy valleys and sun-lit capes. The sun set clear into the sea, and was succeeded by the innumerable stars of a Greek heaven. When the moon rose, about nine o'clock, we had already passed between the northernmost capes of Santorin and Therasia, and were struck with wonder at the walls of rock that were revealed by the moonlight on both sides of the great basin. We wandered on beneath the cliffs of Santorin, sometimes in light, sometimes in pitchy darkness, in search of the landing-place, which we discovered at last from the ships lying there. Owing to the almost unfathomable depth of the water there is no anchorage elsewhere in the bay, whereas at this point a slight rim of shallow bottom gives hold for an anchor. The scene in the neighbourhood of this was most extraordinary. The cliffs rose to all appearance perpendicularly above our heads, and were crowned with what looked in the moonlight like a crust of ice, but was in reality the buildings of the town. Nearer to the water were innumerable caves, and small white structures, resembling chapels, on the face of the rock; these we discovered to be dwelling-houses, and the caves also, we found, were inhabited. It was midnight when we landed, and all was silent as the grave, but we succeeded in obtaining a clean room at the agency of the Greek steamers.

In the morning the appearance of everything was even more strange. The steep cliffs, which line the whole side of this island, as they do that of Therasia in like manner, are marked in horizontal bands by black lava, white porous tufa, and other volcanic strata, some parts of which are coloured dark red; and here and there solitary masses of rock project from the face of the precipices. We ascended by a steep zigzag path, formed of lava-blocks compactly fitted together, an arrangement which is very necessary, for the tufa soon crumbles into cindery dust. As it is, persons are not unfrequently killed at the landing-place by stones that fall from above. The town retains the ancient name of Thera, but the form most commonly heard is Phera, and similarly Pherasia is used for Therasia. It stands 900 feet

Town of Thera.

above the water, and the descent is so abrupt that you seem able to throw a stone into the tiny craft below. The houses run along the crest, and are themselves peculiar, for their foundations and, in some cases, the sides also, are excavated in the tufa, so that occasionally they are hardly traceable except by their chimneys; and, owing to the absence of timber—for, with the exception of the fig, the cactus, and the palm, there are hardly any trees in the island—they are roofed with barrel vaults of stone and cement. It is easy to conceive how strange a sight they present, when seen from above; and moreover the paths and the land in their neighbourhood resemble nothing more than the English 'black country.' Both wood and water have occasionally to be imported from the neighbouring islands, for there are no wells, and the rainwater, which is collected in numerous cisterns, does not always suffice. Owing to the prevalence of fine dust, the women go about as closely veiled as if they were Mahometans, though to some extent this habit prevails in other islands, and may arise from traditional custom. The population here struck us as being the handsomest we had seen, and as retaining more of the old Greek type. The town and the contiguous villages run along the crest for a considerable distance towards the north, until, at Merovuli, the highest point in this neighbourhood is reached; this commands an extensive view, and overlooks the town of Apanomeria near the northern entrance, which is crowded together in a white mass, resembling a glacier rather than houses, while the rocks below it are the reddest that are seen in the island. From this position let us take our survey.

The island of Santorin is crescent-shaped, enclosing the bay on the north, east, and south, while on the western side lies the island of Therasia. The encircling wall thus formed, which is eighteen miles round in its inner rim, is broken in two places; *The volcanic group.*

towards the north-west by a strait a mile in breadth, where the water is not less than 1100 feet deep; and towards the south-west by an aperture about three miles wide, where the water is shallow, and an islet called Aspronisi or White Island, lying in the middle, serves as a stepping-stone between the two promontories. The cliffs, as I have described, rise perpendicularly from the water, in some places to the height of 1000 feet; but towards the open sea, both in Santorin and Therasia, the ground slopes gradually away, and has been converted into broad level terraces, everywhere covered with tufaceous agglomerate, which, though extraordinarily bare and ashen to the eye, is the soil which produces the famous Santorin wine. Towards the south-east rises the limestone peak of Mount Elias, the highest point of the island (1887 feet), and the only part that existed before the volcano was formed. In the centre of the basin lie three small islands, though from this point they seem to form one; the furthest of which is called Palaea Kaumene, or Old Burnt Island; the nearest, Mikra Kaumene, or Little Burnt Island; while that which lies between them, and is by far the largest of the three, bears the name of Nea Kaumene, or New Burnt Island: this last was the scene of the great eruption of 1866. It is hardly accurate, perhaps, to speak of the basin as a crater, for most geologists, including Lyell, support the view that the whole of this space was once covered by a single volcanic cone, the incline of which is represented by the outward slope of Santorin and Therasia, while the position of the crater was that now occupied by the Kaumene islands, only at a much greater height above the sea; and that at a remote period, perhaps about 2000 B.C., owing to some sinking of the strata beneath, the central portion of this, extending over an area which a French writer compares with that included within the fortifications of Paris at the time of the siege, fell in, by

Santorin, Antiparos, and Paros.   99

which convulsion the basin was formed. Lieutenant Leycester in his notice of this volcanic group[1] informs us, that if the gulf, which is six miles in diameter, could be drained, a bowl-shaped cavity would appear with the walls 2449 feet high in some places, and even on the south-west side, where it is lowest, nowhere less than 1200 feet high; while the Kaumenes would be seen to form in the centre a huge mountain 5½ miles in circumference at its base, with three principal summits (the Old, the New, and the Little Burnt Islands) rising severally to the heights of 1251, 1629, and 1158 feet above the bottom of the abyss. The rim of the great cauldron thus exposed would be observed to be in all parts perfect and unbroken, except on one point where there is a deep and long chasm or channel, known by mariners as the 'northern entrance.' Perhaps the imagination may in some degree realize the appearance of this chasm by thinking of the upper valley of Lauterbrunnen in Switzerland.

The principal eruptions of this volcano that have taken place within historic times are, that of 196 B. C., when, as we learn from Strabo[2], flames rose from the water half-way between Thera and Therasia for four days, and the island of Palaea Kaumene was ejected; that of 726 A. D., during the reign of the emperor Leo the Isaurian, when an addition was made to that island, and the pumice-stone that was

Chief eruptions.

---

[1] In the *Journal of the Royal Geographical Society*, vol. xx, quoted by Lyell, *Principles of Geology*, vol. ii. p. 71.

[2] I. 3. 16, p. 57.

cast forth was carried by the waves to the shores of Asia Minor and Macedonia; that of 1573, when Mikra Kaumene appeared; that of 1650, a fearful eruption, which destroyed many lives by its noxious exhalations, and ended in the upheaval of an island in the sea to the north-east of Santorin, which afterwards subsided and became a permanent reef below the sea-level; that of 1707, when Nea Kaumene arose; and, within the recollection of the present generation, that of 1866. Of this last eruption we have a description from an eye-witness, Commander Brine, who ascended on Feb. 28 of that year to the top of the crater of Nea Kaumene, about 350 feet high, and looked down upon the new vent, then in full activity. 'The whole of the cone was swaying with an undulating motion to the right and left, and appeared sometimes to swell to nearly double its size and height, and to throw out ridges like mountain spurs, till at last a broad chasm appeared across the top of the cone, accompanied by a tremendous roar of steam, and the shooting up from the new crater to the height of from 50 to 100 feet of tons of rock and ash mixed with smoke and steam. Some of these which fell on Mikra Kaumene at a distance of 600 yards from the crater, measured 30 cubic feet. This effort over, the ridges slowly subsided, the cone lowered and closed in, and then, after a few minutes of comparative silence, the struggle would begin again with precisely similar sounds, action, and result[1].'

[1] Quoted by Lyell, *Principles of Geology*, vol. ii. p. 70.

In the town of Thera we visited two collections *Collections* of antiquities, belonging to M. de Cigallas and *of antiqui-ties.* Mdme. Delenda. They contained a considerable number of inscriptions, which have been published, numerous antiquities in glass and earthenware, an Egyptian figure in pottery, probably brought from Cyrene, and one of the very large and roughly-painted vases which are peculiar to this island; but on the whole they were disappointing, particularly as there were none of the prehistoric objects which we hoped to find. Most of these have been carried off, and they are said to be very brittle and difficult to preserve. The Spanish names of the owners of these collections are noticeable, for they are descendants of some of the Catalans who in the fourteenth century were the terror of the Aegean, and parts of whose bands settled in various districts. Traditions of Spanish occupation are to be found in several places in Greece, and in Crete Pashley mentions a village still called Spaniako for this reason.

Descending to the landing-place, we started to *The* visit the central islands. As we approached them *Kaumene Islands.* the sea took a sulphurous colour, which deepened as we neared the shore, and the water became warmer and warmer, until at last it was almost too hot for the hand. The passage between Nea and Mikra Kaumene in this part is not more than twelve feet across. In a further part of the channel some Russian ships, which were engaged in the wine trade, were moored to the coast on both sides, the place being chosen for its sheltered position, and giving a forcible proof of the want of anchorage in the harbour. Close to the point where we landed on Nea Kaumene was a hot sulphur spring, from which the steam was evaporating. Mounting over loose blocks of lava and detritus, which yielded to the foot and made the ascent far more difficult than that of the cone of Etna or Vesuvius, we arrived at the summit, which is about 500 feet high. Here there were several small craters, one of which emitted much sulphurous steam, coming out in jets mixed with smoke; and though we stood to windward, the air around us was very oppressive, and the stones beneath our feet were cracked by the heat. The descent on the opposite side required the greatest care, for a leg may easily be broken when treading on large blocks that give with the foot, owing to the loose foundation on which they rest.

Therasia. We had sent round our boat to meet us, and passing on our right hand vast masses of slag that tower from the water, and on our left the island of Palaea Kaumene, which presents a steep face on this side, as if it was broken off, where a strait divides it from Nea Kaumene, we made our way across to the south side of Therasia. In this part, halfway between two capes, there was said to be a prehistoric village. At the end of a very steep scramble upward over the rocks, we found the guide whom we had brought with us from Thera quite at fault, and were glad to meet with a shepherd—a strange being, with boyish looks and complexion, and grey hair—who conducted us to the spot. It was a small level, high above the sea, and close to the deposit of soft white tufa which covers the whole island; here, to our disappointment, we found nothing but heaps of lava-blocks, the materials of the dwellings, which, our informant told us, had been excavated some time before, and afterwards ruined. Originally the whole had been concealed by the tufa, and in the steep face of this we could see traces of the excavations. The *pozzolana* is exported from this neighbourhood and from Santorin in great quantities, and has been much used for the works at Port Said in connexion with the Suez Canal, since, when mixed with lime, it forms a very hard cement, which resists the action of the sea. We regained our boat, and shortly after dark reached the landing-place of Thera, where a bonfire had been kindled for the festival of the Annunciation (March 25, o. s.), of which this was the vigil.

As these prehistoric dwellings have attracted much attention, it may be worth while to notice a few points relating to them. The first explorers[1] say without hesitation, that the buildings were constructed previously to the formation of the layer of tufa; and further, that the eruption, by which they were covered, must have been antecedent to the falling in of the crater, for the layers of tufa are broken off precipitously, in the same way as the lava-rocks of Santorin and Therasia, and this can only be explained by the supposition that they all

Prehistoric dwellings

---

[1] See Fouqué, *Archives des Missions*, 2 sér. vol. iv, and Lenormant, *Revue Archéologique*, nouv. sér. vol. xiv.

fell in together. The foundations of the dwellings rested, not on the tufa, but on the lava below it; and here and there between the stones branches of wild olives were found, according to a mode of building that still prevails in the island, in order to resist the shocks of earthquakes. Part of the skeleton of a man was discovered, and large vases, some containing grain, others stone instruments very carefully worked. Some of these vases were of fine yellowish earth, ornamented with brown bands; others of smaller size were more elaborately decorated, in some cases having lines representing foliage, and in a few instances figures of animals; some were of red earth, without ornament; while others, of pale red earth, were of very large dimensions. No implements of metal were found. At first it was thought that the pottery came from abroad, the red kinds probably from Anaphe, the others from other islands, especially Melos; but this view has been abandoned, since the same sort of earth as that of which they were made has been found in Santorin, though these strata are now covered by the sea[1]. But as some objects in obsidian, which is of foreign importation, have been discovered in these dwellings, it is certain that these early inhabitants must have had some commerce.

Primitive art. It has naturally been the subject of much discussion what was the origin of the very primitive art displayed in this pottery. The late M. Dumont, who was the leading authority on the subject, though

[1] Fouqué, *Santorin et ses Éruptions*, p. 125.

speaking with great caution on account of the insufficiency of the evidence, inclined to the belief that it was partly derived from Phoenician influence, but at the same time that there were evident traces of native originality. Comparing it in respect of date with the other prehistoric developments of art in the neighbourhood of the Aegean, he would place it later than that at Hissarlik, but earlier than those of Ialysus in Rhodes, and of Mycenae[1].

Southern parts of Santorin.

It remained now (April 6) to visit the southern part of Santorin, and with this object we hired a boat to take us to the town of Acroteri, which lies a little within the south-western promontory, and takes its name from it. On the way, the horns of the crescent-shaped island were finely seen. In many places lumps of light pumice-stone were floating on the surface of the water. Shortly after landing below the town we found an intelligent lad, who undertook to conduct us to a prehistoric village in that neighbourhood. This is situated in a similar position to that on Therasia, but facing the harbour. Two of the dwellings that composed it partly remain, but the others subsequently to their excavation have been again covered by a fall of the tufa cliff. These two, which stand side by side, are about 12 feet square, and their walls are composed of black lava-blocks roughly put together, while in one part they are covered with a kind of mortar. These remain to the height of 4 or 5 feet, and in the party-wall is a sort of closet, in which corn was found. The

[1] *Les Céramiques de la Grèce Propre*, pp. 74, 75, 209.

boy described how six large jars (πίθοι) were found in the houses, and fragments of some of these were still lying about. When this village was first discovered, it was believed to be of later date than the one on Therasia, but now it is agreed that it also existed before the crater fell in[1]. Above this place the town of Acroteri forms a conspicuous object, from its old Venetian castle occupying a rocky height, with a square central tower, round which numerous vaulted buildings are ranged. We then directed our steps eastward, in search of an ancient temple, now converted into a chapel of St. Nicolas Marmorites, as the saint is here called, in honour of his marble sanctuary. Our road lay between vineyards, and was so deep in sand from the pulverised tufa, that we found it easier to walk on the top of the rude walls of lava on either side than in the path itself. From this neighbourhood we obtained superb views of the snowy ranges of Dicte and Ida, in Crete, stretching along the southern horizon. The vines presented a most curious appearance, from their branches being twisted round and round and plaited together into what resembles a circular maund or hamper; and as the stock of the trees hardly rises at all above the surface of the ground, the fields from a distance look as if they were covered with gigantic birds-nests. The strangeness was not lessened by the leaves being now in bud: as the summer comes on, the branches are untwisted and spread out upon the ground.

[1] Dumont, *Les Céramiques de la Grèce propre*, p. 29.

We found the temple at a little distance from the road, in the middle of a vineyard. It is a tiny place, only 12 feet long, and somewhat less in breadth, and 10 feet high; and is built of large blocks of grey marble, some of them as much as 3 feet long, put together without cement. Over the entrance, which faces south, is a small pediment, and a narrow cornice runs round the top, but the whole building is almost devoid of ornament. Still, notwithstanding its insignificance, it is extremely interesting, being (as far as I know) the only existing Greek temple in perfect preservation; for here the original roof remains entire, composed of large stone beams reaching from the front to the back, the intervals between which are covered by thin slabs laid across transversely. Inside, the proportions are still more minute, since the thickness of the walls has to be deducted from the dimensions already given. At the inner end, opposite the entrance, about half-way up the wall, is a little niche, flanked by two Ionic columns supporting an entablature and pediment. In this a statuette of the hero must have stood, for it was probably a *heroum*, notwithstanding that an inscription on the wall contains a dedication to the Goddess Queen (θεᾷ βασιλείᾳ). Whether Cybele or some other goddess is meant by this, is uncertain; but, according to Ross, *heroa* were frequently dedicated to deities. On one side, hidden under some church furniture, I discovered a small ancient altar.

Ancient heroum.

After inspecting the temple, we turned northwards towards Megalo-chorion, where the inhabitants were keeping a double festival, for the anniversary of Greek Independence coincides with the Annunciation; they were all sitting in the streets, and were not a little surprised by our sudden appearance. The main street was crossed by two archways, over each of which hung six large bells. At this point we were close under the flank of Mount Elias, on the summit of which we could see a monastery. We then followed the edge of the great basin, obtaining views of the eastern sea with Anaphe, the three peaks of Amorgos, and the distant Astypalaea, which is in Turkish waters; and when we reached the town of Thera, we descended once more through its steep and slippery streets to the harbour.

Names and myths. After seeing what a cinder this island is, we cannot help being astonished at its having been colonised at an early period by the Phoenicians. That this was the case we learn from Herodotus[1], who attributes the foundation of the colony to Cadmus. This story vouches at least for the belief that there was an early settlement of that race in Thera, and the traces of the influence of Phoenician art which have been discovered point in the same direction. It must therefore have possessed some sources of attraction, and one of the names by which it was known to the Greeks was Calliste or 'the Fairest Island.' Unless this was a euphemistic expression, we can only explain it as referring to the fitness of Thera for the cultivation of the vine, and perhaps also to the excellence of the harbour as

[1] Herod. 4. 147.

a shelter, notwithstanding the want of anchorage.
The modern name is derived from its dedication by
the Latins to St. Irene; Tournefort, who sometimes calls the island Sant-Erini, mentions nine
or ten chapels of that saint as existing there. The
classical myth of its origin described it as sprung
from a clod of earth presented to the Argonauts by
Triton[1]. In modern times, as the nature of the soil
prevents bodies from decomposing easily, it is regarded as the especial home of the Vampire, for
according to this superstition, when the soul of a
man after death has assumed this malignant form,
his body refuses to decay. So widely is the par-
tiality of vampires for Santorin recognised, that the
Hydriotes and Cretans believe that they can permanently get rid of those obnoxious visitors, if they
can once be transported thither. The same notion
has probably caused it to be regarded as a place
of purgatorial suffering, an idea which appears in
the following weird story.

'Many years ago, it may be a hundred and fifty, *A weird*
a vessel was on its way to Rhodes, when it was *story*.
caught by a storm in the open sea, and was in
danger, until they found a refuge in a small unknown island. There the crew cast anchor and
went ashore. After a little while, as soon as it was
day, all at once they saw three laden mules coming
down from the mountain above, bending under
the weight of three stones apiece; but as soon as
they reached the beach they turned round with

[1] Apollon. *Argonaut.* 4. 1551 foll.; 1731 foll.

their loads and made for the place they had come from, and then returned again shortly after with the same loads, and did as before. This they repeated several times. Now when the sailors noticed this strange occurrence, how that the mules went to and fro with their burdens without any one appearing to guide or to load them, it attracted their attention, and they perceived that there was something uncanny in the proceeding: and one of them in particular, coming up to one of the mules, struck it with the stick that he held in his hand; whereupon the mule turned round, and with a human voice addressed him thus, " Don't strike me, cousin." And when he stopped, all in a fright, and gazed at him, the mule proceeded, " You think it strange that I call you cousin, so let me tell you that I am no born mule, but a man undergoing purgatory: I am your cousin, Father M., who often took away people's characters by perjury, and these are two other countrymen and friends of ours (and he mentioned their names), and they too are undergoing purgatory. The name of this place is Kaumene, and it is near Santorin. When you return to our country, make offerings for the repose of our souls, if so be we may obtain some alleviation of our sufferings [1]." '

Antiparos. During the two first days of our southward voyage

---

[1] Polites, Νεοελληνικὴ Μυθολογία, pp. 406, 407. M. Polites maintains that, though the doctrine of purgatory is not admitted by the Eastern Church, yet traces of the belief in it are found among the lower classes in Greece: p. 397.

we had been favoured by the north wind; then succeeded two days of perfect calm, and now we were delighted to see the waves begin to ripple from the direction of Crete, from which we gathered that we should have a favourable wind for our return journey. Accordingly we re-embarked at once, and were gently carried back to the strait between Ios and Sikinos; but there towards evening the breeze freshened, and bore us northward with great speed, so that shortly after midnight we landed on the eastern shore of Antiparos, where it is separated from Paros by a narrow channel. This island was the birthplace of our Silenus of a captain, who seemed to regard the famous Grotto as under his especial patronage, and spoke of it with great pride. After sleeping at a village near the coast, we started on foot under his guidance to explore the Grotto, taking with us two donkeys, one to carry the stout rope that was required for the descent, and the other, of course, for Silenus. 'Plenty of wine, and little foot-work' (πολὺ κρασὶ, ὀλίγο ποδάρια) was the maxim of life which he enunciated. Our path led southwards, and in less than two hours we reached the ridge of the island, just beneath which the cavern is situated. The arched roof of the entrance of this is imposing, and behind, rising against the darkness of the interior, a tall stalagmite, resting on a narrow base, reaches nearly to the rock above: on the right hand side stands a small rude chapel of St. John the Evangelist, and opposite to it was a shepherd's *mandra* or enclosure, in which were lying some kids a month old. On the rocks at the back of this is an inscription, containing the names of persons who visited the Grotto in classical times, from which we gather that the vulgarity of writing one's name in celebrated places is not altogether new; but the moderns, it would seem, are worse than the ancients, for across the face of the inscription runs a horrid palimpsest, in the shape of the initials of a man who was here in 1778—probably one of the companions of M. Olivier, the French traveller and author, whose name with the same date is to be seen hard by.

Descent into the Grotto.

The ground descends rapidly into the narrowing cavern, until a stalactitic cupola is reached, where the first steep fall of rock commences; here the water from the roof was brightly dripping into a shepherd's broken cruse, and as we looked back the stalagmite stood out against the light like a huge idol. The rope was then fastened round a stalactite, and without further instructions we were desired to descend. The depth here is about 15 feet, but a fall would be fatal, for there is only just standing room below, and beyond that are precipices; however, I found no great difficulty in letting myself down by the rope while keeping my feet against the rock at right angles to my body. My companion followed, and then our tapers were lighted, and we proceeded to climb round the smooth and slippery cliffs at the side, after which came slopes of *débris*, together with several faces of rock like the former one. It is this steep continuous descent that distinguishes this cavern from others that I have seen, such as that of Adelsberg in Styria, the Corycian cave on Mount Parnassus, and that of St. Michael at Gibraltar. At last we reached a place which looked like Malebolge, for all was darkness below, and our guide disappeared down the rope to a much greater depth than before; but as we had not, like Dante, a Geryon on whose back to descend into the abyss, we swarmed down the face of this precipice also, and then found ourselves in the Grotto. It is a large and lofty hall, ornamented with very fine pendent stalactites, the white forms of which glimmer in the dim light, and if it were brilliantly illuminated, the effect would be striking; but in itself, though curious, it is not the most imposing of caverns. The depth must be several hundred feet. We were shown the altar where mass had been said when King George and Queen Olga visited the place three years before; at that time the descent was made by ladders. Our ascent from Malebolge was facilitated by a rope passed under our arms and hauled from above, and so we regained the daylight. The natives call the place 'The Refuge' (καταφύγι), a name which I have found applied to other *subterranea* in Greece, and which explains the use to which such caverns have been put. On the way back I dug up a variety of orchids, and the natives who assisted me asked many questions about their destination, England. On the other side of the strait which separates Antiparos from Paros a large extent of rich land

Visit of King George.

was seen, while behind rose the central Mount Marpessa, toward which the ground slopes upward from every part of the coast.

Paros. We re-embarked, and in an hour reached Paroekia, the capital of Paros. From the size and fertility of the island we expected to find it a prosperous town, but, on the contrary, it proved the dirtiest place we had visited on our journey: the streets were open sewers, and everywhere full of nuisances. As might be expected in the neighbourhood of the famous Parian quarries, fragments of marble were to be seen in all directions; pieces of cornices served for doorsteps, and triglyphs and other ornaments were built into the walls of the houses. The greatest amount of these relics of antiquity is on a knoll on the north side of the town, on which stood the ancient acropolis; here drums of columns, some Doric, some Ionic, lie in all directions, while others have fallen down the steep hillside into the sea. The white marble of the temples to which they belonged must have looked well from the water in this elevated position. A portion of the wall of the Venetian fortress which occupied one side of this height is curiously composed of drums laid on their sides and slabs unequally fitted together; within this there is a chapel of our Lady of the Cross, and the masonry which now forms the east end of it is almost the only ancient structure which retains its original position. Several churches here have incised ornaments, and other features of the true Byzantine style of architecture, which are rarely found in the islands. At the back of the town is a large church of the Virgin of a Hundred Gates (Παναγία 'Εκατομπυλιανή), adjoining which are extensive buildings constructed of marble: these are new and therefore uninteresting, for the Greek rite is so thoroughly mediaeval in its character that it is unsuited to modern, and especially to Italian, architecture.

The following day we devoted to a visit to the quarries, having first called on M. Damias, the proprietor, who owned the ground in their neighbourhood, though at this time they were not being worked. Our path lay upward along the lower slopes of Mount Marpessa, and in an hour and a half we reached the little monastery of Hagios Minas, which is enclosed by a square white wall, quite Moorish in its appearance from the absence of windows. Inside, the buildings are quaintly packed together at various levels; but it has ceased to be a monastery, and is now used as a farm, and is tenanted by a son of M. Damias. This gentleman undertook to show us the quarries, which are in the immediate neighbourhood; they are entered by openings in the hillside, like the grotto of Antiparos. At the mouth of that which is considered the finest there is a curious sculptured tablet on the rock, containing numerous groups of figures, conspicuous among which is a seated female deity, with a dedication to the nymphs below. This is figured in one of the plates to Stuart's *Antiquities of Athens*, but now a large piece has been broken off the face of it. With deep indignation we learnt that in

The marble quarries.

the year preceding our visit, a foreigner who came to Paros cut this piece off and carried it away with him: but subsequently, on a letter of remonstrance being addressed to him by M. Damias, who at the time was ignorant of the act of vandalism, he returned it, and we saw it at the monastery in the packing-case in which it was sent. When we reached the point where daylight ceases, our tapers were lighted, and the dogs that had accompanied us from the convent first whined dismally, and after proceeding a little further returned to the upper air. I had expected to find the quarry worked in regular shafts, but instead of this the dip of the strata has been followed, and consequently the passage descends at a considerable incline, winding about in different directions, and the roof slopes from left to right. It varies in height from 16 to less than 3 feet, so that sometimes it is necessary to crawl on hands and knees; in these places the passage must formerly have been wider, otherwise the stone could not have been carried out. At one point two hundred bats were hanging from the roof, but fortunately they were not disturbed by our lights: had they been aroused, they would have extinguished the tapers, and we might never have regained the entrance. The marks of the tools of the old workmen were visible everywhere on the roof and sides, the groovings being about two inches apart; the amount excavated must have been immense, for the whole place has the appearance of a labyrinth, and we were told we might wander for a day without

Traces of working.

finding the end. The marble on the surface is not usually white, but where it is broken it is brilliantly pure; in some parts the grain is very fine, and I tested its hardness in breaking a lump in order to bring away a specimen. After being fifty minutes underground, we returned to daylight, and then proceeded to a second quarry, where, however, the marble is somewhat inferior. In places there were stalactites in process of formation, but none were to be compared with those of Antiparos. It is deeply interesting to think that these quarries furnished the material for most of the famous Greek statues that have come down to us, and for several important temples, such as that of Apollo at Delphi, which was rebuilt of this stone by the Alcmaeonidae.

The scirocco (Eurus) had been blowing with considerable force all day, but towards evening it increased to the most furious gale against which I ever have attempted to stand, and corroborated all that our boatmen had told us of its extremely dangerous character. On the morrow, however, it had lulled, and we started on our return voyage with a favouring south-west breeze. After we had passed a dangerous rock in the middle of the sea called 'the Ant' (μυρμίγκι)—the name of which recalls the corresponding ancient name of the rock Myrmex off the Thessalian coast[1]—the wind freshened, and it was a fine sight to see the great deep-blue waves rolling in from the west. Nor less fine was it to watch the steering of our helmsman, Yanni, as we

Return to Syra.

[1] Herod. 7. 183.

raced along with all our sails set, sometimes in the trough of the waves, sometimes on the crest, but never once shipping a sea. At last, when we reached the nearest point of Syra, we suddenly darted into calm water, and shortly afterwards arrived at the town, which had been our headquarters during our various excursions.

CHAPTER VI.

LESBOS.

Storms in the Aegean.

TWELVE years elapsed from the time of my first visit before I was able to renew my explorations in the Greek islands. At last, in the spring of 1886, an opportunity presented itself, and on this occasion I turned my attention to those that lie off the coast of Asia Minor. This group I found it convenient to investigate in due order from north to south, beginning with Lesbos, which, with the exception of the small island of Tenedos, is the most northerly of all. It was my good fortune to be accompanied by the same friend as before, Mr. Crowder, and by the same travelling servant, Alexandros Anemoyannes of Athens, whom we found, notwithstanding the weight of years, to be thoroughly competent and vigorous. Our headquarters for this journey was Smyrna, as on the former occasion it had been Syra; for the former of these two places is not only the most important and most central port on the Asiatic coast, but is also the rendezvous of the numerous steamers, belonging to different companies, which communicate with one or another of the islands. The weather which welcomed our arrival in Greek waters was not less boisterous than that which we experienced in March, 1874, for a rude north-east wind met us as soon as we had rounded the Peloponnese; and during the two days that we spent at Athens snowstorms were trailing over the plain, and whitening the slopes of Parnes. When we steamed down the Saronic gulf on our way from that place to Smyrna, the peaks of Cithaeron, Helicon, and Parnassus, which appeared above the nearer mountains, and the eastern slopes of Mount Cyllene in Arcadia, displayed their maximum of winter snow; and after we had passed the promontory of Sunium, the fine pyramid of Mount Dirphe, in the centre of Euboea, presented all the features of an Alpine summit. Again, the heavy sea that we encountered as we emerged from the strait which separates the north of Andros from Euboea, made us applaud the wisdom of the Homeric heroes, who when returning from Troy declined to cross the Aegean from Lesbos to this point, until they had received a favourable omen from Poseidon[1]. In consequence of this, instead of reaching Smyrna on March 27, as we hoped, we did not arrive at that place till the following morning. As the Egyptian steamer, on board of which we were, was to touch at Lesbos on her way to Constantinople, we continued our voyage in her, and landed after nightfall at Mytilene, the capital, which has now given its name to the whole island. We found a lodging at the Hotel Pittacus (ξενοδοχεῖον Πιττακός), the title of which

Snowy mountains.

[1] Hom. *Od.* 3. 168-179.

is an evidence that Lesbos has not forgotten her wise men of old.

The town of Mytilene is a large place of imposing appearance, and contains a population of 20,000 souls. It is built partly on a peninsula, which here projects into the sea, and partly on the neighbouring ground and the isthmus which connects the two. Like almost all the capital cities of the islands off this coast which occupy an ancient site, it is placed on the eastern side, this position having, no doubt, been determined by two considerations: first, greater safety in respect of navigation, as they were not exposed to the force of the open sea; and secondly, facility of communication with the mainland, for the Greek settlements were everywhere founded with a view to commerce, and especially to the export of the produce of the interior of the country—so much so, that some of these islands possessed a Peraea, or strip of land on the opposite coast, which provided them with a depôt, and rendered the transport more easy. The town is backed by a screen of hills, some of them of considerable height, the slopes of which are clothed with beautiful vegetation, and dotted with country houses. For the present, however, I will defer a more detailed description of the place and its site, in order that we may at once start for the interior of the island; for the chief source of interest which Lesbos affords is a geographical one, since it is penetrated on its southern side by two bays, or inlets of the sea, the entrances of which are so narrow in proportion to their area as to be almost a unique phenomenon. The primary object of our visit was to see these; and as the highest point in this part of the island, Mount Olympus—for Lesbos also boasts an Olympus—stands up between them, and commands a fine panoramic view, we purposed to make the ascent of that mountain.

Bay of Iero. In the afternoon of the day following our arrival (March 29), having hired horses for our journey, we left Mytilene and ascended the heights to the westward on our way to the town of Agiasso, which is situated at the foot of Olympus, five hours distant. Our road lay through olive groves, and continued to do so throughout the whole of our ride. Olive is king in Lesbos as much as cotton in Manchester; the population are devoted to the cultivation of it, and oil is the chief export. Some of the trees were finely grown and of great age. In consequence of this, the island is called by the Turks 'the garden of the Ottoman empire.' At the end of three quarters of an hour we crossed the ridge of the nearer hills, and came in sight of the first of the two bays of which I have spoken, that of Iero (pronounced Yéro)—a lake-like expanse of water, six miles in length by four in breadth, extended at our feet. It is surrounded by fine mountains, and over those that bounded the shore opposite to us the peak of Olympus, now called Hagios Elias, stood up conspicuous. We descended to the eastern side of the inlet, and rode round its head, but were unable at any point to see the entrance, notwithstanding that the dip of the ground in that direction, and the sloping hillsides that formed it, were well marked. This is not surprising, when we consider that the narrow strait by which it is approached from the sea is four miles long. I subsequently met the captain of a merchant steamer, when on my way to one of the other islands, who told me that he had once penetrated into this harbour, in order to bring away a cargo of oil, and that the rocks at the two sides of the entrance, which were clothed with trees, appeared quite close to him as he passed between them. He added, however, that the water was deep, and that he thought a large ship of war might enter without serious difficulty. Just at the head of the bay there is a bathing establishment on the shore, the hot springs of which are much resorted to for a variety of complaints by visitors from Constantinople, Smyrna and elsewhere. After passing this, we turned southwards, near the village of Keramia, which was distinguished from a distance by a number of fine cypresses; and then ascended a lateral valley, partly by the side of a clear torrent overhung by chestnut-trees not yet in leaf, and partly over a steep paved road, until the valley contracted into a deep gorge, and at the highest point of this we entered Agiasso. Here we put up at a sort of church-house or public institute, in which there were rooms for the accommodation of strangers. All along our route during this day's ride, the anemones—white, purple, pink, and crimson—were growing in extraordinary profusion.

Its narrow entrance.

Agiasso. This mountain town—for its height above the sea can hardly be less than 1000 feet—stands at a watershed between the two inlets, for the streams at this point begin to flow in the opposite direction, towards the Bay of Kallone. The inhabitants praise its position, its fine air and good water, and the vegetation by which it is surrounded must make it a delightful summer resort; the same boast was expressed on the cups in which our coffee was served, and which bore the inscription 'Agiassos the beautiful' (ὡραία 'Αγιάσσος). It occupies a curve in the hills at the head of a valley facing south-west, on the further side of which the summit of Hagios Elias rises in a grey mass of limestone, with a buttress clothed with pine-trees intervening. When seen from opposite, the red-tiled roofs and white stone walls of the houses in the town, being clustered closely together, present a striking appearance. Its inhabitants, who number 7000 or 8000 persons, are mostly occupied in the oil trade or the cultivation of the olive; and at the highest point of the town stands a large manufactory, with oil-presses of elaborate construction and a factory chimney. Eight years ago a large part of the place was burnt down; but it has since been rebuilt, though many of the houses are not yet finished. It possesses a boys' and a girls' school. In the former of these, religious knowledge, ancient Greek, and the elements of French are taught; but those who desire any higher instruction for their children have to send them to the town of Mytilene. I observed, as an evidence that the classical spirit, which is so widely prevalent in Greece, has not penetrated here, that their Mount Olympus is only known as Hagios Elias, and that the Trojan Ida, which is visible from many points in the neighbourhood, is always called by its Turkish name of Kaz Dagh.

Early the next morning (March 30) we started to make the ascent of the mountain with a native of the place for our guide. Though an elderly man, he proved a good walker, for he went at a steady pace, and did not stop till he reached the summit. Another of the inhabitants joined our company in making the *pilgrimage*; for in this light the ascent is regarded, since there is a chapel dedicated to the Prophet Elijah near the summit, which is frequently visited by pilgrims from the surrounding country, and service is held there on the festival of the saint. Our guide, who seemed an intelligent man, told us that originally he had been engaged in the oil manufacture; but that, having been ruined by the fire, and having a large family, he had been forced to leave his home for five years, in order to seek employment elsewhere (he had been usher in a school), but that lately he had been able to return. Descending the steep streets, we crossed a stream at the bottom of the town, and mounted on the other side by a winding path in the midst of chestnuts. When we emerged from these, we entered on a region of open pasture land, in which the blue squill (*Scilla bifolia*) was growing, together with the yellow blossoms of a *Gagea*. This extended to the foot of the peak, which rises steep and bare in masses of broken rock.

Ascent of Mount Olympus.

The path, which is well marked throughout, ascends this transversely on the southern side as far as the chapel of the saint, which is built a little way below the summit at the eastern extremity of the ridge. Before reaching the chapel we met an old shepherd, who feeds his flocks here in summer, and throughout the year is employed as a guardian of the sacred place, which he visits occasionally to see that everything is in order. He presented us with a handful of blue hyacinths, which were very fragrant, but proved to be garden flowers, for they were grown in a small enclosure close by the building, which was backed by the rock, and sheltered from the north wind by a low wall. The little chapel is nicely kept, and has pictures of saints on its *iconostasis*, including one of the Jewish prophet.

Names Olympus and Elias. It is worthy of notice, as we have now before us an instance of a mountain, which was called Olympus in antiquity, and at the present time bears the name of Hagios Elias—and the same thing is true of the more famous Thessalian mountain—how frequently both of these names recur in mountain nomenclature. Of the modern appellation this has often been remarked—indeed, no traveller in Greece can fail to notice it; but it is also the fact that in Asia Minor, in continental Greece, and in the islands, there were as many as fourteen mountains called Olympus in ancient times, so that the name seems to have been almost generic. As to the reason which caused Elijah to be associated by the Greeks with lofty summits, the view has frequently been propounded of late years, that this arose, in part at least, from the similarity of the name Elias to that of Helios, a divinity who possessed sanctuaries on many of the Greek mountains. This receives striking confirmation from a passage of Sedulius, a Christian writer of the fifth century, which shows that the two were associated together at an early time, for he argues that there was an especial fitness in the prophet Elijah ascending to heaven by a track of fiery brilliancy, because, if by shifting the accent on his name in Greek you alter one letter (ī into ĭ), he appears as the sun (Helias becomes Helios)[1].

View from the summit.

From the chapel we climbed over rough boulders to the summit, the height of which above the sea is marked in the Admiralty chart as 3079 feet. The ascent had occupied an hour and a half. The view was extensive, and very interesting, on account of the number of places famed in history which were in sight. To commence with Lesbos itself—the inlets of Iero and Kallone were conspicuous on either side of us, two land-locked enclosures of blue water; the latter of these, which penetrates the island for three-fifths of its breadth, was now visible to us for the first time. The surface of the ground is generally mountainous, but the most marked chain is that towards the north, in which another peak named

---

[1] *Carm. Pasch.* i. 184-7; see Polites, 'Ο "Ηλιος, p. 49:—

    Quam bene fulminei praelucens semita caeli
    Convenit Heliae! meritoque et nomine fulgens
    Hac ope dignus erat: nam si sermonis Achivi
    Una per accentum mutetur litera, sol est.

Hagios Elias, the ancient Lepethymnus, forms a fine object. Through a depression to the westward of this, the promontory of Lectum, the southernmost point of the Trojan territory, appeared. In the distant view the object which at once attracted the eye was Mount Ida, rising above the bay of Adramyttium in a lofty range, the upper part of which was clad in snow. In 1861, my companion and I had looked down from its summit on the peak on which we were now standing, and we then noticed that the bay of Kallone is visible from thence between the two heights of Lesbos. In front of the bay of Adramyttium lay the group of small islands called the Hecatonnesi, and following the coast downwards we could see the territory of Atarneus and the deep gulf of Elaea. Towards the south was the bay of Smyrna, which was bounded on one side by the promontory of Phocaea, and on the other by the massive headland of Mimas, the huge proportions of which and its power of attracting storms[1] caused it to be personified by the ancients as a malevolent giant. Westward of this, and separated from it by a strait, rose the lofty Chios, and as an outlier from this again the smaller Psyra, which in modern times has become famous as Psara, on account of its gallantry in the Greek War of Independence, and the massacres which attended its ruin by the Turks. The distant islands towards the north—Imbros, Samothrace, and others in the Thracian Sea—were excluded by the northern ranges of Lesbos. After having studied this instructive view

[1] Its Homeric epithet is ἠνεμόεις.

for some time, we returned to Agiasso by the same route by which we had ascended.

On our return to Agiasso, we were informed, to our surprise, that an Englishman was desirous of paying us a visit. This proved to be Mr. Procopios Constantinides, a native of the place, who had lived for sixteen years in Australia, and had been naturalised there, so that he was a British subject. He had also spent four years in London. Having inherited lands in this neighbourhood from his father, he now resided here; but he assured us that his favourite reading still was English literature, especially Shakspere, Byron, Scott, and Macaulay. He presented each of us with a pretty coin of Mytilene, bearing on the reverse the lyre, an emblem to which that city had a rightful claim as being the birthplace of Alcaeus and Sappho. The poetic art is still represented in Lesbos, for he informed us that M. Demetrios Bernardakis, the author of 'Maria Doxapatri,' a drama of the period of the Frankish occupation of the Peloponnese, and other tragedies, who is one of the foremost poets of modern Greece, and was once professor at the University of Athens, now resides in Mytilene. Of him we shall hear more presently. His brother, M. Gregorios Bernardakis, the editor of Plutarch's *Moralia*, and author of other contributions to classical scholarship, is director of the gymnasium in that town.

A British subject.

The same afternoon we started for the ruins of the ancient Pyrrha, which was one of the most important cities in the island. They are situated on the shore of

Bay of Kallone.

the Bay of Kallone, between four and five hours distant from Agiasso in a north-westerly direction. At first we descended for a long distance through a narrow valley bordered by olive-groves, leading our horses the greater part of the way, on account of the steepness of the road. When at last we reached more level ground, our progress was even more impeded by the stony nature of the surface, the track being often lost altogether, either in a watercourse, or in the midst of broken fragments of rock where horses' feet left no trace. It was an extremely solitary region, and a few shepherds were almost the only persons we met in the course of our ride; but it was rendered picturesque by the pine trees, which once, in all probability, formed part of a dense forest, but now are scattered at intervals over the face of the country, though they are more thickly clustered in the valleys. At last the Bay of Kallone appeared, and we descended to it just where a steep rocky hill rises from the water's edge. This was the site of Pyrrha, and the place still bears that name. The bay is considerably larger than that of Iero, being ten miles long by six wide; and the passage by which it is entered is broader, though still very narrow. In consequence of this it was called, in ancient times, the Euripus Pyrrhaeus. Both these pieces of water have deep soundings; and this harbour, in particular, would afford safe anchorage for a fleet of any size.

Meeting a poet.

As this place is very seldom visited, we enquired before leaving Agiasso whether we should find any accommodation; and were told that there were a few booths or shops by the shore, where we could pass the night. When we reached them, they appeared to be very wretched shanties; and we were glad to find that our baggage-horse, which had preceded us, had been conducted to a good-looking farm, which occupied a slight elevation close by. On our arrival at this, we were welcomed by the owner, who, after our first communications had passed in Greek, proceeded, to our surprise, to talk French with us; and as the conversation continued, I discovered that he was acquainted with the system of study pursued in the English Universities, and had resided in France and Germany, and in former years had been personally acquainted with Fallmerayer, the well-known Munich professor and man of letters. Before long we were engaged in a discussion of the characteristics of the modern Greek language and poetry. It was evident that we were not in the company of an ordinary Greek farmer, and my curiosity was roused to know who our entertainer might be. At last the mystery was solved. By way of turning the conversation on the subject of native talent, I made use of the information which I had received in the morning, and said that I understood that M. Bernardakis the poet was living in the island. 'Probably,' our host remarked, 'you mean me? I am M. Bernardakis!' He then told us that some time ago he purchased this farm, in the neighbourhood of which he possesses vineyards, and that from time to time he comes hither to superintend it. He added, however, that up to that time it had been a dead loss to him, owing to the oppressiveness of the taxation of the Turkish government. For the same reason the cultivation of the olive is carried on with great difficulty; but in this case there is another and more powerful cause of depreciation, in the low price of oil, owing no doubt to the competition of rock oils, which in the South of France also is rapidly causing the olive to be neglected. The agreeableness of an evening spent in such good company was enhanced by a large fire of olive wood, which was lighted in our honour; for, though the day had been cloudless, the wind still blew cold from the north-east. During the whole of our stay in Lesbos, however, I was struck with the purity of the air and the transparency of the sky, which invested objects with a remarkable brilliancy. In ancient times the island was famed for the salubrity of its climate.

Ruins of Pyrrha.

The next morning (March 31) was spent in exploring the site of the ancient Pyrrha. The hill which it occupied forms a narrow rectangular table of land, running from west to east, and gradually sloping upwards from the shore, until it reaches a high point, where the masses of brown rock fall in steep precipices towards the valley at the back. On seeing it from that side on the previous day we had been struck with its suitableness for a Hellenic city. The two sides also are flanked in most parts by sheer walls of rock. In consequence of this the place would seem to have required but little artificial defence; anyhow, but few traces of walls remain. The best preserved portion of the fortifications is in the middle of the eastern face of the acropolis, overlooking the valley already mentioned, at a point where the ascent from below is somewhat easier than elsewhere; here six or seven irregularly horizontal courses of masonry remain. But the most remarkable construction is what appears to be the base of a tower half way down the slope on the north side, where unshaped blocks of enormous size are rudely, but evidently artificially, piled together. The greater part of the area is covered with olive trees, and growing under these I found some specimens of a pretty pink orchis with branching flowers (*Orchis saccata*). This city was ruined and deserted before Strabo's time, and the suburb which he speaks of as then existing was situated on the shore in the direction of the modern booths. Some traces of its buildings are visible near the foot of the hill, and in the water may be seen the remains of a mole, which formed the harbour that he mentions[1]. Pyrrha is now resorted to for the cuttlefish and mollusks which are caught there; and as it was now the season of Lent, numerous boats were lying there in readiness to transport these to other places about the bay. The fishes of the Euripus Pyrrhaeus, especially the shell-fish and polypi, are frequently mentioned by Aristotle in his *History of Animals*. The octopus at the present time is a considerable article of food in the island, and not among the lower classes only. At the *restaurant* which we frequented in the town of Mytilene it was entered

---

[1] 13. 2. 4, p. 618.

on the *menu* as one of the dishes, and we heard it ordered.

During the afternoon we rode back to Mytilene in six hours and a half, the first part of the way being over open country, sprinkled with pine trees, like that which we had traversed on the previous day. From this we descended to the head of the Bay of Iero, and followed our former route to the city.

Modern town of Mytilene.

It remains now briefly to describe the modern town, and to investigate the site occupied by the ancient city. It is a place which deserves our attention, on account both of its former splendour, which caused Horace in a well-known ode to class it with Ephesus, Rhodes and Corinth, and of the important historical events of which it was the scene, especially the Athenian siege, which occupies so prominent a position in the narrative of Thucydides, and the dramatic story of the escape of its inhabitants from massacre on that occasion. It has been already said that a peninsula here projects into the sea, having the opposite coast of Asia Minor full in view, and that it is joined by an isthmus to the ground behind, which rises somewhat rapidly towards the interior of the island. The city is composed of two portions, the mediaeval castle, which covers the summit and a great part of the northern declivities of the peninsula, and the modern town, which is built on the isthmus and the slopes on either side of it. The castle is an extensive and picturesque structure, having inner and outer lines of walls, with bastions, round and angular towers, and battlements. Its fortifications reach to the shore, which they follow for some distance on the north-western side. It is of Byzantine construction; but in 1355 it passed into the hands of the Genoese merchant nobles of the family of Gatilusio, who possessed Lesbos for more than a century, until it became the prize of Mahomet II., in 1462. Its history may be said to be literally written on its face, for in the neighbourhood of the entrance, at the summit of the hill, where the old iron-plated door still remains, a Byzantine eagle, a Frankish coat of arms, and a Turkish inscription, are built into the wall close together. It is now occupied by an Ottoman population, who are chiefly composed of the government officials, and of a considerable body of troops. The greater part of the peninsula is left bare, and descends to the sea in rugged cliffs. The northern portion of the modern town, which is nearest to the castle, is also a Turkish quarter, and contains several mosques; while that towards the southern side of the isthmus, which is much more extensive, is inhabited by the Greeks and the European consuls. The contraction of the coast-line at either end of the isthmus forms two harbours, both of which are protected from the sea by two moles; but owing to long neglect, the northern one of these. which is the larger, has become useless, and is now deserted, while that towards the south, which is the centre of the commerce of the place, is so far silted up as not to admit vessels of considerable size. All these objects, together with the blue waters of the strait, are finely seen in one view from the heights behind the town.

The ancient city. If we desire to understand the appearance of the city in antiquity, we must remember that what is now a peninsula was then an island, and was separated from the mainland by a narrow channel. It is difficult at first to realise this at the present time, because no trace of these features remains; but by following the main street of the town, which runs in a straight line from one harbour to the other, and is perfectly level, we could see that the change might easily have arisen in the course of ages. The canal was a natural one, but was afterwards artificially improved. On this island the original city was placed, and its citadel continued to be the Hellenic acropolis all along; but the walls could not then have descended to the water's edge as they do now, for the northern harbour is spoken of by Diodorus as lying 'outside the city.' As the population of the place increased, it extended to the mainland, in which direction its area must have been much greater than it is at present. The northern harbour, as we learn from Strabo[1], was protected by a breakwater. This is the same which remains, though in a dilapidated condition, at the present day. From the silence of the geographer with regard to any artificial protection of the southern harbour, we may conclude that it was undefended; and it was less in need of a mole, in consequence of its being enclosed within the buildings of the town, and sheltered from the wind. Owing to

[1] 13. 2. 2, p. 617.

its two harbours, and the channel between them, Mytilene had a great advantage in respect of commerce and navigation, since vessels could thus approach in any wind, and could pass from one side of the city to the other. There can be little doubt, also, that at that time the harbours penetrated further into the land, and consequently that the interval between them was less than at present.

Our best authority for the ancient topography of this place is Diodorus, who describes it in connexion with the events that preceded the battle of Arginusae[1]. His account, which is much clearer than that of Xenophon, is evidently derived from one who was well acquainted with the place; and it has been acutely conjectured that this was Ephorus, who was a native of the neighbouring Aeolian city of Cyme[2]. Diodorus says that Conon, in command of an Athenian fleet which was coming from the north, being hard pressed by the Spartans under Callicratidas, took refuge in the port of Mytilene, the entrance to which he obstructed, and defended to the best of his ability. But when his opponents forced their way through, he escaped to the harbour 'within the city,' while the Spartans occupied the harbour which was 'outside,' but still anchored close to the city. In order to explain these proceedings, he describes the channel which separated the old portion of the city from the new, evidently implying that Conon

Descriptions by classical writers.

---

[1] Diodor. 13. 77-79.
[2] See Conze's excellent monograph, *Reise auf der Insel Lesbos*, p. 8.

must have passed through it. This account is corroborated by Strabo, who speaks of an island, which contained part of the city, lying in front of the two harbours [1]; by Pausanias, who, when describing the river Helisson as intersecting Megalopolis, compares it to the channel which ran through Mytilene [2]; and by Longus, the author of the story of *Daphnis and Chloe*, the scene of which is laid in Lesbos, who speaks of the bridges of polished white stone that spanned this channel [3].

At nightfall, on April 1, we embarked on board the *Balkan*, a French steamer of the Fraissinet line, and reached Smyrna the following morning.

[1] Strabo, *loc. cit.*   [2] Pausan. 8. 30. 2.   [3] i. 1.

CHAPTER VII.

CHIOS.

THE vessel on board of which we next started from Smyrna, the *Ianthe*, belonged to a line of small steamers, called the 'Bell' line from the name of the chief proprietor in the Scotch company that owns them, which are engaged in the carrying trade and passenger traffic of the Asiatic islands, and thus afford facilities to the traveller in those parts. Another line, which has its head-quarters at Smyrna, and will be found serviceable in the same manner, though the area of its operations is somewhat more restricted, is that of the Joly-Victora company, which is similarly named from its two proprietors. The *Ianthe* was bound in the first instance for Scio (Chios), but afterwards was to make a special voyage to Tenos in the Cyclades, with a view to the great festival of the Virgin in that island, which is held on March 25, o. s., when pilgrims resort thither from all parts of the Aegean. With these the deck was crowded, as it appeared to us, from stem to stern, but the captain informed us that after passing Scio he would proceed to Scala Nova, a town on the coast near Ephesus, to take in 150

Pilgrims bound for Tenos.

more. We could not trace any outward signs of illness among them, though the object of the pilgrimage is in most cases to obtain the cure of some disorder. The captain's wife told us that once, when they were conducting devotees to this festival from the Macedonian coast, one of the passengers, a woman, was sufficiently crazy to make her timid about her; but that on the return journey she seemed better, and her relations maintained that she was cured. They presented a motley appearance, as they lay about in picturesque groups on carpets and mattresses, or crouched in the most sheltered places they could find to screen them from the cold wind. Great good-humour prevailed among them, even when they had to shift their positions in consequence of the sea washing over them; but later on, when we passed the promontory of Karabournou, the ancient Mimas, and reached more open water, their sickness was a pitiable sight. In really bad weather this human cargo has to be deposited in the hold (there is only one small cabin), and the hatches are battened down over them, the sequel of which proceeding is, happily, left to the imagination. We had started at 3 p.m., and it was midnight before we reached the town of Scio. The vessel lay to in the offing; and, in accordance with the unconventional habits that prevail at these intermediate stations, we let ourselves down her side by a rope into the boat which was to take us ashore—no easy process in a tossing sea. When we reached the harbour we found it full of vessels, which gave evidence of considerable commerce. Later in the night the gale freshened, and we thought with compassion of the pilgrims on their way to Scala Nova.

The day after our arrival (April 3) was the fifth anniversary of the great earthquake in Scio, one of the most terrible visitations of modern times owing to its suddenness, which gave the inhabitants no opportunity for escape. On that occasion the greater part of the capital, and most of the villages on the eastern side of the island, were shaken down, and several thousand lives were lost. A correspondent of the *Times*, writing shortly after the disaster, said :— *Earthquake in Scio.*

'The town looks as if it had been subjected to a terrible bombardment; hundreds of houses have been transformed into a shapeless mass of ruins, under which lie buried an unknown number of victims. A majority of the remaining houses, already cracked and roofless, may fall at any moment.'

We found that the greater part of the place had been rebuilt in the interval, though in some of the streets ruined dwellings were still to be seen. The restoration, however, had not extended to the interior of the island, for the country districts were a scene of universal ruin, for which, notwithstanding all that I had heard beforehand, I was not prepared.

Chios has been indeed a most ill-fated island. During the Greek War of Independence it suffered more than any other spot from Moslem fanaticism; for in 1822 nearly the whole of the inhabitants were either massacred or carried off into slavery. The Chiotes at this time were an *The massacre of* 1822.

industrious and peaceable population, but, unfortunately for them, they were goaded into revolt by a band of Samians who landed there, and besieged the Turkish garrison in the fortress. It was in every respect a most ill-considered attempt, and when the Turkish capitan-pasha, Kara-Ali, appeared near the coast with his squadron, hardly any attempt was made to resist the landing and the advance of the Ottoman troops, who were aided by a body of volunteers from the Asiatic shore. What followed is thus related by Finlay in his *History of Greece*:—

Finlay's narrative.
'The vengeance of the Turks fell heavy on Chios. The unfortunate inhabitants of the island were generally unarmed, but they were all treated as rebels, and rendered responsible for the deeds of the Greeks who had fled. In the city the wealthier class often succeeded in obtaining protection from Turks in authority by paying large sums of money. In the meantime the poor were exposed to the vengeance of the soldiers and the fanatics. The bloodshed, however, soon ceased in the town, for even the fanatic volunteers began to combine profit with vengeance. They collected as many of the Chiots as they thought would bring a good price in the slave-markets of Asia Minor, and crossed over to the continent with their booty. Many Chiot families also found time to escape to different ports in the island, and succeeded in embarking in the Psarian vessels, which hastened to the island as soon as it was known that the capitan-pasha had sailed past Psara.

'Three thousand Chiots retired to the monastery of Aghios Minas, five miles to the southward of the city, on the ridge of hills which bounds the rich plain. The Turks surrounded the building and summoned them to surrender. The men had little hope of escaping death. The women and children were sure of being sold as slaves. Though they had no military leader, and were unable to take effectual measures for defending the monastery, they refused to lay down their arms. The Turks carried the building by storm, and put all within to the sword.

'Two thousand persons also had sought an asylum in the fine old monastery of Nea Mone, which is about six miles from the city, secluded in the mountains towards the west. The Turks stormed this monastery as they had done that of Aghios Minas. A number of the helpless inmates had shut themselves up in the church. The doors were forced open, and the Turks, after slaughtering even the women on their knees at prayer, set fire to the screen of paintings in the church, and to the woodwork and roofs of the other buildings in the monastery, and left the Christians who were not already slain to perish in the conflagration [1].'

These events were followed by indiscriminate pillage and massacre throughout the island, the only part that was spared being the district which furnished mastic to the ladies of the Sultan's harem. Forty-six flourishing villages were reduced to ashes. It was calculated that ultimately 25,000 persons were killed, and 45,000 made slaves, and of these latter not a few were members of opulent families. The archbishop and seventy-five other citizens, who had been retained as hostages before the commencement of the outbreak, were executed on the spot by express orders from the Sultan. Three months later, only 1800 Greeks were left in Chios. The fugitives, also, who escaped from the island, were mostly in a state of total destitution, and many of them perished from

Depopulation of the island.

---

[1] Finlay, vol. vi. pp. 255, 256; compare Gordon, *History of the Greek Revolution*, vol. i. pp. 356-363.

disease and want. This tragedy, the circumstances of which have been described with much pathos by Mr. Bikélas in his story of *Loukis Laras*, produced the same effect at that time as was produced of late years by the Bulgarian massacres, in rousing the indignation of Europe against Turkish barbarity, and thus ultimately promoting the cause of freedom.

The town and harbour.

The position of the town in many respects resembles that of Mytilene, for it lies on the east coast of the island, facing the mainland, and extends for some distance along the shore, with a spit of land, on which stands the old Genoese castle, projecting into the sea in front of it. It is also backed by a range of mountains, but these retire further from the sea and are barer of vegetation than those behind Mytilene, for they form part of the chain which intersects the island from north to south, and which from its steepness obtained for it the Homeric epithet of 'rocky' (παιπαλόεσσα). The harbour, for there is no bay, is formed by a half-ruined mole which runs out from the extremity of the castle on its southern side, together with another which extends towards it from the shore. This is now submerged, with the exception of a lofty broken mass of masonry at the end which the inhabitants call 'The Old Lighthouse' (τὸ παλαιὸ φανάρι). The principal article of export is the spirit called *mastic*, which is famous throughout the Aegean; we afterwards saw huge flasks of this being taken on board the steamer in which we made our return journey. The gum from which it is made exudes from the stems and branches of a shrub which is mostly grown in the southern part of the island, in the same way as I have seen the gum tragacanth in Asia Minor and Armenia dropping from the *Astragalus verus*; and like that plant, the mastic tree is scored with incisions by the natives during the summer that the gum may flow out, with a view to its being collected.

The castle which has been mentioned was the fortress of the Giustiniani, whose Maona, or joint-stock company, governed Chios for more than two hundred years. The constitution and history of this body offer many points of resemblance to those of our own East India Company; and it has been described as the first example recorded in history of a mercantile company of shareholders exercising all the duties of a sovereign, and conducting the territorial administration in a distant country. In the year 1346 the Genoese admiral, Simone Vignosi, fitted out a fleet of twenty-nine galleys, with the object of conquering the island from the Greek empire. The treasury of the republic, however, was at this time so exhausted that the funds necessary for the expedition were subscribed by private citizens, who were guaranteed against loss by the state. After the conquest had been effected, the subscribers were formed into a Maona, and the shareholders in this were recognised as the proprietors and governors of the island for the period of twenty years, during which time it was to be in the power of the republic to pay off the debt and resume the grant of the island. This, however, was never done;

Maona of the Giustiniani.

and the power of administration of the shareholders became permanent. A change also took place in the composition of the Maona. The original society had farmed out the revenues to another Genoese company, but serious quarrels arose between the two bodies, and these reached such a pitch that the government interfered; it was then arranged that the members of the old Maona should be bought out, and that the powers which they possessed should be transferred to the farmers. This body was called the new Maona, and the majority of the shareholders in it assumed the name of Giustiniani.

Its history. During the first century after this system was established the prosperity of the company was very great. The mastic that was produced in the island, and the alum that came from the mines at Phocaea on the mainland, yielded immense profits; and all the most important posts in the administration were filled by members of the Maona. Nor was it for the time injurious to the natives. The population of Chios at this period exceeded 100,000 souls, the Greeks were secured in all the rights and privileges which they enjoyed under the Byzantine emperors, and no tax could be imposed without their consent. The government was less rapacious, and it afforded better securities for the lives and properties of its subjects, than they had enjoyed under the Palaeologi; and it was milder than the governments of the Knights of Rhodes and the Republic of Venice. But in the course of time the great subdivision of the shares tended to impoverish the holders, and the increase in the number of the officials, who were chosen almost entirely from the *ihaonesi*, entailed a much larger outlay on the public service and the imposition of heavier taxes. The Maona became tributary to the Ottoman sultans some time before the capture of Constantinople, but by good management they prolonged their dominion for more than a hundred years after that event. At last, in 1566, Suleiman the Magnificent, to indemnify himself for the failure of his attempt to expel the Knights of St. John from Malta in the previous year, ordered his admiral, Piali Pasha, to annex the island to his dominions, which he did without encountering any resistance[1].

In consequence of the state of politics in the East at the time of our visit—for this was a period of great tension in the relations of Greece and Turkey, and it was feared that war might break out at any moment—we experienced much difficulty in obtaining permission from the Ottoman authorities to visit the interior of Chios. They were in great fear of political emissaries; and we afterwards found that another English party, who shortly before this had been in the island of Icaria, were absolutely forbidden to quit the principal town. After several hours' delay, however, we were allowed to start, but one of the Pasha's officials was sent to accompany us, and, no doubt, to watch our proceedings. Our object was to see the monastery of Nea Mone, which is situated high up among the mountains, and can boast some of the most ancient mosaics in the Levant. The

Interior of the island.

---
[1] Finlay, *History of Greece*, vol. v. pp. 70-79.

first hour of our ride was spent in ascending westwards from the city along watercourses or over rough slopes, which were wholly uncultivated, except here and there where small gardens had been made in the valleys; in these we observed that the vegetation was more advanced than we had found it in Lesbos, and some of the fruit trees were in full leaf. After many windings we reached a gorge, above which rose precipices of grey and red limestone, while the lower slopes were covered with pine trees. The ascent now became extremely steep, and would have presented great difficulties to any but the surefooted horses of the country. These, however, carried us safely at an unusually rapid pace, for we were not encumbered by baggage, and in less than two hours we reached the monastery.

Monastery of Nea Mone. This building is situated on an irregular level at least 1000 feet above the sea. Its position is exquisite, for close at its back rise the highest summits of this part of the island, clothed with beautiful vegetation, and towards the east, in which direction it faces, there is a charming view of the deep-blue sea far below and of the mainland beyond, framed like a vignette between the stern rocks which flank the gorge. In its flourishing days the monastery must have presented an imposing appearance from its extensive structures compactly massed together, and from the houses that form a small village in its neighbourhood; these latter were intended partly for women, who are not allowed to enter the establishment, and partly for those who come to visit, or to worship at, the holy place. Now, alas! it is a sight of dismal ruin, for its buildings have been half destroyed by the earthquake, with the exception of the church and the refectory, which escaped owing to the strength of their walls; and even these are not wholly intact.

The history of the foundation of this convent is as follows. In the middle of the eleventh century three hermits, Niketas, John, and Joseph, established themselves in a cave high up in the mountains of Chios, and while dwelling there frequently saw a light proceeding from a place in the neighbouring forest, which however vanished whenever they approached it; so they determined to set the trees on fire, feeling sure that, if this portent came from God, the tree in which it appeared would not be consumed. This they did, and when the rest of the wood was burnt down, there remained a myrtle-bush, from which was suspended a picture of the Virgin. The pious fathers removed this picture to their cave, but the sacred object refused to remain there, and miraculously returned to the myrtle, near which in consequence they built a humble chapel for its reception. Now it happened at this time that the future emperor of Constantinople, Constantine Monomachus, was living in exile in Lesbos, and it was revealed to the three hermits that he would be raised to the throne. Accordingly they repaired to him, and communicated to him what they had learned with regard to his future destiny. At first he was incredulous, but when they had overcome his doubts,

Story of its foundation.

and had narrated to him their discovery of the icon, which they compared to the history of Moses and the burning bush, he promised, at their request, that if their prediction came true, he would build on the spot a splendid temple to the Virgin. Not long after this, the Empress Zoe, having become a widow for the second time, gave Constantine her hand in marriage, whereupon he fulfilled his vow. The building was finally completed by Theodora, the sister of Zoe. The name of the convent, 'The New Monastery' (Νέα Μόνη), reminds us of that of New College at Oxford, from its permanence in spite of the lapse of ages. At present there are sixty monks, but before the earthquake they numbered a hundred. As they possess considerable property in the lower country, they have hopes of rebuilding their convent, notwithstanding the large sum of money that will be required.

The church.

The Hegumen and some of the superior monks gave us a friendly greeting, and conducted us to see the church, which stands in the centre of the court. It is entered through a modern porch at the west end; this leads into the outer *narthex* or ante-chapel, which is lofty and has three cupolas, but is without ornament, except that in the centre of the floor there are patterns in *opus Alexandrinum*. The second *narthex*, which is entered from this, is low, and the domes in its roof have no windows or other openings; the central dome contains in its upper part a representation of the Virgin, and figures of saints standing in a circle below, while other portions of the roof are covered with heads of saints in circular compartments; all these decorations are in mosaic. A door in the eastern wall of this opens into the body of the church, which is octagonal; its walls were ornamented with marble slabs, and at each of the angles were double columns, also of marble, but of the original thirty-two only four now remain. In the *iconostasis* stands a picture of the Virgin, the whole of which except the face is covered with a sheathing of silver; this is the sacred icon which caused this spot to be selected as the site of the monastery, according to the story which has just been related.

The surface of the upper part of the church was originally covered with mosaics; but owing to the injury done, first by the Turks in 1822, who ruined a great part of the central dome, and afterwards by the earthquake, these only partially remain. The subjects which are best preserved are the Baptism of our Lord, the Transfiguration, the Deposition from the Cross, and the Resurrection. The last-named subject, though it bears that title (ἡ ἀνάστασις), in reality represents Christ delivering Adam and Eve from Hell; this mode of treatment is universally found in mediaeval Greek art, and in the West, also, no painter before Giotto represented the Resurrection as an actual scene. On the bronze doors of the cathedral of Ravello, near Amalfi, which were made by an artist of Trani after a Constantinopolitan original, this subject is treated in the same manner, and whereas the inscriptions for the scenes in the

Its mosaics.

other compartments are in Latin, the title of this one is in Greek, and is the same as that which I have given above. The mosaics throughout the church of Nea Mone are coeval with its foundation, and the figures are stiffly designed in sombre colours on a gold ground. Mutilated though they are, they well deserve a visit, for this mode of decoration is rare in the neighbourhood of the Aegean; indeed, except at Salonica, hardly any other mosaics can be found to rival them. We subsequently saw the refectory, which is now disused. It is a long, bare room, down the centre of which runs a single table, built of stone and brick, and covered with slabs, and the seats on either side of it are constructed in the same way—an arrangement which I had never before seen except in the rock-hewn monasteries of Cappadocia.

The channel of Scio. The island of Scio is singularly destitute of classical remains; in fact, the only relic of antiquity that is found in it is the so-called School of Homer. This object is situated near the sea-shore, about five miles northward of the town, and towards it we now bent our steps. When we had reached once more the bottom of the gorge, we struck along the mountain sides at a great height above the sea, following terrace paths, which commanded views of extreme beauty. The town of Scio and the gardens in its neighbourhood, with the lower slopes of the mountains, lay beneath us, and beyond the blue strait rose the strange peninsula that intervenes between it and the bay of Smyrna, the northern part of which is the range and headland of Mimas, while in the centre is the deep gulf of Erythrae. The northern extremity of the strait is defended by a breakwater of islands, but the narrowest part is towards the south, where lies Cheshmeh, the scene of one of the greatest exploits in the Greek War of Independence. There it was that the Turkish fleet was lying, when Constantine Canaris approached it, and attached his fire-ship to the admiral's flagship, which in the space of a few minutes was a mass of flames. This event appeared like an act of retribution for the massacres in Chios, for it took place in the June of the same year in which they happened. The following account of it is taken from Finlay:—

Canaris and his fire-ship.

'On the 18th of June, the last day of Ramazan, in the year 1822, a number of the principal officers of the Othoman fleet assembled on board the ship of the Capitan-pasha to celebrate the feast of Bairam. The night was dark, but the whole Turkish fleet was illuminated for the festival. Two Greek ships, which had been hugging the land during the day, as if baffled by the wind in endeavouring to enter the Gulf of Smyrna, changed their course at dusk, when their movements could be no longer observed, and bore down into the midst of the Othoman fleet One steered for the 80-gun ship of the Capitan-pasha, the other for the 74 of the Reala Bey. Both these ships were conspicuous in the dark night by the variegated lamps at their mast-heads and yards. The two Greeks were fire-ships. One was commanded by Constantine Kanares, the hero of the Greek Revolution. It is superfluous to say that such a man directed his ship with skill and courage. Calmly estimating every circumstance of the moment, he ran the bowsprit into an open port, and fixed his ship alongside the Capitan-pasha, as near the bows as possible, so as to bring the flames to windward of his enemy. He then lighted the train with his own hand, stepped into his boat, where all the crew were ready at their oars, and pushed off as the flames mounted from the deck. The sails and rigging, steeped in turpentine and pitch, were immediately in a blaze, and the Turkish crews were far too much astonished at the sudden conflagration to pay any attention to a solitary boat which rowed rapidly into the shade. The flames, driven by the wind, rushed through the open ports of the lower and upper decks, and filled the great ship with fire roaring like a furnace. Those on board could only save their lives by leaping into the sea. Kara-Ali jumped into one of the boats that was brought alongside to receive him, but before he could quit the side of his ship he was struck by a falling spar and carried dying to the shore [1].'

This exploit was followed by a second and similar one in the November of the following year, when Canaris set fire to a Turkish line-of-battle ship, that was lying between Tenedos and the mainland, near the anchorage which has subsequently become familiar under the name of Besika Bay. The two daring deeds attracted the attention of Europe, and were celebrated in verse by the German poet, Wilhelm Müller, who in 1824 composed an epitaph on Canaris, which might serve after his death. The hero, however, postponed the occasion until 1877, when he died as Prime Minister of Greece. As the original poem is not as well known, perhaps, as it ought to be, I introduce it here, together with Aytoun's spirited translation :—

Wilhelm Müller's poem.

Konstantin Kanari heiss' ich, der ich lieg' in dieser Gruft,
Zwei Osmanenflotten hab' ich fliegen lassen in die Luft.

[1] Finlay, vol. vi. pp. 258, 259.

Bin auf meinem Bett gestorben in dem Herrn, als guter Christ:
Nur *ein* Wunsch von dieser Erde noch mit mir beerdigt ist:
Dass ich mit der dritten Flotte unsrer Feind' auf hohem Meer
Mitten unter Blitz und Donner in den Tod gefahren wär'.
Hier in freier Erde haben meinen Leib sie eingesenkt —
Gib, mein Gott, dass frei sie bleibe, bis mein Leib sie wieder
    sprengt.

    I am Constantine Canaris,   *Aytoun's*
      I, who lie beneath this stone,   *translation.*
    Twice into the air in thunder
      Have the Turkish galleys blown.

    In my bed I died—a Christian
      Hoping straight with Christ to be,
    Yet one earthly wish is buried
      Deep within the grave with me:—

    That upon the open ocean,
      When the third Armada came,
    They and I had died together,
      Whirled aloft on wings of flame.

    Yet 'tis something that they've laid me
      In a land without a stain:
    Keep it thus, my God and Saviour,
      Till I rise from earth again.

For several miles we continued to skirt the upper *School of Homer.*
slopes of the mountains, but afterwards a very steep
and stony descent commenced towards the lower
ground. Shortly before we left the higher regions
we passed through the village of Karyes, the houses
of which must once have been well built, but were
now all in ruins; the church, however, had been
restored, and a beautiful bell-tower, with several
storeys in the Italian style which prevails in the
Cyclades, had been attached to it. At last we reached
the shore, and were conducted to a spot where

stands a rough mass of limestone rock, the upper surface of which has been artificially levelled, forming a table twenty-five feet across. On one side of this a stone bench is cut, and near the end which is furthest from the sea a mass of rock is left, which looks as if it had formed the base of a statue. In the last century, when Chandler saw it, this supported a seated figure of Cybele, with a lion carved on either side and on the back of her chair. The name of the School of Homer which was attached to it is purely fanciful. At the present time neither the statue nor any trace of ornament remains. From this spot we made our way to the city, which we reached at nightfall; and the next morning, finding that a Greek steamer was in the harbour ready to start for Smyrna, we returned once more to that place.

CHAPTER VIII.

SAMOS.

THE most convenient route by which Samos may be reached is by way of Ayasolouk (Ephesus) and the port of Scala Nova, from which, with a favouring wind, it is three or four hours' sail to Vathy, the capital of the island. Accordingly, as this was the next point for which we intended to make, on the morning of April 5 we took the train by the Aidin railway from Smyrna to Ayasolouk, and after spending some hours in examining the now well-known ruins, proceeded on horseback to Scala Nova. Our road at first skirted the plain of the Cayster, and then turned southward over low hills, commanding beautiful views of the gulf of Scala Nova, from the northern shore of which rise the fine mountains of the mainland, with Chios appearing beyond, while the opposite side is bounded by the lofty broken summits of Samos. It was from these that the island received its name, for Strabo tells us that in early times the word *samos* signified 'a height'[1]; it is in reality of Phoenician origin, and is found in connexion with settlements of that people in Samothrace and elsewhere. The town of Scala Nova lies in a fold of the hills above a

Port of Scala Nova.

---

[1] Strabo, 8. 3. 19, p. 346; σάμους ἐκάλουν τὰ ὕψη.

creek which is protected from the sea by a small headland, while in front of it is an island, surrounded in its whole circuit by a wall, with a square fort occupying the highest point in the centre. Notwithstanding its Italian name it has a thoroughly Turkish aspect, presenting a strong contrast to anything that can be seen in the islands. The houses are closely packed together, but when seen from the hills above it appears a large place, containing at least 6000 or 7000 people; the Mahometans form the majority of these, and occupy the Kastro, or fortified enclosure, and some of the suburbs towards the interior, while the Christian population, including several hundred Armenians in addition to the Greeks, inhabit the steep declivities that overhang the port. This quarter is singularly picturesque, since the houses seem piled on one another, and their upper storeys, which are of wood and sometimes elaborately carved, project above the precipitous streets at a variety of angles so as almost to meet in the middle. The khan in which we were housed was a regular caravanserai, with an extensive court surrounded by stables, above which on two sides ran a wooden gallery, giving entrance to numerous chambers. Within the Kastro was a similar, but more ancient, building with pointed arches of brickwork, which seemed to be frequented by the Mahometan traders.

The Lenten Fast.

Hitherto our visit to these parts had been accompanied by a cold north-east wind, though the sky was cloudless; it now went round to the west—

a change which was agreeable enough in itself, but unfavourable to our voyage, as it blew in the opposite direction to that in which we were going. However, we hired a small vessel with a lateen sail to take us across to Vathy, expecting to reach that place in the course of the afternoon. Our crew consisted of two men and a boy, the last a charming-looking sailor-lad of twelve years old. Shortly after we started they took their frugal midday meal, which consisted of bread, together with three or four small fried fish, which served for a relish. The fish were an unusual accompaniment to their ordinary fare, since it was the Lenten season, when only bloodless fish, such as mussels and the octopus, are allowed to be eaten; but we found that this day was the Lady-day of the Greek Church, and on that festival and Palm Sunday (τὰ βάϊα) the rule is relaxed in favour of fish, though not of meat.

Passage to Samos.

At first we sailed close to the wind in the direction of the northern side of the bay, with the object of making a long tack into the harbour of Vathy, which is not easily reached with a head-wind on account of a promontory which projects on its eastern side; and as we danced along over the crests of the blue waves, with the mountains around us softened by a gentle haze, and the snowy peaks of Mount Tmolus rising far away in the interior above the depression formed by the plain of the Cayster, we had no wish that our voyage should come to a speedy termination. After three hours, however, we had reason to change our minds, for the wind, which had freshened, and dashed the waves over our bows, became too much for our little craft, so that our captain was glad to make for a creek in the northern shore, intending to wait there till midnight, at which hour, so the sailors assured us, the wind would fall. We landed, and wandered about the low hills in the neighbourhood, meeting only a few Turks, the inhabitants of a village on the mountain-side above, who were collecting grass for their cattle; but we afterwards learned that this district is one of the worst in respect of brigandage on the whole of the coast of Asia Minor. The islands, fortunately, are free from this curse, because within a restricted area which offers no outlet a highwayman can easily be hunted down. In the latter part of the day the wind became so violent that we were well contented to be in shelter, but our crew were not mistaken in their weather forecasts. When midnight came, I heard one of them who had been sleeping, rouse himself and say to the others— using the old Biblical Greek expression - 'the sea has ceased' (ἐκόπασε ἡ θάλασσα). We then started, and found the bay so calm that it was a difficult matter to make any way, until towards daybreak a kindly breeze arose and carried us across to Samos, and up the long and narrow fiord, at the head of which Vathy stands.

Town of Vathy. This place, which, like the chief town in modern Ithaca, and several other spots in Greece, takes its name from the deep waters of its harbour, has within the present century become the capital of the island, instead of the town of Chora, which lies on the southern side, not far from the ruins of ancient Samos. It consists of two parts, which are called Upper and Lower Vathy; the former of these is situated on steep slopes at a distance of more than half a mile from the sea, while the latter, which is the centre of commerce, and the place of residence of consuls and merchants, is grouped round the port. Its long and well-built quay is an object of which the inhabitants are justly proud, for, with the exception of that of Smyrna, there is no other that can rival it on the coast of Asia Minor. Shortly after landing, we made the acquaintance of the British consul, Mr. Marc, and in his company we paid a visit to the Prince of Samos. Ever since 1832 this island has been virtually independent of the Porte, for it enjoys a constitution of its own and regulates its own affairs, and its governor, who bears the title of Prince, though he is appointed by the Sultan, must be a Christian, and is not removeable at pleasure, like the ordinary Turkish governors. A small Turkish garrison resides in the place, but it is merely nominal. The island is allowed to have a flag of its own, the colours being red above and blue below, with a cross in the lower part. It pays a fixed annual tribute to the Ottoman Government, but most of this, we were told, is expended on improvements in the island. The experiment of establishing such a principality was an interesting one, and it seems to have thoroughly succeeded : being freed from Turkish misrule the inhabitants are contented and prosperous—this at least is what we were

Constitution of the island.

assured on the spot, and all that we saw tended to corroborate it. The present Prince is Caratheodori Pasha, who was one of the representatives of the Porte at the Berlin Congress, and at one time held high office at Constantinople. He is a thoughtful-looking man of about fifty years of age. We found that he spoke English well, and he conversed with us for some time in that language.

Samian wine. The principal exports of Samos are carobs, oil, and wine—the last-named article being far the most important. This I discovered to my cost on arriving, for some orchid-plants (*Serapias cordigera*), which I had dug up in the course of my wanderings on the previous day, with the view of transporting them to England, were promptly sequestrated for fear lest they should introduce the *Phylloxera*—a proceeding which would not have surprised one on the frontier of France and Italy, where even an orange is not allowed to pass, but which seemed strange in this remote island. The natives, however, depend so much on the proceeds of their vineyards that even potatoes are forbidden to be imported. All the Samian wine is somewhat sweet with a slight muscat flavour, and it bears mixing with a large quantity of water; it is exported to Genoa, and also to Hamburg and Bremen, and is used for doctoring other wines. Some old wine with which Mr. Marc regaled us was of a splendid quality, and almost a liqueur. When Byron, in his song, 'The Isles of Greece,' exclaimed—

Fill high the bowl with *Samian* wine—

he evidently intended to select the choicest of all the beverages of these islands. After this it is surprising to learn, as we do expressly from Strabo[1], that Samos did not produce good wine in ancient times.

The primary object of our visit to this island was to see its classical antiquities, all of which are to be found in the neighbourhood of the city of Polycrates, and with this view we left Vathy the same afternoon (April 7) for Tigani, a village which is built round the ancient port. The island is narrowest in this part, and the lofty mountain-chain that runs through it forms a low *col* immediately at the back of the capital; in consequence of this it only requires two hours and a half to ride from one of these places to the other. Passing through the upper town of Vathy, we mounted by a staircase rather than a road, which commanded fine views of the narrow harbour behind, and in no long time found ourselves on the ridge, and began to descend towards the southern coast. Where the country was cultivated, the ground was covered with olives and carob-trees; but the greater part of it was clothed with aromatic shrubs, which exhaled delightful odours under the influence of the genial warmth. As we approached the sea, beautiful views opened out of the strait of Mycale, which separates Samos from the mainland, dotted over with a few white sails, with the two peaks of the magnificent promontory of that name rising behind; then, turning westwards, we rode through pine-forests, until Tigani came in view, lying at our feet

The southern coast.

Strait of Mycale.

[1] Strabo, 14. 1. 15, p. 637.

on the shore. Before descending to it, we left our horses for a while in order to explore some ruins which were close at hand; these belonged to the acropolis of the original city, before its circuit was extended so as to include the loftier heights towards the west. The portion of the walls which is best preserved is on the eastern side, and this is in some parts composed of polygonal stones carefully fitted together; in one place there is a gateway, the head of which is formed by courses of masonry approaching one another.

Village of Tigani.

The inhabitants of Tigani have shown their enterprise by constructing a handsome quay round their harbour, and are now engaged in repairing and completing the two ancient moles which protected it; the longer of these, which faces the open sea, is the breakwater of which Herodotus spoke in terms of admiration in a passage which will be quoted hereafter[1]. It was no doubt the shape of the enclosed port that suggested its modern name of the 'Frying-pan' (τηγάνιον), a descriptive appellation which is found applied to a headland in Lemnos, and to a small peninsula west of the Taenarian promontory in the Peloponnese; in ancient times also, according to Pliny[2], there was a small island near Rhodes called Teganon. The warmth of the climate is shown by the palm-trees which grow there, and during the night a few mosquitoes made their appearance. We were lodged in a large disused warehouse belonging to Mr. Marc; and here we had the

[1] Herod. 3. 60.   [2] *Hist. Nat.* 5. 31, 36.

pleasure of meeting Mr. and Mrs. Theodore Bent, who occupied other rooms in the same building; they were engaged in excavating some of the tombs that lie outside the city walls. The warehouse apparently had been originally intended for storing oil, for in the court behind it there were lying thirty-nine earthenware oil-vessels of such dimensions that, had they been set upright, they might easily have accommodated forty thieves save one.

Directly after our arrival we started to visit the ancient city of Samos, the walls of which we had seen from the old acropolis on the opposite side of an intervening valley, reaching in a long line down the north-eastern side of a lofty hill. The line of this hill runs parallel to the shore, and the city was built on the slopes which descend from its broad flank to the water, but the fortifications enclosed the whole of the ridge, including the summit at the western end, the height of which is between 700 and 800 feet. The point which we first made for was the little monastery of 'Our Lady of the Cave' (Παναγία Σπηλιανή), which forms a conspicuous object with its white walls and dark cypresses high up on the bare south face of the hill. On reaching it we were welcomed by an old monk, who told us that this convent is a dependency of a larger monastery in Amorgos, and showed us the cave, which descends for some distance into the rock behind, and was evidently an ancient quarry. Within it is a little chapel, from which the place derives its name. We then mounted to a depression in the ridge, where was another quarry,

The ancient city.

and immediately on crossing it came upon the city walls, which are twelve feet thick and have towers at intervals. These we followed up to the summit, where, near the north-west angle of the fortifications, are the finest remains, consisting of numerous courses of masonry, the massive blocks of which almost rival the work of Epaminondas at Messene. From this point the walls descend the mountain side, and are traceable at intervals until they reach the sea; at one point, not far below the summit, a large tower, the best preserved of all these outworks, now stands alone, though it once formed part of the fortifications.

The theatre. In returning to Tigani, we made our way down the rough hill-side until we reached the theatre, which is situated a little way below the monastery; the form of this is clearly traceable, and the arches remain which supported the scena, but few of the seats are in their original position. The dimensions are small, considering the size of the city. It commands a wonderful view over the Sporades and the neighbouring coast of Asia Minor. Looking from it, we can picture to ourselves Polycrates proceeding from the harbour in his galley to drop in the sea the ring, which has added so great an element of romance to his story; or, extending our view a little further, we can make ourselves present at the battle of Mycale, which was fought on the shores of the strait. Immediately below the theatre, the hill-side breaks into easier declivities, and it was here that the upper part of the ancient city stood, for the ground above is too steep to allow of being built over. This is what Strabo meant, when he described the place as 'lying for the most part on level ground, and washed by the sea, though part of it runs up the mountain-side above [1].'

The next morning (April 8) was devoted to exploring the aqueduct and tunnel of Eupalinus, the discovery of which has been one of the greatest archaeological triumphs of our generation. But before proceeding thither, it may be well for me to quote the passage of Herodotus in which the historian has described it together with the other wonders of Samos. It runs thus in Canon Rawlinson's translation:— *Tunnel of Eupalinus.*

'I have dwelt the longer on the affairs of the Samians, because three of the greatest works in all Greece were made by them. One is a tunnel, under a hill 150 fathoms high, carried entirely through the base of the hill, with a mouth at either end. The length of the cutting is seven furlongs, the height and width are each eight feet. Along the whole course there is a second cutting, twenty cubits deep and three feet broad, whereby water is brought, through pipes, from an abundant source into the city. The architect of this tunnel was Eupalinus, son of Naustrophus, a Megarian. Such is the first of their great works; the second is a mole in the sea, which goes all round the harbour, near twenty fathoms deep, and in length above two furlongs. The third is a temple; the largest of all the temples known to us, whereof Rhoecus, son of Phileus, a Samian, was first architect [2].'

About the position of two of these works, the mole and the temple, there never has been any doubt, but this remarkable tunnel is not mentioned by any other ancient author, and all trace of it seemed to *M. Guérin's exploration.*

---

[1] Strabo, 14. 1. 14, p. 637.   [2] Herod. 3. 60.

have disappeared. The first person who attempted a systematic exploration was M. Guérin, the author of a book on Patmos and Samos, who visited this island about 1853. He rightly judged that the source of water should be made the starting-point in the investigation, and discovered that there was a copious spring about half a mile from the northern foot of the lofty hill on which the city was built— that is, towards the interior and away from the sea. By digging in the neighbourhood of this he found an underground passage, leading in the direction of the hill-side, in which were earthern pipes intended for the passage of water; and though it was much blocked up from the soil having fallen in, he traced it nearly to the foot of the hill. He was forced, however, to discontinue the work before arriving at that point, and consequently did not reach the tunnel which Herodotus describes. After all, the real discovery was made by accident, and on the opposite side of the mountain.

The discovery. Seven years ago a priest from the neighbouring monastery of Hagia Triada, called Cyril, who possessed a piece of ground not very far from the ancient theatre which I have described, chanced to find an opening, which led into the tunnel near the point where it issued from the mountain-side; and so great was the enthusiasm aroused in Samos by this discovery that a large sum of money was soon forthcoming with the object of clearing it out and restoring it. As yet, owing to the magnitude of the task, this has not been fully accomplished, but enough has been done to give an accurate idea of the work, and to confirm the statements of Herodotus. We now know that the water was carried underground the whole way from the spring to the heart of the city; first by the passage which M. Guérin explored, then by the tunnel through the bowels of the mountain which Herodotus describes, and finally by another passage in the direction of the port. There were also independent entrances at either end of the tunnel. The first intelligence of this discovery was sent to the ACADEMY by Mr. Dennis from Smyrna shortly after it was made; and the place has since been described by Mr. Bent both in the ACADEMY and the ATHENAEUM[1]; and with great fulness of detail by M. Fabricius in the *Mittheilungen des deutschen archäologischen Institutes in Athen*[2]. The following account is that of a passing traveller, and for more exact information I may refer the reader to the authorities above mentioned.

We started for the tunnel in the company of a *Chorophylax* or *gendarme*, who proved to be a most painstaking guide. Before reaching it we found sitting under some trees two monks, one of whom was Cyril, the discoverer of the entrance; they volunteered to join us, and with this admirable escort we arrived at the opening, which I have mentioned. Candles were now lighted, and when we had descended a little way into the ground, we entered a narrow passage constructed with large

Description of it.

[1] *Academy*, June 9, 1883; *Athenaeum*, June 12, 1886.
[2] Vol. ix. pp. 163 foll.

hewn stones, the upper of which were cut angularly so as to form an arch; after passing through this, in a short time we found ourselves in the tunnel. This was an excavation seven or eight feet wide, the sides of which curved somewhat outwards; and about two-thirds of its width was occupied by a footway, which ran along by the wall on our left-hand as we proceeded north-westwards in the direction of the source, while the rest of the space was taken up with the channel for the water, the sides of which descended perpendicularly to a depth of thirty feet. This was not open throughout, for spaces remained at intervals where the rubbish which had choked it had not been removed. In the process of clearing it the pipes which served to convey the water were found at the bottom. The height of the roof of the tunnel varied in different parts, for in some places it was eight feet high, or even more; while in others we had for some distance to stoop in walking. The roof was not arched but flattened, though rounded at the angles; and its surface, though, like that of the rest of the tunnel, it had been cut to a fairly smooth face, was often ridged owing to the character of the rock, as we discovered when our heads came into contact with it in places where our attention was diverted by the risk of slipping into the water-course.

Its course underground.

The *Chorophylax* and the second monk did not accompany us for any great distance, but Cyril conducted us as far as a point where a considerable quantity of water had collected on the path, and about which were the remains of stalactites. When the place was first explored a great quantity of these had to be broken away before the passage could be cleared. Here, also, strange to say, a large piece of a fluted column was lying half-immersed in the water, showing apparently that at one time a small *sacrarium* must have existed on the spot. We now proceeded alone, until we reached a place where the height of the tunnel was greater than before, and both tunnel and water-course made a bend ; on the further side of this the passage was obstructed, the clearing not having been continued further in this direction. As our progress thus far had occupied twenty minutes, we could not have been far from the middle of the tunnel, for its length is probably less, certainly not more, than the seven furlongs at which Herodotus estimates it. The change in the elevation which has just been mentioned, coinciding as it does with an alteration in the course of the tunnel, renders it almost certain that this was the meeting-point of two working parties, and that the excavation was carried on simultaneously from the two ends. In the case of the conduit of the pool of Siloam at Jerusalem—a smaller undertaking than this, but one that affords a singularly interesting parallel—this is known to have been done, from its being recorded in the famous inscription which was lately found there. A comparison of the two gives proof of greatly superior engineering skill in the execution of the Samian work, and suggests that it cannot date from a period of very remote antiquity.

Other features.

We now retraced our steps, but before we reached the entrance we noticed a number of cuttings or niches in the side of the rock, which probably were resting-places for lamps, since earthenware lamps were found in them; and in one place a deeper hollow had been made, concerning which it has been conjectured that it was intended to receive the tools of the workmen. Near the point where the transverse passage by which we entered meets the tunnel, a section of the rock was left, so as to form a wall across the passage; here no doubt there was originally a gate, for at the side it was pierced by a hole, through which a person desiring admission might call. During the forty minutes that we remained underground we found the air warm, but nowhere close or foul. The tunnel is continued by a subterranean passage, which runs parallel to the mountain-side in the direction of the port; this has been excavated as far as the theatre, but its exit into the city has not yet been found. Its course may be traced above ground by the stone-cased openings, resembling large vents, that form the heads of the shafts, through which, both in ancient and modern times, the earth and rubbish were removed from below.

The northern entrance.

The point that we next made for was the northern entrance of the tunnel; and in order to reach this we crossed the mountain under the guidance of the *Chorophylax*, and descended to a point beneath the north-west angle of the city walls, where another opening had been made. By this the roof of the underground passage leading from the spring has been broken through from above, just where it makes a sharp turn at its junction with the tunnel; the tunnel itself is blocked with *débris* a little way beyond its mouth. In the steep hill-side close above, an arched entrance, flanked with stone walls, has been discovered, corresponding to that through which we had first passed on the southern side, only here the gallery is longer, and runs at first above the tunnel, instead of striking it transversely. We penetrated into it for a quarter of an hour, until the passage became extremely narrow, and the water that had collected in it reached nearly to our knees; here it appeared useless to proceed further, and turning round with some difficulty, we returned to our starting-point. In one place a hole in the floor, which in the dim light of our candles required to be passed with great care, seemed to communicate, through a shaft or otherwise, with the tunnel below; but we had no means of discovering where is the ultimate point of junction of the two. The underground passage which brought the water from the spring has been completely cleared out, so that it is possible to pass from one end to the other. Owing to the nature of the ground its course was very irregular, for it was carried round the heads of two small valleys, where we traced it from outside by the openings of the shafts, which were constructed in the same way as those which I have already described. The fountain, which is close to the commencement of the passage, but has now *The fountain.*

no communication with it, lies beneath a small chapel of St. John the Baptist; the reservoir which contains it, is of ancient construction. In the middle of the floor of the chapel there is a square wooden cover, and when this is removed the water can be seen welling out in a large volume.

Questions connected with it.

Two questions naturally suggest themselves in connexion with this interesting work. First; what was the object of boring such a tunnel, with enormous expenditure of labour, through the rock, when, so far as the position of the ground is concerned, the water might have been carried in an open channel round the flank of the mountain into the city? We naturally conjecture that it was to secure the water supply in case of war; but then we are met by the difficulty that the spring was situated some way outside the walls, and consequently was in the power of an attacking force. I can only suggest that the source may have been completely concealed from view, and at the time of M. Guérin's visit it was so, for in order to discover it one of the flags of the pavement had to be removed. This idea is rendered probable by the fact that the water was carried underground to the foot of the mountain. If this was the case, the existence of the source, and probably that of the tunnel also, must have been a state secret, confined to a few persons; otherwise the city would have been at the mercy of every traitor. Secondly; what explanation is to be given of the extraordinary depth of the water-way, which so far exceeds all the requirements of the supply? To this question the only satisfactory answer is to be found in the suggestion of M. Fabricius, that as the depth is more remarkable in the southern part of the channel, which is furthest from the source, it may have been deepened as the work proceeded in consequence of insufficient allowance having been originally made for the fall of the water [1].

Leaving the spring, we descended the valley in which its water now runs, and at its narrowest part passed the broken arches of a Roman aqueduct which here crossed it; this would seem to have been constructed at a time when the supply of water that was brought into the town by way of the tunnel was found insufficient. Hence we emerged into a wide rich plain extending to the sea, at the head of which stands the town of Chora, which until recently was the capital of the island; this plain we crossed diagonally in the direction of the Heraeum, which is situated on the seashore, about four miles west of Tigani, its position being easily traceable from a distance by the single column that is now standing. The ruins have been partially excavated, the work having been begun by M. Paul Girard in 1879, and resumed for a time by M. Clerc in 1883 [2]; but the progress hitherto made is not sufficient to enable us to speak with confidence either of the dimensions or the character of the building. The portion which has been chiefly laid bare is the wall and the bases

The temple of Hera.

---

[1] A practical engineer, to whom the facts were mentioned, at once, and without hesitation, assigned this as the cause.

[2] *Bulletin de Correspondance hellénique*, vol. iv. pp. 383-394; vol. ix. pp. 505-509.

of the columns of the eastern end, and especially of the north-eastern angle; part of the white marble floor, and the bases of some of the columns that belonged to the interior of the building, have also been uncovered. It seems to have faced east and west, and to have been a dipteral octastyle of the Ionic order, with a frontage of 165 feet; it must thus have been one of the largest Greek temples—probably the largest existing in the time of Herodotus, if the building which he mentions corresponded in size to this one. The remains which we see appear to be of a later date, with the exception of the standing column, which may have formed part of the original structure. This object, however, forms a very puzzling feature, for it is not fluted, and its broad, bulging base, together with part of the drum above it, are channelled with a number of horizontal flutings varying in size. It consists of twelve white marble drums without the capital, while the base is of grey marble. A peculiar effect is produced by the drums being irregularly super-imposed on one another, having been shaken out of place by an earthquake, or—according to an old story which Tournefort mentions, and which still finds its supporters—by cannon balls fired at it by the Turks.

Rivers Imbrasos and Chesios.

A small vessel happened to be lying off the beach close by, having just been laden with carob-pods, which were destined to be exported to Savona, near Genoa. As this was on the point of starting for Tigani, our *Chorophylax* preferred to avail himself of this mode of transit, while we ourselves returned on foot along the seashore. At no great distance from the temple we reached a clear stream, which was of sufficient width to render wading necessary. This is now called Potoki, and was in ancient times the Imbrasos, on the banks of which, according to the local legend which is given by Pausanias, Hera was born beneath a bush of agnus castus[1]. Further on, as we approached the site of the ancient city, we crossed two others, both of which admitted of being jumped. They belonged to the ancient Chesios, from the neighbourhood of which river the western quarter of the city was called Chesias, while the eastern portion, which included the original acropolis, was named Astypalaea. Between these streams and the city walls lay the tombs, which Mr. Bent was at this time exploring. In the course of the afternoon we once more reached our head-quarters at Tigani.

[1] Pausan. 7. 4. 4.

CHAPTER IX.

PATMOS.

Voyage to Patmos.

IN passing from Samos to Patmos we leave a land of classical archaeology for one the interest of which is wholly Biblical and ecclesiastical. Before the Christian era the name of Patmos only occurs in a few passages of ancient writers, and of its history, if it had one, nothing is known; it was when it became the place of banishment of St. John the Divine, and the scene of his apocalyptic vision, that it once for all attracted the attention of mankind. At the present day it is one of the least accessible of the Aegean islands, for owing to its remote position and the unproductiveness of its soil no steamers ever touch there. In order to reach it we engaged a good-sized decked vessel, for though we hoped after visiting it to arrive at the neighbouring island of Leros in time for the Austrian packet which touches there on its way from Smyrna to Rhodes, yet it was necessary to be prepared for a longer voyage, since, if the weather was unpropitious, we might be forced to continue our course southwards to Calymnos, or even to Cos. Early on the morning of April 9 we left the harbour of Tigani; and a favouring breeze carried us along the southern coast of Samos, where the two highest summits were in view—Mount Ampelos, which rises behind the Heraeum, and descends to the cape which is called Colona from the standing column of that temple; and, towards the west, Mount Kerkis, the ancient Kerketeus, which is the loftiest point in any of the islands on this side of the Aegean, excepting Samothrace, being 4725 feet above the sea. After this we sailed between groups of islands unknown to fame, and at last in the course of the afternoon passed Cape Geranos, the north-eastern headland of Patmos. We then penetrated into the harbour, which forms the innermost part of a deep bay on the eastern coast, and is so landlocked that frequent tacking was required in order to enter it. Long before we arrived, the monastery of St. John, which is the most conspicuous building in the island, had been in sight, crowning the summit of a high hill, like a vast sombre castle, with the white houses of the town clustered round it; behind this rose the peak of Hagios Elias, which reaches the elevation of more than 800 feet. The *scala*, or village at the landing-place, has a very peculiar appearance, for each of the small two-storeyed houses of which it is composed resembles a square, flat-topped box, as white as whitewash can make it. This mode of building prevails throughout this island, and, as we afterwards found, in those that lie to the southward of it.

In shape Patmos may be roughly described as forming a crescent, the horns of which face eastward; *Description of the island.*

but its outline is broken up by innumerable promontories enclosing landlocked creeks, so that, when seen from above, it presents somewhat the aspect of a strange polypus. Its length from north to south is about eight miles, and its area is rugged and broken; but the most marked peculiarity is that it is almost divided in two in the middle, for in this part, within

a distance of little more than half a mile from one another, are two isthmuses only a few hundred yards wide, and rising but slightly above the sea-level. On the southernmost of these the *scala* is situated, while between the two stands the steep hill on which the acropolis of the Hellenic city was built. The narrow waist thus formed serves for a boundary line to determine the domain of the monastery, for while the southern half of the island belongs to the monks, the northern part is the possession of the civil community. At the time of the foundation of the convent no women were allowed to pass this limit, but within a short period the restriction had to be abandoned. The soil of which the island is composed is everywhere volcanic and very barren, and its coasts are flanked by red and grey rocks, which ever and anon break into quaint pinnacles. The absence of running water is shown by the numerous windmills, and there are only three or four wells in the whole area; the want of these, however, is made up for by cisterns, and the inhabitants are never obliged to import water, as sometimes happens in Santorin. The male population are chiefly employed in the sponge fishery, which is carried on in many of the Sporades. The island is most commonly known by its mediaeval name of Patino, in like manner as Astypalaea is still called Astropalaea, and Carpathos Scarpanto. *Volcanic soil.*

Leaving our baggage to be carried up to the monastery of St. John, which is a mile and a half from the *scala*, we ourselves proceeded to the smaller monastery of the Apocalypse, which occupies a steep position on the mountain-side about one-third of the distance in the same direction, and is the spot pointed out by tradition as the scene of the Revelation. It is entered from the back, and from this point the visitor descends among a variety of buildings by numerous stone staircases, the steps of which are forty in number. At the lowest point, though still at a con- *Monastery of the Apocalypse.*

The cave. siderable height above the valley below, is the cave which forms the chapel of the Apocalypse. This is entered through a church dedicated to St. Anne, which is built outside and parallel to the mouth of the cave, and consists, like the chapel, of two parts—a *narthex* or porch, and the sacred building itself. The *iconostasis* at the further end of this church is ornamented with pictures of St. Anne, of our Lord, and of the Panagia, and is surmounted by an elaborate rood-screen, while against the outer wall a representation of the Entombment, richly embroidered on velvet, is hung in a glass case; this was a gift from Russia. The chapel of the Apocalypse, which is formed by the bare sides and roof of the cave, is about twenty-two feet in length by fifteen feet in breadth. In one part of the roof a rent is pointed out, where the rock was broken at the commencement of the Revelation, and from a somewhat deeper cleft in this the Divine voice is said to have proceeded; nor does the process of identification stop here, for a hole in the wall close below this is believed to have been the place where St. John's head lay.

Pictures in the Chapel. The pictures in the *iconostasis* of this chapel are worthy of notice. In the left hand compartment is a Jesse tree, in which the Virgin and Child are the most prominent objects; but figures of prophets and saints are seen in the branches. The central picture represents our Lord appearing to St. John, who lies at his feet as dead. In this, Christ is seated in the midst of seven angels, who bear in their hands seven churches, while a candlestick stands in front of each of them. A sword proceeds out of his mouth, and in his right hand are seven stars, in his left hand the two keys of hell and of death. The third is divided into three sections, the first of which presents a figure of the founder of the great monastery, St. Christodoulos; in the second the disciples of St. John are represented as laying his body in a tomb, while he himself is being taken up to heaven, such being the tradition of the Greek Church with regard to his death; while in the third St. John is listening to the divine inspiration, and a disciple is writing from his dictation. The monk who pointed out these objects to us was a simple, pleasant man, and had a full belief in the genuineness of the local traditions. Though he belonged to the great monastery, he had lived here, together with some members of his family, for the last eight years, and they were the sole occupants of the building. To their credit be it said, the whole place was scrupulously clean.

Before proceeding further, I must make mention of a work which has exercised a great influence on the traditions of Patmos, the 'Acts of St. John' attributed to Prochorus, one of the seven deacons. This narrative, the text of which is given in full in Zahn's *Acta Johannis*, was probably composed in the first half of the fifth century; for a time it was much used in the Eastern Church, and its popularity is attested by the numerous versions of it that exist—in Latin, in Old Slavonic, in Coptic, and in Armenian. Of its apocryphal character there can be no doubt, for, not to mention other proofs, the writer was wholly

The 'Acts of St. John.'

ignorant of the position, size, and nature of Patmos ; he makes it nine days' sail from Ephesus, and conceives of it as a large and populous island, hardly smaller than Sicily. The story commences with the departure of John from Judaea on a mission to the province of Asia, on which Prochorus accompanied him, and after describing his sojourn at Ephesus, relates in full detail his banishment to Patmos and residence there. Two of the incidents that are mentioned deserve notice here, because they will be referred to later on.

Story of Kynops the magician. The first of these is the contest of St. John with Kynops, a magician who inhabited a cave in a desolate part of the island. It runs as follows. When the priests of the temple of Apollo in Patmos found that John was converting all the leading men to Christianity, they came to Kynops to request him to put an end to his influence; and in consequence of this, Kynops, in the presence of a great multitude, displayed his magical powers in a variety of ways as a challenge to John, and finally cast himself into the sea, intending to reappear from it, as he had done on several former occasions. But John, extending his arms in the form of a cross, exclaimed, 'O thou who did'st grant to Moses by this similitude to overthrow Amalek, O Lord Jesus Christ, bring down Kynops to the deep of the sea; let him never more behold this sun, nor converse with living men.' And at John's word immediately there was a roaring of the sea, and the water formed in an eddy at the place where Kynops went down, and Kynops sank to the bottom, and after this reappeared no more from the sea. The name of the magician is now attached to one of the southern promontories of Patmos, a wild and precipitous locality, and in one part of it a cavern is shown which is reported to have been his dwelling-place.

The other incident relates to the composition of St. John's Gospel, which is associated with the Apostle's departure from the island at the end of his term of banishment. When the people of Patmos, whom he had converted, found that he was about to leave them, they begged him to deliver to them in writing a narrative of the miracles of the Son of God which he had seen, and of His words which he had heard, that they might remain steadfast in the faith. Prochorus then narrates how he went with John to a tranquil spot by a low hill a mile distant from the city; and, after long fasting and prayer, John caused Prochorus to seat himself by his side with paper and ink, and then, standing and looking up steadfastly into heaven, dictated to him the Gospel, commencing with the words, 'In the beginning was the Word.' The interest of this story—which is in direct contradiction to all the early traditions relating to this Gospel—arises from its having been a suggestive subject for early works of art. The figures of an aged man, who is standing, dictating to a youth who is seated, in the midst of rural surroundings, are found, for instance, in a Greek MS. of the Gospels in the Vatican, figured in Agincourt's *History of Art* (Painting, pl. lix), in the Codex Ebnerianus in the Bodleian, in the facsimile

John dictating his Gospel.

Treatment in art.

from an Armenian MS. in Professor Westwood's *Palaeographia Sacra*, and in one of the MSS. in the monastery at Patmos. Strange to say, in the narrative of Prochorus in its original form, there is not a word about the Apocalypse. In some of the later MSS. of the 'Acts of St. John,' however, there is an interpolated passage, evidently adapted from the story of the composition of the Gospel, in which that book is said to have been dictated by the Apostle to Prochorus in a cave in Patmos. It was thus, no doubt, that the grotto which we have visited was fixed upon as the scene of this event, and it is possible that the picture on the *iconostasis* is intended to describe it. It is noticeable, that in the *Guide to Painting* of Dionysius of Agrapha, which from an unknown period of the Middle Ages to the present day has determined the mode of treatment of sacred subjects in art in the Eastern Church, it is prescribed that the scene both of the Revelation and of the composition of the Gospel shall be a cave ; but whereas in the latter subject Prochorus is to be introduced as the scribe, in the former the Apostle is to be represented alone [1].

Ruined school buildings.

Just outside the entrance gate of the convent of the Apocalypse stand the ruined buildings of a school which formerly was resorted to by numerous students from the neighbouring islands. About thirty years ago it was given up, owing to the competition of schools that had sprung up elsewhere. Leaving this, we now proceeded upwards by a rough road

[1] Didron, *Manuel d'Iconographie chrétienne*, pp. 238, 304-307.

composed of blocks of trachyte until we arrived at the town, and, passing through it by a succession of steep zigzags, reached the entrance to the great monastery of St. John. The likeness of this to a castle increases as you approach, owing to the massiveness of the walls and buttresses, and the projections, resembling towers, at the angles. Here we were welcomed by the Hegumen, and conducted to a simple monastic chamber, which was destined for our reception.

With the exception of one or two Greek monasteries which are built in the interior of caverns—such as those of Megaspelaeon in the Morea and Sumelas at the back of Trebizond—none that I can remember is so closely and strangely packed together as that of St. John on Patmos; its staircases are quite a puzzle, and passages occur in the most unexpected places, and diverge in a variety of directions. The court round which it is built is very irregular in shape, and several pointed arches are thrown across it to strengthen the buildings on either side: within it are numerous cisterns for storing water and troughs for washing. The upper part is a wilderness of chimneys, bells, domes, and battlements. A pavement of tiles or flags covers the flat roof, or rather roofs, for different parts have different levels, and the communication between these is made by steps constructed at various angles. Among them the domes of chapels project at intervals, and at one point stand three large bells, one of which has an inscription in Latin, another in Russian. The voices

Monastery of St. John.

of these we heard in the middle of the night, calling the community to prayers, after the door of each chamber had first been vigorously knocked, and the *semantron*, or alarum used in the Greek Church, had been sounded in the corridors. The number of monks is thirty, and they are all natives of Patmos. They possess farms in Crete, Samos, and Santorin, but at the present time they complain of poverty. The foundation of the monastery dates from the latter half of the eleventh century, when a monk named Christodoulos, who had been an inmate of several convents, and found none of them sufficiently strict in their rules to satisfy his own ascetic temperament, obtained from the Emperor Alexius Comnenus a concession of the island of Patmos, confirmed by a golden bull, that he might establish there a community regulated according to his ideas of monastic life. We are expressly told that for some time before the island had been uninhabited, and this fact must be taken into account in estimating the value of the local traditions.

Panorama seen from it. The panorama from the roof of the monastery, to which I ascended on the morning after my arrival, is truly wonderful. The greater part of the strange island, with its varied heights and irregular outline, is visible, and, along with it, the wide bay, which is embraced by its rocky arms. Toward the north appeared the level line of Icaria, the peaks of Samos, and the promontory of Mycale; and, in the opposite direction, the island of Leros, beyond which rose the fine summits of Calymnos; while in the open expanse of the Aegean to the west lay Amorgos, and the distant volcano of Santorin. In addition to this, the sea was studded with numerous islets, and these, together with the intervening spaces of deep blue water, formed the pervading feature of the scene. Such was the view which, with frequent changes from day to night, and from sunshine to storm, must have been present to St. John at the period of his banishment; and it is an interesting question whether the impression which it made upon him is traceable in the imagery of the Revelation. The subject is one which may easily lead to fanciful speculation; and Dean Stanley, whose mind was singularly open to local influences, and could trace their working with great felicity, in this instance seems to have yielded to the temptation in an eloquent passage on Patmos in the Notices appended to his *Sermons in the East*[1]. There he goes so far as to suppose that the dragon, and the beasts with many heads and monstrous figures, were suggested by the serpentine form of the island and its rocks contorted into fantastic and grotesque forms. Still the references to the sea in the Apocalypse—even if we exclude from consideration, as we ought to do, those passages where the sea is introduced, like the earth and sky, as one of the constituents of creation—are frequent and striking; and still more so is the introduction of the islands (Rev. vi. 14: 'Every mountain and island were moved out of their places;' xvi. 20: 'Every island fled away'); for these objects rarely occur in Biblical imagery,

Suited to the Apocalypse.

[1] p. 230.

and in the Old Testament the expression 'the isles' signifies rather a region than a feature in geography or landscape. But even if we hesitate to admit the direct suggestiveness of such points as these, we may, at least, feel that the scenery of this island, from its grandeur and wildness, and the sense of space and solitude which it conveys, was well suited to form a background in the mind's eye of the seer for the wonderful visions of the Apocalypse.

The Library. The first place of interest in the monastery which we visited was the library. This is a spacious and airy room, and the books are arranged in cases along its walls, so that it presents a very different appearance from what Dr. E. D. Clarke described, when he saw it at the beginning of this century, and carried off some of the most valuable of the works that it contained. At the present time its most precious *Codex N.* treasure is the famous Codex N., a quarto MS. of the sixth century, with double columns, written on purple vellum in uncial letters in silver, with the names of God and Christ in gold. The portion which is here preserved consists of thirty-three leaves, and contains the greater part of St. Mark's gospel; but its interest is increased by the fact that other fragments of the same MS., containing portions of the other gospels, exist elsewhere—six leaves in the Vatican, four in the British Museum, and two at Vienna. Strange to say, the MS. which resembles it most nearly, both in its externals and its text, is the Codex Rossanensis (Σ), which belongs to the monastery of Rossano in Calabria, not far distant from the site of the ancient Sybaris. So close is the correspondence between the two in respect of their peculiar readings, that it is thought they may both have been copied directly from a common original[1]. The Rossanensis also is a *codex purpureo-argenteus*, a kind of manuscript which is very rare—rarer even, according to Professor Westwood, than those which are written entirely in gold letters.

Next in importance to Codex N. is a MS. of the book of Job, which is attributed by Mr. Coxe to the seventh or eighth century[2]. It is a very large folio, and is written on vellum in uncial letters, with illustrations inserted in the pages; these appeared to me of great value for the study of mediaeval art, having much more originality than is usually found in Byzantine work. Among them are groups representing Job's sons and daughters, figures of stags and other animals, and scenes from Job's history; and these were not illuminated on the conventional gold ground, and in some parts were drawn in outline. There are also two Books of the Gospels in small quarto, with the original binding, one of which has the emblems of the evangelists in silver gilt at the corners, with the figure of Christ on the cross in the centre, while the other, which is bound in red silk, has the heads of the evangelists in silver. Both possess full-page illuminations of the evangelists, but

Other MSS.

---

[1] See Prof. Sanday on the Cod. Rossan. in *Studia Biblica*, No. VI.
[2] *Report to Her Majesty's Government on the Greek MSS. yet remaining in the Libraries of the Levant*, p. 27.

in the latter of the two the picture of St. John is wanting: in the former he is represented, as I have already described, as dictating the gospel to Prochorus. We were also shown a semi-uncial MS. of the works of St. Gregory of Nazianzus with the date 942; this was much defaced by damp. Not the least interesting object is the original bull of Alexius Comnenus, authorising the foundation of the monastery. The dimensions of this are about 9 ft. long by 16 in. wide, and it is on paper, which has been mounted on linen; the writing is large, and the emperor's signature, and words inserted by him, are in red ink.

Bull of Alexius Comnenus.

Let me now describe the great church of the monastery. This is entered through an outer porch, or *proaulion*, which runs the whole length of the west end of the building, and is open to the court, being supported on the outer side by marble columns. In one part of this there is a rude font, intended to contain the holy water that is used on the festival of the Epiphany. Its walls are frescoed with sacred subjects, among which may be seen the warrior saints, St. George and St. Demetrius, and St. Artemius with Constantine and Helen. In one part stands Alexius Comnenus in robe and crown, bearing a cross in his hand; in another the magician Kynops is throwing himself into the water, while on the opposite side of the picture is the aged St. John with his followers. In the eastern wall of this corridor there are three doorways, two of which lead into the church, and the third into a chapel of St. Christodoulos. The

The great church.

church is entered through a *narthex*, and is extremely dark, the only light being that which is admitted from the cupola and through a side chapel. The central dome is supported on four pillars, and contains a fresco of the Saviour; the floor beneath is ornamented with stone mosaic. The *iconostasis* is richly carved with figures, fruit, and flowers, and the lecterns are inlaid with tortoise-shell and mother-of-pearl. There are two ancient paintings of St. John—one large and the other small—but both much defaced by time and the devotion of worshippers; and a small triptych of the period of the founder is shown, with very delicate paintings of Scripture subjects. In the chapel the body of St. Christodoulos lies in a niche which has been hollowed out in the side wall; it is enclosed in a case, but the face is visible. His shoes and his staff are preserved as relics; the former are made of coarse brown leather, and much worn, while the latter—a *pateritsa*—is in two parts, one of which has the cross-piece attached to it, which is sometimes used for leaning on during service in the monasteries. The monks also show the chain by which St. John was bound as a prisoner; but the spurious character of this, as of all the memorials of St. John in the island, is made more conspicuous by the genuineness of most things connected with the founder. *Relics of the founder.*

The refectory is a large and lofty room, with a vaulted roof and central dome, and a long stone table runs down the middle, resembling that which we noticed at Nea Mone in Chios; but the seats *Refectory and kitchen.*

here are of wood, resting at intervals upon stone supports. It is now disused, owing to the system of common meals having been given up, but some frescoes remain to testify to its former grandeur. Adjoining it is a kitchen of equally massive construction, with a single fireplace surmounted by a chimney running up to the top of the monastery, like a rude funnel of irregular shape.

'The Garden of the Saint.' When we left the monastery we descended towards the western coast of the island, until, at the end of half an hour, a creek came in view, and on its shore a small level of cultivated land, which is known by the name of 'The Garden of the Saint' (ὁ κῆπος τοῦ ὁσίου). It measures about a quarter of a mile each way, and contains a chapel and a few dwelling-houses; but the fame which it enjoys is due to its possessing one of the few fountains in the island, and this is said to have issued from the ground in answer to the prayers of St. Christodoulos. From this point we made our way along the rugged slopes until we reached the inlet at the back of the *scala*, on the further side of which rises the height

The acropolis. that was occupied by the acropolis of the ancient city. The situation of this, as I have already described, is remarkable, since it stands between two isthmuses and two seas. When we arrived at its foot, we proceeded to climb its steep south-western face, and not far from the summit came upon the remains of fortifications, which were mainly formed of polygonal blocks roughly put together; but when we had crossed over to the opposite side, we found a line of walls and towers in much better preservation, as many as six courses of masonry remaining in many parts. The site was well chosen on account of its inaccessibility and its central position in the island.

We now re-embarked in our Samian vessel, and started for Leros, in hopes of catching the Austrian steamer, which touches at that island once a fortnight on her way from Constantinople to Alexandria. The voyage was a tedious one, for the wind was light at first and afterwards adverse, so that we did not reach our destination till shortly before daylight the following morning. We were fortunate in arriving at all, for within a few hours so strong a gale arose from the south-east that all progress would have been impossible in the face of it. The little town is composed of square white houses, like those of the *scala* at Patmos, and, like that place, it lies in the recesses of a landlocked harbour. After sunrise we obtained *pratique*, and having landed, took up our abode in an upper room belonging to a very dirty *café*. In the course of the morning, while we were sitting there, we suddenly heard a shout peal forth from every side, as if the whole population of Leros had risen in insurrection. This was caused by the Lloyd's steamer having come in sight—the fortnightly excitement of the island. The shout was followed by a general rush of the inhabitants to the shore, some embarking in boats, while others crowded the pier; and when the vessel had taken up her position in the harbour,

Island of Leros.

she was surrounded by a swarm of little tubs, most of them manned by three boys apiece, all of whom screamed at the top of their voice, apparently in the hope of disembarking some stray passenger. So numerous were the boats and so tightly packed, that we had some difficulty in forcing our way on board. It seemed strange enough that so fine a packet as the 'Vesta' should put into so insignificant a port as this, but during our stay in Rhodes the anomaly was explained to us. It appears that the inhabitants of Leros are possessed of some wealth, and that latterly many of them have settled in Alexandria, and have become shopkeepers there; and in consequence of this, the community in Egypt have found it worth their while to guarantee the Lloyd's company a sum equivalent to £1000 sterling annually, on condition that they carry on communications for them with their native island. This is a good instance of the commercial enterprise of the insular Greeks.

Connexion with Egypt.

Satires on Leros.

In ancient times the citizens of Leros were the victims of a malicious epigram, which was aimed by the poet Phocylides against one of their number, called Procles. It ran thus:—

> 'They are bad to a man, are the people of Leros;
> To a man, except Procles—and he too's from Leros[1].'

A poet of their own, Demodocus, attempted to

[1] The gnomic poems of Phocylides were subsequently quoted in this form, Καὶ τόδε Φωκυλίδεω; hence the epigram runs—
Καὶ τόδε Φωκυλίδεω· Λέριοι κακοί· οὐχ ὁ μὲν, ὃς δ' οὔ·
πάντες πλὴν Προκλέους· καὶ Προκλέης Λέριος.
Strabo, 10. 5. 12, p. 487; compare Bergk's note in his *Poet. Lyr. Gr.*, p. 338.

divert this so as to apply to the people of Chios, but apparently without much effect. We are told that if you throw plenty of dirt, some of it will stick, and satirical epigrams seem from their nature to be the form of literary dirt which sticks most easily and most permanently. This appears to be true in the present instance, for this gibe, which was uttered by Phocylides in the sixth century before Christ, is recorded against Leros by Strabo, who wrote in the Augustan age. The Greeks of the present day have not been less malicious than their predecessors. *Lera* is the modern word for 'filth,' and consequently 'Leros, filth' (Λέρος λέρα) has become a regular proverbial expression. It came naturally to the lips of our Athenian travelling-servant, as we approached the island.

Our voyage to Rhodes carried us past many interesting objects. At first our view was attracted by the islands on our right, those which form a chain between the extremity of Samos and the Triopian promontory. The northern portion of these is formed by Patmos and Leros; then follows Calymnos with its long and graceful line of summits; and at the end of the chain lies Cos in a transverse position to the others. This splendid island is intersected throughout its whole length by a backbone of mountains, which rises to a number of lofty peaks in the centre; and its northern slopes, which are cultivated to a great height, appear remarkably fertile. The houses of the city line the shore for a considerable distance at its eastern extremity.

Voyage to Rhodes.

The remark which has been made with regard to Lesbos, that the site of its capital was chosen with a view to its facing the mainland, is true also of all the larger islands off this coast—of Chios, Samos, Leros, Cos and Rhodes. On the left hand we pass the headland within which lay Halicarnassus; and shortly afterwards the huge towers of the castle of Budrum, which was built by the Knights of Rhodes on the site of that city, are clearly seen, notwithstanding that they are twelve miles distant. Then the land recedes, where the deep bay of Halicarnassus—one of those remarkable inlets in which the multiform coastline of the west of Asia Minor seems to reach its highest development towards this angle — intervenes between the promontory just past and the Triopian headland. The last-named cape is by far the most prominent feature in all this region owing to its magnificent succession of broken heights. On its extremity the ancient Cnidos was situated; so that at this point we are in the midst of one group of the towns which formed the Dorian hexapolis—Cos, Cnidos, and Halicarnassus, and the three others we are about to visit in Rhodes. During this part of the voyage the steamer is forced to pursue a devious course, in consequence of the eastern extremity of Cos being thrust in between the two promontories. The sun now set, and night had fallen some time before we approached the port of Rhodes.

CHAPTER X.

RHODES.

THERE is an element of excitement attending a voyage to Rhodes, arising from the uncertainty which exists with regard to reaching that island. It is easy to secure your passage thither, but it is a further question whether you will be able to land, for the harbour is too much silted up to admit large vessels, and when a high sea is running, it is impossible for boats to reach the steamer. When we left Leros in the Austrian packet, the captain threw out ominous hints that this might happen on the present occasion; in which case we should have been carried on to Alexandria—a fate which has frequently overtaken other travellers. In the island we heard of one person who left Smyrna with the intention of passing Christmas at Rhodes, and after making several journeys to and fro between Smyrna and Alexandria, during which it was impossible to land, ultimately reached Rhodes at Easter. It was therefore a relief to us when the strong south wind abated towards nightfall, and rendered it possible for us to leave the vessel. We were rowed ashore in a tossing sea by two Turks, two Greeks,

Arrival at Rhodes.

and a Jew—a crew that well represented the nationalities which inhabit the place. The languages that may be heard at the port are very motley, for the Jews, as in Salonica, are descendants of those who were expelled from Spain in the time of Ferdinand and Isabella, and speak a corrupt form of Spanish; and Italian, which, during the last thirty years, has been rapidly superseded by French in the Levant, is still prevalent here. On landing, we were conducted to the suburb of Neo-Maras, which lies to the northward of the city, and is the residence of the foreign consuls and the Roman Catholic population. The gates of the city are closed at night, and no Christians are allowed to remain within the walls, so that the Greeks, who occupy shops there, are obliged to quit the place at sunset. Until about forty years ago there was a further regulation, that on Fridays all Christians should leave before noon, in consequence of a prediction, or a prevalent idea, that the city would sometime be retaken by the Christians on a Friday, when all the faithful were at their prayers. We were at once struck with the balminess of the climate, and the air was laden with the scent of orange-blossom. The next morning (April 12) we found that even the plane-trees were partially in leaf, and the numerous palms testified to the temperature of the South. A resident informed us that he had only once had a fire lighted in his house during the previous winter. The pleasant climate, no doubt, was one of the chief attractions of the place in Roman times.

Its mixed population.

The city of Rhodes is situated close to the northern-most extremity of the island, facing the mainland, with a north-eastern aspect. In front of it are three harbours, which were originally separated from one another by small spits of land; but these were subsequently improved and strengthened by moles so as to afford protection against the sea. From the shore the ground rises gradually in the form of an ancient theatre, the highest point being towards the west, where it overlooks the sea in the opposite direction. This hill—which now bears the name of Mount Smith, because the house that stands on its summit was the residence of Sir Sydney Smith in 1802, at the time of Napoleon's Egyptian expedition—was the position of the ancient acropolis. But it is by no means a commanding height, and this is probably the reason why no city was built here at an early period; for the site was unoccupied until towards the close of the Peloponnesian war (B.C. 408), when the inhabitants of the three leading cities of the island, Lindos, Ialysos, and Cameiros, agreed to abandon their homes and found a city in common. In other respects the position is admirable for a commercial station, on account of its harbours, its nearness to the mainland, and its being a natural point of departure for Egypt and the East. The later glories of the place, when it became the stronghold of the Knights of St. John, and one of the bulwarks of Christian Europe against the Ottomans at the height of their power, have almost eclipsed its ancient fame. Yet Strabo speaks of its

Position of the city.

Its ancient grandeur.

grandeur as being surpassed by no other city, and hardly equalled by any[1]. Its commerce, its political institutions, its school of oratory, and its school of sculpture, enjoyed a world-wide renown[2]. Its strength was so great that it endured a siege by Demetrius Poliorcetes in B.C. 304, and triumphantly repulsed him, though he brought all his force against it for the space of a year. Nor can we forget that it became the residence of many great men; that Cicero studied there, and that Tiberius chose it as his place of voluntary exile. Of the magnificence of that time little remains beyond the Hellenic foundations of the moles, and the numerous sepulchral monuments of grey marble—resembling small round altars or pedestals of statues—which are met with in the city and the suburbs.

The fortress of the Knights.

But as a specimen of a mediaeval fortress the existing city is almost unrivalled; and the objects that remain there, notwithstanding the ravages of time, illustrate in an impressive manner the organisation of the Order of the Knights of St. John. The enormous moat, wide and deep, and faced on both sides with stone; the solid walls, with towers at intervals, forming sometimes a double, and at the highest point, where the palace of the Grand Master stood, a triple line of defence, and drawn in a horse-shoe form over the sloping heights from either side of the central harbour, and along the line of the

---

[1] Strabo, 14. 2. 5, p. 652.

[2] An interesting account of the mercantile law of Rhodes, its system of arbitration, and similar points, will be found in Prof. Mahaffy's *Greek Life and Thought*, ch. xv.

harbour itself; and the fortifications by which the moles themselves were protected—all remain unchanged, to attest the strength of this bulwark, on which for centuries the attacks of its powerful foes broke in vain. And in like manner the names of saints attached to the various gates, and their figures sculptured in relief above them ; the Priories, which formed the headquarters of each nationality or Tongue, as they were called, while the affairs of the Order at large were discussed in their common place of meeting ; the bastions, or portions of the wall which were permanently assigned to each nationality to defend ; and the escutcheons over the dwellings or the gateways, denoting either the possessor or the person by whom they were erected, but all of them containing the cross of the Order; all these bear witness to the religious character of the institution. and to the principle according to which the independent position of each people was recognised.

Within the memory of the present generation, however, two objects, which were among the greatest glories of the place, have been destroyed. One of these was the Tour de Naillac, which bore the name of the Grand Master by whom it was constructed, and formed a conspicuous object in views of the place as seen from the sea, rising, as it did, on the northern side of the central harbour ; this was ruined by an earthquake in 1863. The other was the church of St. John, the Sanctuary of the Order, of which no trace now remains; it was destroyed in 1856 by an explosion of gunpowder, which was set on fire by a

Objects recently destroyed.

Church of St. John.

flash of lightning that struck an adjoining minaret. The neighbouring palace of the Grand Master, which was already in a ruinous condition, was still further damaged by the same catastrophe, so that now only the lower storey remains.

The deposit of gunpowder. It is an interesting question at what period, and by whom, the powder was stored in this neighbourhood, for the Turkish authorities at the time of the explosion were ignorant of its existence. At first it was suggested that it was deposited there when Rhodes was besieged by the Ottomans in 1522; and that this was the act of Amaral, the chancellor of the Order, who turned traitor through jealousy in consequence of L'Isle Adam being preferred to him as Grand Master, and might have concealed a quantity of the gunpowder belonging to the besieged, in order to hasten the fall of the place. To this view, however, there are two objections, which appear to be fatal. In the first place, there is no historical evidence of the concealment of the powder, and without that we are in the region of conjecture[1]. Secondly, the doubt not unreasonably suggests itself, whether it is possible for gunpowder to retain its explosive power for more

[1] M. Guérin, who propounded this explanation of the existence of the gunpowder in the preface to the second edition of his *Île de Rhodes*, speaks of having found contemporary mention of the concealment of the powder, but he gives no authorities for this statement. Mr. Torr, the author of *Rhodes in Modern Times*, tells me that he has read through every contemporary record that he could find, but has been unable to discover anything to this effect. The charge against Amaral was, not that he had concealed any powder during the siege, but that he had been remiss in bringing in powder beforehand.

than three centuries. This question has been submitted to Sir F. Abel, the highest authority on explosives in this country; and his opinion is that, though gunpowder may retain its explosive properties for an indefinite period, provided that it is so packed and enclosed that moisture cannot have access to it, yet it is scarcely probable that packages such as were available at that period, even if they were in the first instance fairly impervious to moisture, could have preserved this essential feature for so long a time. It follows that the attractive view which would invest this gunpowder with a historical interest must be set aside; and we must content ourselves with the more prosaic supposition, that it was deposited in the vaults underneath the church at some comparatively recent period, and was subsequently forgotten.

An account of a walk which we took one day through the city may serve, better than any detailed description, to illustrate the characteristics of the place. Starting from our Christian suburb on the northern side, we have on our left the first harbour, that of the galleys, which was outside the *enceinte* of walls, but was defended by a strong round tower at the extremity of the mole, called the Tower of St. Nicholas, which was erected by the Spanish Grand Master, Zacosta. It has been conjectured that this fort occupies the site of the famous Colossus[1], but Mr. Torr[2] inclines to the view that that statue stood on the low ground at

The harbours.

---

[1] Newton, *Travels and Discoveries in the Levant*, vol. i. pp. 176, 177.   [2] *Rhodes in Ancient Times*, p. 97.

the south-west corner of this harbour. The notion that it bestrode the harbour is purely fabulous. We next pass through the gate of St. Paul, over which stands a figure of the saint, holding in one hand a sword, in the other the volume of the Gospel; like all these figures and escutcheons, it is carved in low relief on a slab of bluish grey marble. This gate leads, not into the city itself, but into the circuit of walls which enclose the great harbour, or harbour of commerce; of the moles that defended this, the nearer formerly bore the tower of Naillac, already mentioned, while from the further, on the eastern side, rises the tower of St. John.

Gate of St. Catharine. Through the wall which borders this harbour the city is entered by the finest of all the gates, that of St. Catharine, which is surmounted by a figure of that saint, standing between St. Peter and St. John the Baptist; it is flanked by two round towers, and has fine machicolations, and a place for the portcullis. Immediately within this, on the right hand as we enter, is the cross wall, which separated off the northern portion of the city, or Castello, which was reserved for the Knights, and occupied about one-third of the entire area, from that part which was inhabited by the citizens. Not far off, on the left was the Chancery, or Palais de Justice, part of the façade of which remains; it is approached by a flight of steps. The architecture of this, as of all the other buildings, is Gothic, and forms a strong contrast to the Byzantine style of the ecclesiastical structures, and the Saracenic military architecture, which prevail elsewhere in Turkey; throughout the city pointed and ogive arches, cable mouldings, and ornamental finials and carved heads of doorways in that style, are found.

Our course now lies through the district that was occupied by the civilians, following a line of streets which penetrates it transversely, the Jewish quarter being on our left hand. This contains many of the handsomest of the old dwellings, which are solidly built and elaborately decorated, and is especially picturesque on a Jewish festival day, as in one of our rambles we saw it, when its occupants are dressed in their rich holiday costumes. The Jews are allowed to reside within the walls, because the Turks regard them as too timid to be dangerous, and also to some degree as being their allies from their traditional animosity to the Christians. In one part of this quarter, where there is an open space of ground, stands the Admiralty, the purpose which it served being shown by the emblem of three flags which is sculptured on a shield. Ascending gradually we reach the walls, and pass through them by the southernmost of the two gates on the land side, the gate of St. John, close to which a number of stone shot, such as were used in the siege, are ranged in a line against the wall. *The Jewish quarter.*

After crossing the moat, we find ourselves at the point where the portion of the wall which was defended by the English met that which was allotted to the 'Tongue' of Provence; for the latter and that of Italy extended from this gate to the sea on the further side of the great harbour, where the third *Moat and walls.*

harbour, that of Acandia, lies, while the English reached from St. John's gate to the tower of St. Mary. The defences in this part are especially strong, the second or outer line, and the bastions, being of very solid construction. Outside the moat is an old Turkish cemetery, where lie the bones of those of the besiegers who fell during the siege. Traversing this, and skirting the moat, we pass first St. Mary's tower, which is distinguished by a relief of the Virgin and Child built into the outside of the masonry; then the Spanish tower and that of St. George; and finally reach the Amboise gate, which received its name from the Grand Master, Emery d'Amboise, who erected it. The intermediate space was defended successively by Spain, Auvergne, and Germany, while the French were responsible for the long line which reached to the sea at St. Paul's gate, and Portugal undertook the defence of the harbour and its adjacent towers.

Street of the Knights. Re-entering the city by the Amboise gate, and passing through successive lines of fortification by winding ways, intended to protract the defence, we find ourselves in the upper part of the Castello, or city of the Knights, where stood the church of St. John, the palace of the Grand Masters, and, between them, the Lodge of St. John, in which was the common hall of council; the last-named building faced directly down the street of the Knights. This famous street, which descends in a straight line by a gradual slope towards the port, is disappointing in the effect which it produces on the eye, owing both to the rough brown stone of which the buildings are composed, and to the projecting latticed frames of wood, which have been thrown out by the Turkish families who dwell there. But from a historical point of view it is the centre of interest in the place, since it contains the Priories, which were the headquarters and places of meeting of the different nationalities, and their escutcheons and those of their most distinguished men can in many cases be seen on the façades. By far the handsomest is that of France, which occupies a central position on the northern side of the street, and is adorned with the arms and cardinal's insignia of D'Aubusson, who successfully defended the city against the attacks of Mahomet II, and with those of the not less heroic, though less fortunate, L'Isle Adam. To an Englishman, however, the most interesting monument in this street is one of the least conspicuous—a little chapel, only the outer wall of which is visible, together with a groined niche for a statue reached by a flight of small steps; this was called the English chapel, and has the arms of England sculptured on its walls. It is now a mosque. This stood higher up than the French Priory, and quite separate from that of England, which was at the bottom of the street, and had a church of St. Catharine attached to it; but of these little remains in its original condition. Opposite to the English Priory was the Hospital of the Order, a large building of rude but massive construction, with a deep Gothic portal, and a court inside. This has been converted into a barrack. The small back

The Priories.

streets also, that run off from the street of the Knights, present a variety of interesting features. Here numerous flying buttresses are found, which were intended to resist the shocks of earthquakes, and vaulted passages, and winding alleys, with shields and quaint bits of ornamental work appearing at intervals. The photographer or the lover of the picturesque might find a greater charm in these than even in the more dignified buildings.

Difficulties in the way of sight-seeing. Sight-seeing in Rhodes at this time was not altogether an easy matter. For three or four years before we visited the island great difficulties had been placed in the way of travellers who wished to view the interesting objects there. It was forbidden to walk on the walls, and any one who stopped for more than a minute to notice an object was hailed by a sentry. To attempt to sketch was dangerous. The ancient buildings also within the city were not allowed to be entered. The explanation of this was, that since the war with Russia the Turks had been suspicious of plans being taken of their first-class fortresses, and orders had at last been issued, which should render this impossible. Rhodes, though incapable of serious defence, was ranked among these, and therefore these rules and restrictions were made to apply to it. At the period of which I am speaking the feeling of jealousy was unusually strong, because of a report which had been circulated in some European newspapers, that England was negotiating to have the island of Rhodes ceded to her; and the ferment which this had created on the spot was such as people in England had little idea of.

The antiquities in the immediate neighbourhood of the city may be visited in the course of a walk of three hours. They lie in the neighbourhood of a place called Simbulli, between two and three miles to the southward of Rhodes, which is a favourite resort for pleasure-parties among the inhabitants. Here there is a deep and narrow ravine flanked by perpendicular rocks, at the bottom of which a thin stream of water flows, and this continues in a sinuous course nearly to the sea. High up on one side of it stands a platform of rock, which has been levelled and carved out by the hand of man, though huge boulders at the sides prevent it from appearing artificial. In the middle a large shallow basin receives the water of two fountains, and both this and the whole locality are overshadowed by plane-trees of enormous size. The ravine immediately below is spanned by a massive bridge of two round arches, which may possibly date from Roman times; and this is surmounted by an aqueduct supported on numerous arches of less solid work of the period of the Knights, by which the water of Simbulli is still conducted to the city. The double tier of arches, together with the ravine and the umbrageous vegetation, form a delightful picture. *Antiquities in the neighbourhood.*

Not far from this place there are numerous sepulchres excavated in the rocks, some of which are surmounted by ornamental façades, resembling those that are found on the Lycian tombs. One of these, *'Tomb of the Ptolemies.'*

which has received, though without much reason, the name of the 'Tomb of the Ptolemies,' deserves especial notice on account of its size. It forms in fact a mound to itself, the ground-plan of which is a square, and it must have been piled up with earth so as to form a pyramid. The surface of the rock out of which it was formed was originally ornamented on all four sides, but owing to portions of it having fallen away, the northern face is the only one at all perfect. That towards the south is completely ruined, and an immense mass of it, which was probably detached by an earthquake, lies face downwards in a neighbouring ravine with one of its colonnettes still visible. What remains of the ornamentation of the northern side is a row of columns half engaged in the rock. As the entrance door does not stand in the middle of this face, the idea has been suggested that there may have been other chambers entered from the other sides. This door leads into a vestibule with a large sepulchral niche cut in the rock both to right and left, and this again conducts into a spacious square inner chamber, containing ten smaller, but deeply cut, niches at the sides, though some of these are now almost destroyed. It is natural to suppose that such a vault was the burial-place of some great family.

Ancient bridge.   After examining this we descended towards the sea, where the same ravine which is spanned higher up by the aqueduct is crossed by another and older bridge of two very solid arches, only one of which could have been used for the passage of the water.

It is constructed of large rectangular stones, fitted together without mortar, and for this reason has sometimes been regarded as Hellenic work. The use of the arch, however, was so rare among the Greeks, that it is perhaps safer to refer it to Roman times.

CHAPTER XI.

RHODES (*continued*).

The western coast.

OF the ten days that we spent in Rhodes, five were devoted to the interior of the island, our object being to visit the sites of the ancient cities of Ialysos, Cameiros, and Lindos, and to ascend Atabyron, which is the highest and most central mountain. For this expedition we hired mules—for horses are rarely found in Rhodes,—and each of these was accompanied by his owner, for they were very careful of their beasts, and declined entrusting them to any one of their number. During the first day of our journey (April 13) we were in the neighbourhood of the western coast. Leaving our suburb, we followed the shore, from which rise huge blocks of conglomerate rock; and further on we passed by the road-side rows of tall cactuses, which in this island, as in Sicily, are used for hedges. The men whom we met coming to the town with their asses and mules all wore high boots reaching to the knee, like the Cretans; and some even of the women and children used them. An hour's riding from the city brought us to a place called Trianda, where a space of level ground was covered with olive groves, and fig, orange, and cherry plantations; the houses which stand in the midst of these are the summer residences of the wealthier inhabitants of the city of Rhodes, but at this time they were untenanted. On the further side of this rises a steep, flat-topped mountain, called Phileremo, on the summit of which, in many places, the remains of a Frankish castle may be seen; this was the acropolis of Ialysos, called in ancient times Ochyroma, or the Stronghold, and pieces of Hellenic work are said to be found imbedded in the walls. The city lay in the plain between the foot of this hill and the sea, and here we saw a Corinthian capital by the road-side, and a few fragments of columns in the neighbouring fields; these are all the traces that remain, but the site has been identified by means of an inscription which was discovered on the spot. In the time of the Knights the castle above possessed an image of the Virgin, which was the object of great veneration, and on important occasions—as, for instance, at the commencement of the final siege—was conducted in solemn procession to the city. In the neighbouring village of Cremaste there is a ruined castle of this period; and its church is dedicated to the Panagia Katholike, and is the scene of a great festival on August 15. As this title is an unusual one, and *Katholikos* is the Greek word for a Roman Catholic, it is not unnatural to suppose that we have here a reminiscence of the alien worship of the Knights. Another place, some way further on, Villa Nova, perhaps derives its name

Site of Ialysos.

from Hélion de Villeneuve, the second Grand Master. The name is undoubtedly ancient, for it is mentioned that the Turkish forces put in there before the final siege.

Kalavarda. Near Villa Nova we made our midday halt in a hollow of the hillside, where a number of fountains gush out from beneath a group of fine plane-trees, while in front the eye ranges over mulberry-trees and other fresh vegetation to the blue sea, with the bold coast of Caria in the distance. The heat of the sun was now sufficiently great to make rest welcome in so pleasant a spot. When we resumed our journey, our route led across an extensive plain, for the hills here recede to some distance from the sea: a great part of the country was rudely cultivated, but the villages appeared poverty-stricken. At the end of six hours from the town we reached Kalavarda, which is the nearest village to the ruins of Cameiros. Our entertainer at this place, to whom we had an introduction from our obliging Vice-Consul, Mr. Biliotti, had served as superintendent of the works to Mr. Alfred Biliotti, now the British Consul in Crete, when, in company with a French gentleman, M. Salzmann, he devoted several years to the exploration of this site. We found him an intelligent man, for he spoke French, having been in Paris with M. Salzmann during the siege, and he had also been in Mr. Alfred Biliotti's employ when he was Consul at Trebizond, and had travelled with him as far as Van in Armenia. Notwithstanding this, he seemed to have returned with perfect contentment to the life of a simple peasant, and his house, which he and his family gave up to us for the night, consisted, like all the country houses in Rhodes, of a single room.

As this house was a favourable specimen of the native dwellings, it may be worth while for me to describe it. *A Rhodian peasant's house.* It was lofty, and nearly square, with massive stone walls and a clay floor. In the centre stood a strong upright pole, with a long cross-beam resting on it, and the roof was formed by poles laid across from this to the two walls, while above these again smaller branches and rods were placed transversely. The whole was covered with a layer of clay, stamped down. Against two of the side walls were erections of wood, five feet above the floor, on which the family sleep, so that they literally 'climb up' into their beds: beneath these, and also in other parts of the room, were cupboards, the woodwork of which was neatly carved in patterns. At one angle was the fireplace, with a large hearth in front of it, raised nine inches above the floor; round this the family sleep in the winter. A basket suspended from the roof contained the bread, which is thus preserved from the inroads of mice and ants. Mattresses and coverlets made up the furniture. There was also a rack for plates, but, as it happened to be cleaning day, these had temporarily been put away. The use of plates as wall-ornaments, which is characteristic of the famous Rhodian ware, is quite a Rhodian custom, though those which the peasants now possess, since they have parted with their ancestral treasures, are modern and of no value. In a house which was in no respect superior to this one I counted seventy plates hung on one wall.

Site of Cameiros.   At the time of our arrival our host was absent, working in the fields, so we engaged another native, who had taken part in the excavations, to act as our guide. The site of Cameiros is at a place called Hagios Minas, three miles to the west of Kalavarda. In order to reach it, we first crossed by stepping-stones a stream, which, to judge from the width of its bed, must, at certain seasons, be a violent torrent, and after two miles came to some excavations, where there had been tombs in the clayey soil; similar graves appeared at intervals for another mile, forming a sort of necropolis. The light colour of the earth throughout this neighbourhood seems to have suggested the Homeric epithet of the place, 'white' (ἀργινόεις). At last we came to the site itself, which is thickly strewn with fragments of pottery, while at the highest point Hellenic walls have been excavated; from this the ground slopes in terraces towards the sea. At the back of the acropolis passages flanked by massive walls, which meet at an angle above, are visible at several points at a considerable depth below the level of the soil; these seem to have belonged to a watercourse which supplied the city. An inscription containing the name of Cameiros was found on the spot, and, like that of Ialysos, is now in the British Museum. The discovery of it was of great importance, for, previously to this, two other localities— one on the eastern, the other further south on the western side of the island—had been suggested as the site of this city, but nothing had been certainly known. The tombs which have been mentioned yielded a rich harvest of works of art, the finest of which have been figured in M. Salzmann's splendid book of illustrations, entitled *Nécropole de Camiros*. We returned to Kalavarda by a different route over the heights, in the midst of pine-trees, with the grand bare peak of Mount Atabyron in view towards the south.

The following day (April 14) we directed our course toward that mountain. In order to reach it we had to cross another ridge, called Hagios Elias, which runs in a long line parallel to the coast, and from its grey precipices, interspersed with trees, reminded me of the Salève as seen from Geneva. During the first part of the way the banks were clothed with cistus plants, which were covered with blossoms, both white and red; and as we ascended we met with white cyclamens and white peonies. After passing the ridge we descended for awhile, and then mounted again for a long distance through forests on the slope of Atabyron, until we reached the little monastery of Artamiti, which stands at the foot of the peak of that mountain. The position of this is excellently chosen, for it occupies a small level in a clearing of the pine-trees, and commands a beautiful view over the eastern side of the island, where one range of hills succeeds another, as far as the sea. The hegumen, who is the only monk, occupies the building together with some members of his family and a few lay-brethren, about fifteen

Monastery of Artamiti.

souls in all. The name of the monastery suggests the idea that it may stand on the site of a temple of Artemis; and this has been corroborated by the recent discovery of an inscription to a priest of Artamis (this is the Doric form of Artemis) at a place only a mile and a half distant [1].

Ascent of Mount Atabyron.

The hegumen provided us with a room for the night, and then at our request procured for us a boy who might act as our guide to the summit. This lad, though he was only from twelve to fourteen years of age, proved to be an excellent walker, for he was as active and surefooted as a goat, and he seemed to find the way by instinct. There was no path beyond what our young companion extemporised, and for the first hour the ascent was very steep and rugged; at one period a grove of ilexes must have covered this face of the peak, but now only sparse copses and isolated trees remain. When we arrived at the shoulder of the mountain, the ground became more level; and from this point to the summit, which we reached in another half-hour, the surface of the soil is simply a wilderness of rocks and fragments of hard grey stone. In two or three places there were small basins filled with soil which afforded scanty herbage, and besides sheep and goats we met with a few cattle, and on the summit itself were a horse and half-a-dozen mules. We also put up several partridges. On a lower summit, a quarter of a mile distant from the highest, and but little inferior to it in elevation, are the rude remains of a temple of grey limestone, consisting of

[1] *Bulletin de Correspondance hellénique*, vol. ix. pp. 100, 101.

the foundations of the outer walls and part of the cella, but hardly more than its shape can be traced. It was dedicated to Zeus, of whom Pindar speaks as 'holding sway on the ridges of Atabyrion[1].' At one time a part of it was converted into a chapel of St. John the Evangelist, but now this also is in ruins. The height of the summit, according to the Admiralty Chart, is 4070 feet. The name Atabyron, or Atabyrion—now corrupted into Ataïro—is also found in Sicily, and is of Phoenician origin, being, in fact, the same as Tabor, which mountain is called Atabyrion by Greek writers.

The view from this point is very striking, for it comprises the whole island of Rhodes, set in the sea. The area over which the eye wanders is a very undulating one, being intersected by ranges of varied form, among which three mountains stand up conspicuously; and three rivers can be seen winding their way to the coast, two on the eastern, and one on the western side. Beyond the southern extremity of Rhodes the long broken outline of Carpathos was visible; but the Cretan mountains, which in clear weather are within view, were now concealed. During our ascent we saw three fine snow-clad summits at three separate points on the mainland of Lycia, and also the island of Syme and the coast beyond it; but these were obscured by gathering mist before we reached the top. The interest of the view detained us longer than was prudent, and when we started to

View from the summit.

---

[1] *Ol.* 7. 160.

return, we were for a time enveloped in clouds. These soon dispersed; but as we were on the eastern, and therefore the dark, side of the peak, and the sky had been clouded over, we found that the light was rapidly failing us. However, when we were in the middle of the worst part of the descent, where owing to the sharp edges of the rocks, and the loose fragments that lay about, the utmost care was required to avoid an awkward accident, the moon shone out brightly, and by her favouring light we at last arrived at the monastery. We had the more reason to rejoice at this, when, a little before midnight, we heard a violent storm of thunder and lightning raging on the summit, and the hail and wind battered the shutters of our dwelling.

The church. The church, which stands in the middle of the square enclosure of the monastery, resembles in its appearance and arrangement most of the churches that we had hitherto seen in Rhodes, and these are different from the ordinary type of churches that is found in the islands. In shape it is a simple rectangle, with four plain walls, except that a small apse projects at the east end, and at the west there is a porch which runs the whole width of the building. The roof is a single vault,—a feature which in the villages forms a contrast to the flat roofs of the houses,—and a sort of clerestory is formed by round-topped dormer windows, three of which rise on either side. Within there are stalls for worshippers all along the side walls, and over the porch stands a women's gallery, with a screen to separate them from the rest of the church. In front of the altar is the usual *iconostasis*.

At breakfast the next morning the hegumen provided us with excellent honey; and afterwards, when I was wandering about at some little distance from the monastery, I found myself within a rude enclosure where the beehives were in which it was produced. At first sight it appeared as if they were actually inside masses of rock which protruded from the ground, and the bees were to be seen crowding in and out of a vertical slit in the front. The hegumen, however, informed me that the hives are of wood, and that they are covered in and faced with stone, in order to protect the bees from cold during the winter. *Beehives cased in stone.*

This day (April 15) was spent in journeying to Lindos on the east coast. It was a beautiful ride, for the path led over hill and dale, mostly through pine-forests, where our muleteers were unacquainted with the track, which is very rarely followed. In these woodland regions fallow deer are said to be found. There was hardly any cultivation, except here and there by the side of the watercourses. After winding about for two hours we reached Laerma, a poor village, and from that place descended a long valley to the sea. At this point the character of the scenery changed with extreme suddenness; for as we followed the coast northward, the red and grey precipices that rose above us were absolutely bare—indeed, this whole neighbourhood is one of the wildest and most sterile in the island. We *Woodland regions.*

crossed the neck of a promontory, which projects far into the sea with a tower at its extremity, and some little way beyond this, in ascending a low height, we caught sight, first of the conspicuous castle-rock of Lindos, and shortly afterwards of the dazzlingly white buildings of the town, lying in a depression immediately beneath us. This place, which retains its ancient name, is the most striking in its position and appearance of all the cities of Rhodes. In some respects it recalls Ragusa, since it reaches from one to the other of two harbours, and is enclosed between the mountain-slopes on the land-side and a peninsula, which juts into the sea, and bears the towering castle-rock. The harbour toward the north is the larger, and is partly defended from the east wind by two islands that lie in front of it; the southern harbour is a small basin with a very narrow entrance. The flat-roofed town, when seen from above, lying between these, presents a peculiar appearance. Many of the houses date from the time of the Knights, who are known in the island as Cavaliers (Καβαλλιέροι), and occasionally as Crusaders (Σταυροφόροι). These mansions can be distinguished by their ornamental doorways and windows, with pointed arches and Gothic ornaments, but not a few are partially ruined, for Lindos has greatly shrunk in size, and now contains less than 800 inhabitants. As in the town of Rhodes, substantial flying buttresses are thrown across the streets as a defence against earthquakes.

The Rhodian ware.

We were conducted to the house of a native

gentleman, M. Vasiliades, to whom we had an introduction from Mr. Biliotti. The courtyard round which this was built was covered with a tessellated pavement of pebbles, a mode of ornamentation which is common in the island; in some dwellings even the rooms are floored with them, and the patterns in which they are arranged are often elaborate. In several of the rooms also the walls were hung with plates of the Rhodian ware, which is so highly prized by collectors; they were for sale, but most of them were damaged, and the owner was well aware of the money value even of these, as in fact is the case with the possessors of such articles, including the peasants, wherever they are to be found. This ware has often been called Lindos ware, in consequence of a large proportion of the specimens having been obtained from that place or its neighbourhood. The correspondences which it presents with the earthenware of Damascus, especially in respect of the flowers which recur on these pieces, prove clearly that the art was introduced into the island from further east; and the period of the Knights seems to have been the time at which it flourished there, but it continued to exist for a century and a half after their departure. These plates were regarded all along by the inhabitants as an heirloom in their families, and they were suspended on the walls, but were never used. Each plate is pierced with two holes with a view to hanging; and it is a curious fact that this custom existed in antiquity, for the earliest dishes from Cameiros, dating from about 700 B.C.,

Rhodian embroidery.

are pierced in just the same way[1]. The other form of ornamental work which was produced in Rhodes, and of which specimens may still be obtained there, is embroidery of silk upon linen. The articles which are enriched in this manner are chiefly curtains, hangings, table-covers and the like. These works of art are also thought to have been produced in the time of the Knights. The patterns introduced are often beautiful, and though the linen is usually stained and sometimes worn from age, the colours of the silk retain their richness.

Remains of the ancient city.

The classical antiquities of Lindos, which we visited the next morning in the company of M. Vasiliades' son, are found, partly in the town itself, and partly in the acropolis above. In the southern part of the town towards the smaller harbour are the substructions of a temple, consisting of a massive wall, finely built of rectangular blocks of a closely grained limestone; half-a-dozen courses of this remain, but of the temple itself there is no trace. Immediately above this stood the theatre, which was in part carved out of the rock in the hillside, a plan adopted by the Greeks whenever the ground allowed of it; and portions of the curved rows of seats may still be seen. On the landside of the town, opposite the acropolis, the lower part of the cliffs is broken into caverns, and one of these has been converted into a burial-place. Above the entrance a Doric entablature, with triglyphs, was carved, below which stood a number of small columns, engaged in the rock, but the central

[1] Torr, *Rhodes in Modern Times*, p. 86.

portion of this ornamental front has fallen down. In one part a number of sepulchral monuments of grey marble, resembling those which are found in the city of Rhodes, must have stood, for several of these—round in form, and decorated with bulls' heads and wreaths—lie about on the ground in front. The rocks at the side and back of the chamber within have been excavated, so as to form sepulchral niches. The inhabitants call this place Campana. It bears a strong resemblance to the Tomb of the Ptolemies at Rhodes. The remains of the famous temple of Athena of Lindos are situated near the highest point of the acropolis, which is at the southernmost angle; they consist of part of the wall that supported the entire building, and part of that of the cella. In its neighbourhood lie numerous stones bearing inscriptions, and one of these, which records a victory at Olympia, has an especial interest, because Pindar's seventh Olympic Ode was composed in honour of Diagoras, a boxer of Rhodes. On the summit itself there are considerable remains of Hellenic walls.

The castle of Lindos, however, deserves a more detailed description, because it was converted into an important stronghold by the Knights of Rhodes. It is now deserted, and the traveller can roam about there at his pleasure; but when Ross visited it in 1843, it was still occupied by a Turkish garrison, and was not allowed to be entered by strangers. The rock on which it stands rises precipitously on every side, but especially so towards the south, where it overhangs the sea at a height of 200 feet. The

Castle of Lindos.

Knights, however, did not do things by halves, and their fortifications were carried all round the summit, without reference to the inaccessible nature of the cliffs. The approach was on the northern side, where the fall is least abrupt; here there are three gateways, which lead successively through three lines of walls, and the third of these, by which the castle itself is entered, is very deep from back to front, and has pointed arches inside; within this, two drums of ancient columns are placed on either hand, and appear to have served for the stations of soldiers on guard. It is a curious feature that another entrance at this point led to the upper storey of the gateway, for a long flight of steps is attached to the outer wall, and from the top of this it would seem that a drawbridge or wooden ladder afforded an entrance. Close to this gate stood the most important buildings—a church of St. John the Baptist, and the residence of the commander of the fortress, below which are extensive subterranean chambers. In one of the rooms a hearth remains, the plaster over which bears a central figure of St. John in fresco, with shields of various dignitaries on either side of it. At several points within the castle there are vast cisterns, and a passage for the defenders runs round inside the battlements. The rest of the area is a mass of ruins. The palm-tree, which forms a conspicuous object in the view of Lindos in Sir Charles Newton's *Travels and Discoveries*, is now reduced to a bare staff, having been struck by lightning during the year preceding our visit.

Our return journey from this point occupied two

days, during which the route lay through the eastern rocky coast, but we soon struck inland, and during the remainder of the first day were traversing a richer country than we had yet seen, for the streams were numerous, and the level land through which these flowed was laid out in olive groves and orange gardens, and we passed through several villages in their neighbourhood. These were built with curious uniformity, each being composed of one or two perfectly straight streets, the houses of which were contiguous, and corresponded exactly to one another. They were one-storeyed and flat-roofed, and contained a single room; every doorway was surmounted by a pointed arch, and the window and chimney of each occupied the same position, so that they resembled the cells of a Carthusian monastery. At last we ascended to an upland plain, the whole of which was under cultivation, and on one side of it lay the large village of Archangelos, which we had noticed as forming a conspicuous object in the view from Mount Ataïro. Here we obtained a lodging for the night in the house of a peasant woman, which resembled in shape and arrangement that at Kalavarda which I have already described, except that here the roof was supported by a stone arch across the middle of the room. The hill above the village is crowned by a fort built by the Knights; but it is of no great strength or size, and the interior is much ruined: on the side towards the entrance an escutcheon has been let into the wall.

The eastern district.

Return to Rhodes.

The scenery through which we passed on the last day of our journey, though it was neither wild nor rich, was always varied, and from every point mountains of striking form were in view. As we descended from the plain of Archangelos, we passed a place where the rocks for some two hundred yards had been carefully cut in ancient times so as to form a road. At midday we rested under a plane-tree in the neighbourhood of a vaulted building, which seems to have been intended to serve for a halting-place, for water has been conducted to it from a point a little distance off by means of a covered conduit, and here pours forth into a marble basin. A neighbouring height bears the name of Eremokastro, and is said to have ruins upon it. Our approach to the city was betokened by the increasing luxuriance of the vegetation, and this sign was confirmed by the appearance of mosques in the villages, for the Turkish population of the island is almost entirely congregated in the capital and its neighbourhood. At last we caught sight of the circuit of walls, with numerous minarets; and threading our way, first through lanes gay with the blossoms of the judas-tree, and afterwards between high walls, the gateways in which revealed the handsome houses and pleasant gardens of the wealthier inhabitants of the suburbs, we reached our resting-place in Rhodes, and the end of our expedition.

CHAPTER XII.

LEMNOS.

IN the course of the journeys which have hitherto been described I had visited the most interesting of the islands which lie in the centre and south of the Aegean, and of those which fringe the coast of Asia Minor. It now remained for me to explore those which lie in the northern portion of that sea, and which are the most difficult of access, and consequently the least known. This part of my task I accomplished in the spring of 1889. On this occasion I was without a companion, and my travelling servant, Alexander, had died in the interval that elapsed since my last journey; but I had engaged the services of a Greek dragoman of Constantinople, George Stamos by name, whose excellent qualities I had put to the proof in the course of long wanderings through some of the wildest parts of European Turkey in 1861 and 1865. It was arranged that he should meet me at the Dardanelles, which place was to be my starting-point for this expedition, bringing with him a camp-bed, a few cooking utensils, and other simple appliances, such as are required for a rough tour. Accordingly, on Saturday, March 16, I embarked at

The northern islands.

Marseilles on board one of the French *Messageries* steamers, which was bound for Constantinople, and after touching at Syra and Smyrna, before daybreak on the following Friday reached the town of the Dardanelles, which lies halfway up the famous strait. After the vessel had obtained *pratique*, I was being rowed ashore, somewhat depressed by the chilly air and the ashen colour of sea and sky, when by the dim light of dawn another boat was seen approaching in the opposite direction, and as we came abreast of it a cheery voice shouted my name in an interrogative tone. To this I responded as cheerily, for I knew that it proceeded from my old servant, and that thus far my arrangements for a start were successful. I was soon established at the *Xenodocheion*—one of those shabby hostelries which are found in most of the trading-ports of Turkey, and which, despite their unpromising appearance, usually have clean beds.

Means of communication. Here I was informed of another circumstance which greatly facilitated my proceedings. As none of the main lines of steamers touch at any of the islands which I proposed to visit, I expected to be altogether at the mercy of the winds and waves in reaching them; moreover, the Thracian sea, as I knew both from its traditional character and from what I had read in books of travel, is apt to be dangerous at this season of the year, and the prospect of being wind-bound for a long spell of time is never an attractive one. But of all these islands Lemnos was the one in reaching which I anticipated the greatest difficulty, on account of its remoteness, and of the wide spaces of sea which separate it from any of the ports on the mainland. It was therefore an agreeable surprise to learn, that two years before this the steamers of an Ottoman company had begun to touch there, and that one of these vessels would leave the Dardanelles on the following morning. Of this I at once determined to avail myself, and the remainder of the day was spent in obtaining *teskérés* or Turkish passports, in providing myself with some Turkish money, and in making other preparations. I may mention, as the result of my experience, that for an expedition such as I was about to undertake the notes of the Bank of France are the best medium of exchange, for even where money-changers will not accept them, they can be negociated at their full value at the agencies of the steamers. In the town of the Dardanelles—a long, straggling succession of houses— the only thing of interest is its manufacture of earthenware, which is famous throughout the Levant. Specimens of this ware may be seen in the shops, and the forms of the vessels are often graceful, though they hardly rise to the level of works of art. The Turkish name of the place, Chanak-kalesi or Pottery Castle, is derived from this industry, and from the powerful fortress which here guards the narrowest part of the strait.

The steamer which we were expecting, the 'Plevna,' had been delayed on its way from Constantinople by a violent *scirocco*, which had been blowing for twenty-four hours, and it was midday on March 23 before we started. The deck was crowded with Turkish

The Dardanelles.

soldiers who were bound for Salonica, and with other passengers of various nationalities. It was an unpleasant day, for the wind had shifted to the northeast, and was accompanied by an overcast sky and driving rain; but its direction was favourable to our voyage, and by its aid the swift current carried us rapidly down through the gradually widening channel. Often as I have passed this ocean-stream, I never cease to wonder at its strangeness as the connecting link between two great seas; and the numerous vessels, carrying the flags of different countries, which sail on its waters, remind the traveller what an important route of commerce it has been in all periods, but especially since the foundation of Constantinople. Of the two shores, that towards the Thracian Chersonese rises somewhat steeply, while the slopes of the Asiatic coast are more gentle, though they are backed by high hills at no great distance off. At last the heights of Rheteium and Sigeium appeared on the left, and between them the Trojan plain was visible, the Ujek-tepe, or so-called Tumulus of Aesyetes, on its western side being the most conspicuous object in its neighbourhood. Here, at the edge of the plain near the mouth of the Scamander, where Homer describes the Grecian fleet as being stationed, now stands the fort of Kum-kaleh, which together with its European sister form the warders of the entrance. We passed through the outlet which is guarded by these, and were soon tossing on the open Aegean.

At first the view on every side was grey and misty;

only the bare slopes and rounded heights of Imbros were visible to our right. But as we coasted along the southern shore of that island the sky gradually cleared, and in front of us Lemnos arose from the water like a fairy vision, its mountains appearing at intervals in delicate outline, while the lower ground that intervened between them was still concealed below the horizon, and only after a time emerged to view. Though the area of Lemnos is less than that of the Isle of Wight, yet the space of sea which it seemed to cover produced the impression of great extent, and the long line thus formed completely justified the descriptive epithet *tenuis* which a Roman poet has applied to it[1]. A still more impressive object revealed itself toward the north, as soon as we had cleared the westernmost point of Imbros. This was the grand mass of Samothrace, which stood up from the sea like one great mountain broken into several peaks, with flecks of snow lying in the rifts of its steep ridges, and now diversified by a long bar of cloud, which hung halfway up its heights throughout its whole length. Again, far away to the north-west the summits of Thasos were dimly seen; and thus in one view I had before me all the islands which were the objects of my present tour. The relative importance of these in history was determined by their geographical position; for those that lay near the mouth of the Hellespont, Imbros and Lemnos, were of necessity brought more into connexion with the commercial and political life of Greece than those

Imbros and Lemnos.

---

[1] Valerius Flaccus, *Argon.* 2. 431.

which were more remote. The current of the Hellespont itself contributed in no slight degree to that result, for it sets with great force in the direction of those islands. A native of Lemnos, with whom I conversed on this subject on board the steamer, further remarked, that with a north wind it is carried towards Lemnos, but towards Imbros when the wind is from the south.

Their conquest by Miltiades.
In passing from the mouth of the Hellespont to Lemnos we have been following in the wake of Miltiades, and are forcibly reminded of the quaint story of the proceeding by which he brought that island under the dominion of Athens. One of the atrocities, which caused 'Lemnian deeds' to be a by-word throughout Greece, was the massacre by the Pelasgians of Lemnos of the Athenian women whom they had carried off from Attica, and their children. In consequence of this the Lemnians fell under the curse of heaven, and when they consulted the Delphic oracle on the subject, they were ordered to give the Athenians whatever satisfaction they required. They came to Athens, and expressed their desire to make amends for the wrong that they had done; whereupon the Athenians replied by an acted parable, and spreading a table with an abundance of good things, desired them to surrender their country to them in a similar condition. To this unqualified demand the answer of the Pelasgians was, 'When a ship comes with a north wind from your country to ours in a single day, then will we give it up to you.' Years rolled on, and these negociations were probably

half forgotten, until the Thracian Chersonese became a possession of Athens, and Miltiades, who resided there, conceived the idea of conquering this valuable island. In order to provide himself with a pretext for doing this—were it not for the peculiarly sophistical character of the Greek conscience, which rejoiced in quibbles of this nature, we might regard the whole transaction as a grim jest—he took advantage of the Etesian winds to sail from Elaeus in the Chersonese to Lemnos; and then, proclaiming to the inhabitants that he had fulfilled his part of the agreement, since the Chersonese was Athenian soil, required that they should surrender according to their promise. They refused and resisted, as Miltiades had no doubt anticipated, but were subjugated without much difficulty[1].

Connexion with Athens. From this time onward Lemnos and Imbros were more closely associated with Athens than any other islands in the Aegean. Their population furnished her with mercenaries. When Cleon boasted to the Athenians of the ease with which he could subdue the Lacedaemonians in Sphacteria, he offered to accomplish this with the Lemnians and Imbrians who were then in the city, together with a few other light-armed troops[2]. Even in the Sicilian expedition we find them employed on the Athenian side[3]. The islands themselves, together with Scyros, formed stepping-stones in the line of communication which led from Athens to her possessions in the Chersonese, and secured to her the trade of the Black Sea: in which respect (to compare small things with great) they held the same

---

[1] Herod. 6. 138-140.   [2] Thuc. 4. 28.   [3] Thuc. 7. 57.

position in the colonial and mercantile policy of that state, which is occupied by Gibraltar and Malta at the present day in securing the transit of vessels and troops from Great Britain to India and Australia. Athenian colonists established themselves there in great numbers; and at last these dependencies were so completely identified with the mother country, that in the Attic law-courts 'a suit in Imbros or Lemnos[1]' became another name for a fictitious plea to justify non-appearance in a suit at Athens. So, too, in the most amusing of Terence's plays, the Phormio, which was adapted from one of the Greek plays of the New Comedy, the story turns on an Athenian citizen having two wives, one at Athens and the other in Lemnos, the latter of whom he used to visit on pretence of superintending the farms which his Athenian wife possessed there. The coins of Imbros bear the familiar Athenian emblems, the head of Pallas and the owl; and at the present day almost the only attraction which that island offers to visitors—except woodcock-shooting, which in the season occasionally draws sportsmen from Constantinople—are the ancient inscriptions, built into the walls and pavements of churches and private dwellings, which in the majority of cases bear the names of Athenian citizens, together with that of the deme of Attica to which they belonged.

Northern coast of Lemnos. We were now approaching Cape Plaka, the north-eastern promontory of Lemnos, which is separated from the nearest point of Imbros by an interval

[1] Ἰμβρία, Λημνία δίκη.

of twelve miles. Before reaching it, my Lemnian fellow-passenger pointed out to me the position of the Mythonaes shoal, an extensive submarine reef which projects into the sea for several miles along the eastern coast. This serves as a protection to the island by forming a barrier to resist the current of the Dardanelles, which otherwise would break violently on its shores; but at the same time it is a source of danger to vessels, which are liable to be carried on to it owing to the force and the irregular movement of the stream. The promontory is a low bluff, far from imposing in its appearance; indeed, as regards height, it is one of the least striking points in Lemnos. This is noticeable, because this spot has usually been fixed upon as the position chosen for the fire-beacon which intervened between those on Ida and Athos, in the chain of signals by which Agamemnon announced the taking of Troy to Clytaemnestra at Argos. The neighbouring cliffs have also been regarded as the site of Philoctetes' cave, in which that suffering hero endured his ten years' exile during the war of Troy; and the two questions hang together, for the Hermaean Mount, which was the station of the beacon, is invoked by Philoctetes as one of the objects in his neighbourhood[1]. But these points I will not anticipate, for they can be discussed more satisfactorily on a later occasion, when we have taken a survey of the island.

The sun now descended in glory into a mass of filmy cloud, when suddenly from one side of this

View of Mount Athos.

[1] Aesch. *Ag.* 283; Soph. *Phil.* 1459.

there arose a peak which had not appeared before, and the height and steepness of which caused me to exclaim with wonder. I knew it could be nothing else than Mount Athos, but for the moment this seemed impossible, for that mountain was fifty miles distant, and the object that I now beheld, being cut off by the surrounding mists both from land and sea, looked huge in its proportions. The people of Lemnos seem to take their weather forecasts from Athos, for they told me that when the clouds rest on its summit they expect the north wind, but the south wind when they hang halfway up the peak. It was dark when we rounded Cape Murtzephlo, the north-western point of Lemnos, and about an hour before midnight we caught sight of the glimmering lights of Kastro, the chief town, which is situated near the middle of its western side. As soon as our vessel had cast anchor in the little harbour, and we were rowed ashore, we obtained practical evidence that Lemnos is but little visited, for we could hear of no inn, and a long debate ensued among the officials at the landing-place as to where we could pass the night. Ultimately we were installed in a half-empty house at some distance off, one room in which was occupied by a young Greek, a merchant's clerk, while the rest, though somewhat dilapidated in respect of windows and shutters, was at our disposal.

Kastro, the ancient Myrina. The town of Kastro, or rather the fortified enclosure from which it receives its name, occupies a striking position, which marks it out as the natural capital of the island. It is situated on a rocky peninsula, which projects westward into the sea from the recesses of a bay, and rises steeply in its centre to a height of 400 feet. On either side of the narrow isthmus which joins it to the mainland there is a rather exposed harbour, and that which lies towards the north is flanked by the Greek, that towards the south by the Turkish, quarter. This peninsula was in ancient times the site of the city of Myrina, and is no doubt the place which is meant by Homer when he speaks of the 'well-built town of Lemnos[1].' The inhabitants of the modern city amount to 3000, while the population of the entire island is reckoned at 30,000, of whom 5000 are Turks. The people generally, I was assured both by natives and by other Greeks who are resident among them, are peaceable and orderly. 'Lemnian deeds' are now at all events unknown. My own subsequent experience taught me that they are everywhere friendly to strangers, and not 'rude of speech,' as Homer says their predecessors were[2]. I may mention that the name of Stalimene, though in most modern maps it is given as the appellation of the island, is now wholly unknown, and only that of Lemnos is used.

As I was desirous to visit the castle before proceeding into the interior of the island, on the morning after my arrival I called on the British consular agent, Mr. Lambiris, who is also the vice-consul for the kingdom of Greece, in order to obtain an introduction to the Turkish governor. I found him occupying

A Lemnian family.

---

[1] Λῆμνον, ἐυκτίμενον πτολίεθρον. *Od.* 8. 283.
[2] οἴχεται ἐς Λῆμνον μετὰ Σίντιας ἀγριοφώνους. *Od.* 8. 294.

a spacious and well-furnished house in the middle of the Greek quarter, and he also owns a country house, situated in a pleasant garden in the outskirts of the town. He received me warmly, and offered me the usual refreshments of sweetmeats, cold water and coffee, which were handed, according to the graceful custom which prevails in Greek families, by the daughter of the house. This young lady and her brother spoke English, having both resided for a year in England, while the father and mother were only acquainted with Greek. She was married, but her husband was at this time absent in Smyrna; her two pretty children, Helene and Gregorios, were very English-looking, and one of them, who was six years of age, was soon to be sent to England for education. To my surprise I discovered that their governess, who was living in the family, was an English girl. It appeared that she had left England some years before from the desire of visiting foreign countries, and had resided three years in Smyrna, after which she accepted the offer of this engagement: but, as Kastro is a place of few resources, and she was the only English person there, I was not surprised to learn that she found it inexpressibly dull, and was most anxious to return to England.

Connexion with Egypt. All the information respecting Lemnos which I had gathered from books of travel had led me to suppose, that owing to its remote position it was a poverty-stricken island, and behindhand in all the arts of life. This, I have no doubt, was formerly the case, but it certainly is not so at the present time. I soon discovered that a good many of the inhabitants are prosperous people; and, as regards education, not only are there elementary schools in the principal villages, but in Kastro and at Mudros, which is the second place in importance, there are higher or 'Hellenic' schools, in which ancient Greek is taught. The cause of the change is the same which I have already noticed in speaking of Leros, namely, that the inhabitants have established a connexion with Egypt. Sir John Antoniades, the wealthy banker of Alexandria, who is father-in-law to Mr. Lambiris, is, if I mistake not, a native of this island; and many of the Lemnians now betake themselves to that port, and make large fortunes there. Much of the money that is thus obtained finds its way to Lemnos, for these emigrants with praiseworthy patriotism have established a society in Alexandria for the advancement of their native country, and contribute funds for the support of the schools. Besides this, it is a point of honour amongst them to take Lemnian girls to wife; and not unfrequently they continue to regard Lemnos as their home, and leave their wives and families there, returning to them when the heat of summer renders Egypt an undesirable place of residence. Another curious result of this connexion is that many of the inhabitants of Lemnos are Freemasons, having become members either of English lodges or of French associations in Alexandria. The treatment of the people by the Turkish government has also changed for the better. The sound of church bells which I heard seemed to show that they enjoy greater freedom in religious worship than is found in most parts of Turkey, for the use of these is generally forbidden; and whereas in former times the erection of handsome places of worship was not allowed, the present metropolitan church at Kastro is a spacious and imposing edifice.

Lemnos a place of banishment.

Another English-speaking person whom I met in Lemnos was M. Jourdain, to whom I was introduced by Mr. Lambiris. He was the son of a French father and a Greek mother, but he seemed to regard himself as Greek by nationality. He informed me that at one time he had been a correspondent of the *Daily Telegraph* in Bulgaria, and he had been employed on Mount Athos in connexion with the dispute that arose between the monasteries and the Roumanian government, in consequence of the confiscation of the properties which the monks had previously possessed, or at least administered, in the Danubian Principalities. From him I learned that Lemnos has long been a place of banishment for political offenders in Turkey. The most important exile who is now living there is Sadik Pasha, who was Grand Vizier at Constantinople some ten years ago. His banishment was connected, I believe, with the fall of Midhat Pasha, some letters of that minister having been found, or said to have been found, in his possession. He has now resided in Lemnos for eight years, and is almost forgotten at the capital. Another person in the same position, who came to visit me during my stay in Kastro, was once a dragoman and travelling-servant of some repute at Beyrout, in which capacity he had been in the service of many Englishmen. His name is Assad Smart, and he is a native of Syria, and a member of the Orthodox Church. His own account of the circumstances of his banishment was this: that on suspicion of complicity, which he entirely denies, in some plot for an insurrection of the Christians in Syria, he was seized, and, without any trial or the statement of any definite charge, was put on shipboard and conveyed to this place. It is curious to find that there is still in the Aegean an island which performs the same office which Gyara did under the Roman empire, though happily it is a less dreary abode than that desolate spot.

Accompanied by the consul's son, I now proceeded to visit the Turkish governor, to whose jurisdiction Samothrace, Imbros and Tenedos are also subject, while he is himself subordinate to the Pasha of Rhodes, who is governor-general of the Turkish islands in the Aegean. I explained to him my desire to see the castle, in order to explore the site of the ancient city, but for this he said it was not in his power to give leave, since admission to that place depended on the military commandant who resided within it. Accordingly a messenger was despatched to that functionary to obtain his permission. We waited nearly an hour for a reply, during which time coffee was served, and I was able to obtain some useful information from the governor and his retinue, especially about the 'Lemnian earth,' which was famed for its medicinal qualities both in ancient times and throughout the Middle Ages, and the locality of

Site of Myrina.

which I hoped to examine. At last, when our conversation and our patience were exhausted, I determined to proceed to the castle, on the chance of being allowed to enter. The approach to the fortifications is very striking, for the granite rocks of which the peninsula is composed rise steeply and stand out in the most fantastic forms, and in many places are stained bright yellow by patches of lichen. The mediaeval walls, of Genoese construction, enclose a wide area, running round the peninsula at about two-thirds of its height from the sea, and above this, at the summit, there is an upper castle or keep: on the northern side, where the slope of the ground is least precipitous, a lower line of strong fortifications is carried along somewhat above the level of the water. The isthmus between the two harbours forms a ridge where it abuts against the rocks, and at the back of this there rises a conspicuous knoll, which falls abruptly on its eastern side toward the level ground where the Greek and Turkish quarters meet one another. Close to this ridge, and not far from the entrance gate, stand the only remains of the ancient city of Myrina—a splendid piece of cyclopean masonry, occupying a steep position on the hillside. The huge blocks of which it is composed are laid in irregular courses, ranging from three to five, and between these at intervals smaller masses were introduced. I measured one of the blocks, and found it to be six feet and a half in length by three feet in height. Immediately below this wall there is a curious wide-mouthed cavern, covered in by one enormous rock which forms a natural arch.

When we reached the entrance of the fortress, one of the sentries who were on guard undertook to convey to the commandant my request for admittance, and after a little time returned with a favourable reply. The approach, which is flanked by high walls, winds in such a manner as to impede an attacking force, and is defended at intervals by three gates, the two outermost of which are still covered with rusty plates of iron. On the face of the wall inside the first of these there is a short dedicatory inscription, bearing in its centre the monogram of the Palaeologi, which is similarly found in inscriptions in Samothrace. In both instances this is the emblem of the Genoese family of the Gatilusi of Lesbos, who intermarried with the imperial house, and whose principality during part of the fourteenth and fifteenth centuries included Lemnos, Samothrace and Imbros. Our perseverance after all was poorly rewarded, for the commandant, though he received us politely and entertained us with the inevitable coffee, allowed us only to go a certain distance round the *enceinte* within the outer walls, and declined to give us permission to ascend to the upper castle. The defences throughout are strong for a mediaeval building, and even as late as the year 1770 this fortress successfully resisted a three months' siege by the Russians under Count Orloff; but it could not stand for a moment against modern artillery, and the precautions which are taken to prevent strangers from seeing it are ridiculous.

The modern fortress.

View from it.

In the part which I visited the only objects of interest were a large plain sarcophagus of white marble, and pieces of columns of the same material, apparently of the Byzantine period. I was rewarded, however, by the striking view which even the lower slopes of the peninsula command. Towards the north the coast of Lemnos was visible as far as the headland of Murzephlo, while to the south beyond the nearer promontories the island of Aï Strati (Hagios Eustratios) was in view. This island was called Neae in ancient times[1], and though it forms an insignificant object on the map, as seen from this point it has an imposing appearance. On the landside fields and vineyards extend in the immediate neighbourhood of the town, and behind these rise bare rocky heights, among which that of St. Athanasius, with a chapel on its summit, is the most conspicuous. Towards the north-west Athos towers above the sea, but at this time it was half shrouded in cloud.

Shadow of Athos.

The sight of this peak recalls the statement which was widely circulated in antiquity, that its shadow reached as far as Myrina, or, to give it in the circumstantial form with which Sophocles invests it, that it overshadowed the back of the bronze cow which stood in the market-place of that city[2]. The same idea is introduced by later poets[3]; and ultimately it passed

---

[1] Some authorities maintain that it was Halonnesus.

[2] Ἄθως σκιάζει νῶτα Λημνίας βοός. Soph. *Fragm.* 348, ed. Dind.

[3] Apollon. *Argonaut.* 1. 601—4:—

ἦρι δὲ νισσομένοισιν Ἄθω ἀνέτειλε κολώνη
Θρηικίη, ἣ τόσσον ἀπόπροθι Λῆμνον ἐοῦσαν,

into a proverb, concerning those who damage the reputation of others by their own eminence. Considering that the interval which separates the two places is about forty miles, the thing is an impossibility; but it is not difficult to conjecture how the idea arose. The shadow of every high and solitary mountain of conical shape is projected to a distance in the morning and the evening when the sky is clear; and having been on the summit of Athos at sunrise, I have seen that effect produced by it in a distinctly marked pyramid stretching far to the west over sea and land. This feature could hardly fail to have been remarked in ancient times by those who navigated the neighbouring seas. Again, at one period of the summer the sun is seen from this part of Lemnos to set behind Athos: of this I was assured by a resident in Kastro who had noticed it; and it may be inferred from Conze's remark, that on July 2 he saw the sun go down a little to the right of that mountain[1]. This also must be a striking sight, and one that would appeal to the imagination. In these

ὅσσον ἐς ἔνδιόν κεν εὔστολος ὁλκὰς ἀνύσσαι,
ἀκροτάτῃ κορυφῇ σκιάει καὶ ἐσάχρι Μυρίνης.

Stat. *Theb.* 5. 51 (speaking of Lemnos) :—

      Ingenti tellurem proximus umbra
  Vestit Athos.

[1] Conze, *Reise auf den Inseln des Thrakischen Meeres*, p. 108. Belon, writing in the sixteenth century, affirms that he saw the shadow of Athos fall on Lemnos on June 2.—*Observations de plusieurs singularités*, pp. 58, 59.

two facts we have the data from which the belief may have arisen. The desire of completeness, which is characteristic of the human mind, would readily supply what was wanting to amplify the fable.

CHAPTER XIII.

LEMNOS (*continued*).

ON my return from the fortress I found three *The warm baths.* horses, which my servant had hired, waiting in readiness to take me into the interior of the island. When we had issued from the town, we began to ascend gradually, passing between fields which flank the lower slopes of the bare stony mountains. These are outliers from the main chain, which runs from north to south, and separates the west coast from the inland districts. At the end of an hour and a half we reached a valley, in which are situated the Therma Loutra, or warm baths, which are much resorted to on account of the medicinal properties of the water. The building which contains them is of solid construction, and encloses a central court paved with stone and open to the roof. At the four angles of this there are rooms in which visitors can be accommodated, and opposite the entrance are two chambers for bathing, with marble baths. In both of these I found the temperature of the water at the point where it enters to be 100° Fahr. The baths are especially beneficial for rheumatism and skin diseases. The patients also drink the water, which has a great effect in increasing appetite; and it is said that, when once a person has drunk of it, he desires to drink more. At the time of my visit there were no bathers; but during the summer, I was told, a great number come, and those who cannot be accommodated within the building are lodged in rude tenements attached to the baths.

Interior of the island.

At this point a steep ascent commences, which leads to the watershed of the western part of the island, and when we had reached this, we wound about among the declivities of the mountains for more than an hour before we began to descend. From these uplands the water flows in three directions, for we had followed up one stream from the neighbourhood of the town, and shortly after leaving this we crossed another that runs southward in the direction of the inlet of Kondia, which penetrates the island near its south-west angle; later still we passed a third, which finds its way into the bay of Mudros. The mountain of Hagios Elias, which rises behind the baths, here forms a conspicuous object, and far away to the south is seen the still loftier Mount Phakos, which intervenes between the two inlets just named. None, however, of the mountains in Lemnos attain a great elevation, for the highest is that in the neighbourhood of Cape Murzephlo, which only reaches 1400 feet. At last the great undulating plain, which occupies the centre of the island, opens to view, bounded by lower heights in the direction of the eastern coast. Towards its further extremity it is almost divided in two parts by the bays of Mudros and Purnia, which penetrate far into the land from the southern and the northern seas. In the distance the imposing forms of Samothrace and Imbros are visible. Numerous villages lie scattered over this area, and the windmills which stand on the low hills in their neighbourhood betoken the absence of running water. Some of the farms are the property of the monks of Athos—a fact of which I first became aware in an unpleasant manner many years before, from the staleness of the eggs which were set before me in the monastery of Lavra; for these, as I discovered on enquiry, had been imported from Lemnos, since hens, like other female creatures, are excluded from the Holy Mountain.

Throughout this plain the ground is extensively cultivated, corn, wine and tobacco being the chief products; and in some places the land had been rendered so moist by irrigation, that it was necessary to deviate from the path in order to secure a safe footing for the horses. The soil is light and powdery, and appears remarkably fertile; but, notwithstanding this, the entire absence of trees—with the exception of a few fig-trees and other fruit-trees in the neighbourhood of the villages I did not see one in the whole island—imparts an aspect of great desolation to the scenery. In consequence of this the houses are everywhere built of stone, and stone walls are used in place of hedges. The wood that is required for burning is imported from Thasos; but generally in the country districts braziers are employed for heating the apartments, and for these small brush-

The central plain.

wood is used. The peasants were now busily employed in tilling the soil; and wherever the ground was newly turned, numerous large gulls were flying about, and gave evidence by their presence of the proximity of the sea. In all the waste lands flocks of sheep and goats were feeding. The dress of the shepherds who accompanied them was peculiar, consisting of a white turban wound round the head, a white shirt and baggy trousers with a black woollen belt fastened round the waist, a jacket of sheepskin with the wool turned inside, leather leggings, and mocassins of hide.

Village of Atziki.

At the end of four hours' riding from Kastro I reached the village of Atziki, which is situated in the middle of the plain. Here I obtained night-quarters in the school-house, a place of abode which is often available in these islands, for the building is the property of the community, and there is usually a vacant apartment in addition to the school-room and that occupied by the master. After I had settled in, some of the inhabitants hospitably offered to provide me with a more comfortable lodging; but I was too well satisfied with the position of my humble quarters at the extremity of the village, and the independence which I thus enjoyed, to be persuaded to leave them. One of the chief men, however, who was desirous of showing me a bas-relief of Byzantine workmanship which had lately been discovered, conducted me to his house, and I was surprised at the appearance of its neatly furnished rooms, which were altogether superior to what is usually found in

Greek villages. The young schoolmaster was a favourable specimen of a class of men who have contributed more than any other, perhaps, towards the advancement of the Greeks. Though occupying a single room, which contained little more than a bed, a table, a few chairs, and his books, he was an intelligent man, and had received his education at Athens. I observe that the village teacher, who was always known as *Dascalos* when I first travelled in Greece, owing to the influence of the Hellenic revival has now risen to the dignity of *Didascalos*. The spread of instruction has brought it to pass that the instructor receives his full title.

In visiting this part of Lemnos I had two objects in view; first, to investigate the spot from which the 'Lemnian earth' is obtained, and to gather any information which could be discovered relating to it; and secondly, to explore the site of the ancient city of Hephaestia. These are situated in the same neighbourhood, near the head of the northern inlet, the bay of Purnia, from one to two hours distant from Atziki. The following morning (March 25) I proceeded in this direction, together with the schoolmaster, who at the last moment offered to accompany me; his scholars, who had already assembled, were dismissed with the welcome news of a holiday. The continuance of north-east wind and drifting rain rendered the weather 'melancholy,' to use my companion's expression (μελαγχολικὸς καιρός): indeed, during the whole of my stay in Lemnos I hardly saw the sun, and the impression of the outward aspect of the

Bay of Purnia.

island which I carried away with me was a gloomy one. As we crossed the low heights at the back of the village, we soon reached a point where both the remarkable inlets are visible; that of Mudros is by far the deeper of the two, and is distinguished by its windings, and by the numerous small headlands which project into it from either shore. At last we descended to the hamlet of Kotchino[1], in the innermost recesses of the bay of Purnia, where a number of shops (μαγάζια) have been erected on the seashore; in the neighbourhood of these stand the remains of a considerable mediaeval castle, which is mentioned by Chalcocondylas, the Byzantine historian of the fifteenth century, as having been successfully defended by Constantine Palaeologus, the future emperor of Constantinople, against a Turkish force which besieged it by land and sea[2]. While we were there we were overtaken by a guard, who had been sent by the Pasha to serve as an escort. I dismissed him with compliments and thanks, since perfect security reigned in the island; but on the following day two others met me when returning from Atziki to Kastro, and accompanied me on the way. I shrewdly suspected that they were intended to spy out my proceedings, for at the present day every traveller from Western Europe is regarded by the Turks as entertaining designs for excavation, which is strictly forbidden unless specially authorised by the govern-

---

[1] So pronounced, though the proper spelling of the name is Κόκκινο.

[2] Chalcocond., Book vi. p. 306. ed. Bonn.

ment; and this I found to be the view taken by the natives of my military escort.

As the scene of the digging for the Lemnian earth is near to Kotchino, I now enquired for some one who could conduct us to the place; and I was fortunate in securing the services of an old man who had passed his life in this neighbourhood, and was consequently familiar with the traditions respecting it; also, being a potter by trade, he was accustomed to make vessels of this material. Notwithstanding his years, he was an excellent walker, and he afterwards accompanied me to the site of Hephaestia. I found that he had visited Mount Athos, and was acquainted with several of the monasteries. Under his guidance we now made our way to the spot. Before proceeding further, however, in my narrative, it may be well for me to give some account of this earth, to which an extraordinary interest attaches owing to the permanence of the belief in its medicinal qualities, and of the customs which have been associated with it. There is the more reason for dwelling on the subject now, because within a few years the local knowledge of it is doomed to extinction. *Kotchino.*

The principal ancient writers who have given an account of the Lemnian earth are Pliny, Dioscorides, and Galen[1]: but the two former obtained their information at second-hand, while Galen, in a truly scientific spirit, investigated the matter for himself, *The 'Lemnian earth.'*

---

[1] Pliny, *Hist. Nat.* 29. 5, § 33, and 35. 6, § 14; Dioscor. *De Mater. Med.* 5. 113; Galen. *De Simpl. Med.* 9. 2, vol. xii. pp. 169-176, ed. Kühn.

S

and voyaged to Lemnos in order to make his enquiries on the spot. So great was his interest in it, that after failing in his first attempt to reach the place on his way from Asia Minor to Rome—the captain of the vessel in which he sailed having landed him at Myrina, and refusing to wait while he visited the interior of the island—he included Lemnos in his return journey, and on this occasion directed his course to Hephaestia, in the neighbourhood of which city he was informed that this material was found. By Dioscorides it is called simply 'Lemnian earth' (Λημνία γῆ); but Galen and Pliny apply to it the names of 'Lemnian red earth' (Λημνία μίλτος, *Lemnia rubrica*), or 'Lemnian seal' (Λημνία σφραγίς), the latter of these terms being derived from the stamp which was impressed upon it, and without which it was not allowed to be sold. The three writers mention a great variety of disorders for which it was a remedy, but they all agree in regarding it as an antidote to poison, and as a cure for the bites of serpents. According to one tradition Philoctetes, whose wound arose from the last-named cause, was healed by using it[1]. It was both taken as a medicine, and employed in external applications.

Galen's account.

Galen, who lived in the second century after Christ, has left us a circumstantial account of the place from which the earth was taken, of the ceremonies observed on the occasion, and of the mode of its preparation as a drug. He describes the hill on which it was found as having a burnt appearance,

[1] Philost. *Heroica*, 5. 2.

from its surface being of the colour of ochre, and destitute of all vegetation. On certain occasions (and one of these coincided with the time of his visit) the priestess of Artemis came to this spot, and after performing a number of rites, the chief of which consisted in casting offerings of wheat and barley, as a compensation, into the cavity from which the earth was dug, carried off a cart-load of it to the city. That which was thus removed was considered sacred, and might be touched by no other hand than hers; but she mixed it with water, kneaded it, and then strained off both the moisture and the gritty particles: after which, when it had assumed the consistence of soft wax, she divided it into small pieces, and impressed upon them the seal of Artemis. Dioscorides affirms that goat's blood was mixed with it; and Galen tells us that his anxiety to discover whether this statement of his predecessor was true was his chief motive for enquiring thus minutely into the origin of the drug. When, however, he interrogated the most intelligent of the inhabitants on the point, their only answer was a burst of laughter, which satisfactorily settled the question.

The exportation of this earth and its use in pharmacy must have continued throughout the Middle Ages, for we find its reputation undiminished at the expiration of that period. In the sixteenth century it was in so great request as an antidote to the plague, to dysentery, and to other disorders, that ambassadors, when returning from Constantinople to their native countries, were wont to bring pieces

Its use in pharmacy.

of it as a present to distinguished men[1]. When Lemnos was regained by the Turks from the Venetians in the year 1657, Mohammed Kiuprili, who commanded on that occasion, sent word to Adrianople to the Sultan that he had won the island where the 'sealed earth' was found[2]. A further proof of the value which was attached to it is given by its being largely counterfeited. Belon speaks of some kinds as being 'sophistiquées'; and Thevet in his *Cosmographie du Levant* (date 1554) remarks[3], 'Les Juifs la falsifient beaucoup, quand ils la vendent à ceux qui ne la connoissent.' In Western Europe it was known from an early period as *terra sigillata*; but the original Greek term *sphragis* also found its way into the pharmacopoeias of the West, where it appears in such corrupt forms as *lempnia frigdos*, and even *lima fragis*[4].

Belon's account. We are fortunate in possessing, for the sixteenth century, a description of the digging of the earth, and of the circumstances attending it, from the pen of a writer not less observant than Galen was in his time. This was the French traveller, Pierre Belon, whose name has been already mentioned, and who,

[1] Belon, *Observations de plusieurs singularités*, p. 51.
[2] Von Hammer, *Geschichte des Osmanischen Reiches*, vol. iii. p. 483 (2 ed.).
[3] p. 52.
[4] *Alphita, a Medico-Botanical Glossary*, ed. Mowat, in the *Anecdota Oxoniensia*, pp. 96, 219. The compiler of the *Glossary* remarks, '*Lempnia frigdos terra est sigillata.*' 'Frigdos' is a corruption of σφραγῖδος, the genitive case being used, as Mr. Mowat has pointed out to me, on account of the form employed in a doctor's prescription.

like the Greek physician, came to Lemnos with the
express purpose of investigating this subject [1]. Then,
as now, the locality was a hill in the neighbourhood
of Kotchino, which place he names, though he was
under the mistaken impression that the castle there
formed part of the ruins of Hephaestia. On the hillside were two fountains, of which the one on the
right hand of the ascent was perennial, while that to
the left dried up in the summer time. No trees grew
upon it, except a carob, an elder, and a willow, which
overhung the perennial spring; nevertheless, the
corn flourished which was sown upon it. This last
statement is in direct contradiction to that of Galen
on the same point; but it is quite conceivable that in
the course of so many centuries a covering of mould
may have formed there. The earth was dug from
the upper part of the hill, but this took place only on
one day of the year, the sixth of August, in the
presence of the Turkish governor of the island and a
large concourse of people. The ceremony commenced with a mass, which was said by the Greek
priests and monks in a little chapel at the foot of the
hill; and at the conclusion of this they mounted the
declivity, and the soil was removed by which the
opening in the ground, leading to the peculiar vein
of earth, was closed. This entrance was so deep,
that from fifty to sixty men were required to clear it.
When the medicinal earth was reached, the monks
filled a number of sacks with it, and made these over
to the Turkish authorities, after which the soil which

[1] Belon, *Observations*, chaps. 22, 23, 28, 29.

had been removed was once more replaced. The greater part of the earth was despatched to the Sultan at Constantinople, but a certain portion was sold to merchants on the spot, and those who took part in the digging were allowed to carry off a small quantity for their private use. In no case, however, was any one allowed to sell it until it was sealed. It was made into small cakes, and of these Belon saw numerous specimens of various shades of colour, but the prevailing tint was dull red. In his book he gives representations of the seals that were used.

Modern customs and beliefs. Let me now describe the place which I saw, and the observances of which I received an account. The excavation to which I was conducted by my local guide is situated on a small space of nearly level ground, somewhat below the summit of a hill about two hundred feet above the sea, and less than a mile to the southward of Kotchino. At the foot of the last ascent before it is reached there is a spring called Phtelidia, over which an ogive arch of stone has been cut at the point where it issues from the rocks. When I enquired whether there was another fountain in the neighbourhood, my informant mentioned one called Kokala, which rises on the opposite side of the hill. The ground is everywhere clothed with turf, but is otherwise devoid of vegetation. The cavity from which the 'sacred earth' (ἅγιον χῶμα, as it is universally called by the Greeks) is taken, is an insignificant hole, about fifty feet in circumference and ten feet deep, the bottom of which is now filled up with dry stalks of thistles. The sacred earth is found at a depth of three feet below this. In the neighbourhood there is another spot which seems to have been excavated, and it is believed that the vein extends for some distance below the soil. The earth, however, is not the same as that which Galen and Belon describe; for while they speak of it as red in colour, the specimens which were shown to me resembled ordinary clay[1]: either the original vein has been exhausted, or they no longer dig deep enough to reach it. As in Belon's time, it can only be dug on the sixth of August; and unless this takes place before sunrise all its efficacy is lost. It is also confidently believed in the island (I heard it both at Kastro and at Atziki) that when the ground is opened, the sacred earth wells up of its own accord —'leaps up,' 'boils up,' were the expressions used; but when I questioned my local authority, who had often been present, on this point, he replied much in the same way as Galen's auditors did to his enquiries about the admixture of goat's blood in the drug. His account of the customs observed on the occasion, which continued in full force until five or six years ago, was as follows. On the appointed morning the governor or his representative proceeded to the spot, accompanied by the Mahometan *khodjas* and the Christian priests, both of whom took part in the ceremony: the former of these offered a lamb as a

---

[1] The same thing was remarked by Dr. Sibthorp, who says, 'The hole [from which the earth was dug] had been filled up, but we observed some of the earth, which was a pale-coloured clay.' Walpole's *Turkey*, p. 281.

sacrifice (*kourban*), of the flesh of which they afterwards partook, while fish was provided for the Christians, who were prohibited from eating meat at that season, owing to its falling in the fast of fourteen days which precedes the festival of the Virgin. Tradition, he said, affirmed that sometimes two or three thousand persons were present, and in his father's time as much as seven mules' load of the earth was carried away, to be sent to Constantinople. It was there made into pieces of the size of tablets of soap, and was stamped with the government seal.

An antidote to poison.   The locality which I have mentioned is evidently the same which Belon visited, and probably corresponds to that described by Galen. The resemblances between the ancient and the modern customs and beliefs are also very striking. The sacred character attached to the earth and the religious auspices under which it was removed, the offerings made on the occasion, the guarantee of genuineness provided by the seal, and the confidence which was placed in its efficacy as a medicine, are features common to the earlier and the later accounts, and seem to point to an unbroken tradition. To these one more may be added, which is not the least curious. I have mentioned that the ancient authorities agree in regarding it as an antidote to poison. At the present day small bowls are made on the spot of this material, and are bought by the Turks, who believe that a vessel made of this clay neutralises the effect of any poison that is put into it. I purchased several of these from the potter, and each of them is stamped in five places with the government seal, which bears in Arabic characters the same inscription which Belon mentions as being used in his day—*tin machtum*, i. e. 'sealed earth.' This seal, he informed me, was obtained for him from Constantinople twenty years before by an exiled Pasha, who desired that a number of these bowls might be made for him.

Notwithstanding the long duration of this time-worn belief, it is evident from the neglect into which it has lately fallen, that ere long it will be a thing of the past. For several years the Turkish governor has ceased to attend, and, following his example, first the *khodjas* and then the priests absented themselves, and no lamb is now sacrificed. Last year only twelve persons were present. Though the tablets were to be bought in chemists' shops in Kastro at the time of Conze's visit to the island[1] in 1858, I enquired in vain for them; and neither the existing governor, nor any persons of the younger generation, had heard of this remedy. In the eastern parts of Lemnos, however, it is still in use for fevers and some other disorders, for the women possess nuts of it, which they string like the beads of a rosary; these they grate in case of illness, and take a teaspoonful of the powder in water. Not long ago the proprietor of the hillside applied for leave to plough over the spot and sow it with corn; and though for the time this was not allowed by the government, yet, when the annual celebration has come to an end, the prohibition will safely be ignored,

An expiring superstition.

---

[1] Conze, *Reise*, p. 121.

and from that time forward the locality itself will be forgotten. This sudden eclipse of what was once an important medicine is partly due, no doubt, to the progress of medical science even in these remote regions; but perhaps it may also have been caused by the discovery that it is devoid of efficacy. That this is the case at the present day has been proved by an analysis of its component parts[1]. Whether it was so with the original *rubrica* we have no means of learning.

The eastern district. Returning to Kotchino, we now struck off northwards over the hills in the direction of a place which is known as Palaeopoli. As we rode along I noticed a village with a minaret rising above it, and found on enquiry that it was called Aïpati, i.e. Hagios Hypatios: it is a rare instance of a Christian village having passed into Turkish hands, for until lately it possessed a mixed population, but the Christians gradually withdrew, and now but few families remain. Further on, the eastern coast came in view, at a point where a large shallow salt-lake, which is separated by a bar from the outer sea, displayed its white surface; this my guide at first called by its Turkish name of Touzla (*touz*, Turk. for 'salt'), but

---

[1] Dr. Daubeny (*On Volcanos*, p. 373) makes the following statement: 'On analysis it is found to consist merely of—

Silex	66.0
Alumina	14.50
Oxide iron	6.0
Water	8.50
Natron	3.50

Lime and Magnesia an inappreciable quantity.'

he knew it also as Megale Alike. At this place salt is collected. Towards the south, between the bay of Mudros and the open sea, the ground reaches a considerable elevation. It was in this district that the famous inscription was found, which is written in primitive Greek characters, but in a language which is not Hellenic, and is supposed by some eminent authorities to be Etruscan[1]. At a distance of two miles from Kotchino, not far from the shore, we came on some ancient graves, one or two of which had been opened. They were plain rectangular stone chambers, and bones and broken fragments of glass were strewn about in their neighbourhood. Close by, a rude excavation had been made of what looked like a house of the Roman period, and amongst the *débris* lay part of an unfluted column, a capital, and numerous large tiles. The neighbourhood of these remains was called by our guide Palaeopoli.

The ground at this point begins to form a peninsula, which projects into the bay of Purnia, and is flanked on its eastern side by the winding harbour of Hecatonkephalais, or 'the Hundred Heads,' which penetrates deeply into the land. Here is the place which since Conze's time has been recognised as the site of Hephaestia. A long and gradual ascent brought us to the highest point of this, which bears the name of Klas; on the further side the ground

Site of Hephaestia.

[1] The inscription, which was discovered by MM. Cousin and Durrbach, and was first published in vol. x. of the *Bulletin de Correspondance hellénique*, will be found, together with a disquisition on the questions raised in connexion with it, in Pauli's *Eine vorgriechische Inschrift von Lemnos*.

falls abruptly, and the peninsula terminates in a low rocky promontory, called Tigani or 'the Frying-pan.' There are no remains of an acropolis at Klas, but all along the ridge the foundations of a wall are traceable, and this I followed down the slope from west to east, until it came to an end just where there is a steep descent to the entrance of the little bight which forms the innermost portion of the harbour. Through the greater part of its course only one layer of stones was visible, and nowhere more than two; the width at the point where I measured it was four feet and a half, and the blocks of which it was composed were of no great size. These, no doubt, are slight traces, but they are sufficient to identify the city to which they belonged with Hephaestia. We know that formerly Lemnos possessed only two towns[1], and one of these, Myrina, is certainly to be placed at Kastro: the only other locality in the island where remains of an ancient city have been found is Palaeopoli, and most of the marble blocks, which have been used for building in other parts, are said by the inhabitants to have been brought from thence. This, we may naturally conclude, was the site of the second of the two, Hephaestia; and the majority of the coins which have been found on the spot bear the name of that place[2]. The position, though not very strong for defence, was serviceable for purposes of commerce, since it lay in the recesses of a fine bay, and possessed a commodious harbour of its own.

[1] The epithet δίπολις was applied to it for this reason.
[2] See Conze, *Reise*, p. 118.

On the following day I returned to Kastro, after *Horned cocks.* passing another night at Atziki; but before leaving that village I had an opportunity of seeing a specimen of what are regarded as among the greatest curiosities of the island, its horned cocks. When first I heard of these I treated the story with some incredulity; but this morning one of them was brought for my inspection by the children of the place. Undoubtedly it had two horns, growing one above the other; and these are nothing else than the spurs, which, by a process which must involve some cruelty, are removed from the legs and planted in the head. The fowls that are treated in this manner are called capons (καπόνια), and are famed for their size and flavour. They are exported to Constantinople, where they fetch as much as a *medjidié* (3s. 6d.). In the sixteenth century, on the other hand, Lemnos was noted for its chestnut ponies, which are specially mentioned by Belon[1]: the breed, however, must have become extinct, for I did not see one of that colour during my stay.

It remains now to notice the reputation which this *A volcano in Lemnos.* island enjoyed in antiquity as a centre of volcanic agency, and to enquire how far this is reconcilable with what we find at the present day. It is difficult to doubt that volcanic phenomena displayed themselves here in some shape or another, owing to the various forms of testimony which imply it. One of the early names by which Lemnos was called

---

[1] Belon, *Observations*, p. 58.

is Aethaleia, or the 'Fire-island.' It was closely connected with the worship of the fire-god, Hephaestus; on it he was reputed to have fallen, when cast down from heaven by Zeus[1], and it became his favourite place of abode on earth[2]. Hence he was frequently styled the Lemnian god, and the island was regarded as sacred to him, and one of its two cities, Hephaestia, bore his name. Three of the Attic dramatists make mention of its fires. By Aeschylus it was regarded as the place from which Prometheus stole the fire which he gave to mankind[3]. Sophocles in one passage of his 'Philoctetes' represents that hero as calling its flames to witness his wrongs[4], in another as praying that he may be delivered from his agony by being cast into them, and even pointing to them, as if they were within view[5]. In Aristophanes a violent flame is spoken of as a 'Lemnian fire[6].' We must not forget that at the time when these authors wrote Lemnos was an Athenian possession; so that, even allowing for the idealism of the Attic drama, there is considerable probability of a groundwork in fact for these poetical conceptions. The name of the burning mountain

---

[1] Hom. *Il.* 1. 594.   [2] Hom. *Od.* 8. 284.

[3] Cic. *Tusc. Disp.* 2. 10, 23, 'Veniat Aeschylus ... Quo modo fert apud eum Prometheus dolorem, quem excipit ob furtum Lemnium;' and the quotation from Accius which follows.

[4] Soph. *Phil.* 986, ὦ Λημνία χθὼν καὶ τὸ παγκρατὲς σέλας Ἡφαιστότευκτον.

[5] Ibid. 800, τῷ Λημνίῳ τῷδ' ἀνακαλουμένῳ πυρὶ ἔμπρησον.

[6] Ar. *Lysist.* 299, 300, κἄστιν γε Λήμνιον τὸ πῦρ τοῦτο πάσῃ μηχανῇ.

which is here alluded to was Mosychlos[1]. Now at the present day no extinct volcano exists in the island, nor do there seem to be any evidences of volcanic agency. The contrary of this, I am aware, has been maintained; but the statements to this effect seem all to be based on a remark of Dr. Hunt, who says, 'The whole island bears the strongest marks of the effects of volcanic fire: the rocks in many parts are like the burnt and vitrified scoria of furnaces[2].' This, however, is unconfirmed by any other traveller, and I myself saw nothing that could justify such a description[3]. The hot spring which I have mentioned hardly deserves to be adduced as evidence, for similar phenomena are found in other islands, which have never been supposed to be volcanic. Even earthquakes, as I was assured by the inhabitants, have now become extremely rare.

Choiseul-Gouffier was the first writer who proposed to explain the difference between the ancient and the modern condition of Lemnos by supposing that the volcano which existed in antiquity had been submerged in the sea[4]. He noticed the Mythonaes

Its supposed disappearance.

---

[1] Antimachus ap. Schol. ad Nicandri *Theriaca*, 472: Καὶ Μόσυχλον δὲ τὰ ὄρη τῆς Λήμνου, ὡς 'Ἀντίμαχος,

Ἡφαίστου πυρὶ εἴκελον, ἥν ῥα τιτύσκει
δαίμων ἀκροτάτης ὄρεος κορυφῇσι Μοσύχλου.

[2] Hunt, in Walpole's *Travels in various countries of the East*, p. 59.

[3] The specimens which I brought away with me are pronounced by a competent authority to be granite and quartzite, which are not volcanic rocks; fragments of the latter of these are widely spread over the face of the ground in various parts of the island.

[4] *Voyage pittoresque de la Grèce*, vol. ii. pp. 130, 131.

shoal, which lies off the eastern coast, and believed that in this he had discovered the traces of Mount Mosychlos. A conjecture such as this, if unsupported by other evidence, would carry little weight with it; but in the present instance there are certain facts which corroborate the hypothesis. In the story of Philoctetes mention is made of an island called Chryse[1], and this is stated to have been in the immediate neighbourhood of Lemnos[2]. This island had disappeared before the time of Pausanias, who gives the following account of the occurrence. 'The island of Chryse, in which Philoctetes is reported to have suffered from the bite of the serpent, was at no great distance from Lemnos; this they say was submerged by the sea, and disappeared in the depths[3].' He then describes how another island called Hiera, a name which was commonly applied to land which rose from the sea, subsequently emerged in its place. Now the shoal just mentioned, which is delineated in Choiseul-Gouffier's plan, and with greater accuracy in the English Admiralty chart, corresponds in its outlines to a considerable promontory projecting from the eastern coast, and an island lying beyond it. These would not unsuitably represent Mount Mosychlos and the island of Chryse. Unfortunately, up to the present time neither the shoal, nor any part of Lemnos, has been examined by a scientific geologist, and in

[1] Soph. *Phil.* 269, 270.
[2] Soph. *Fragm.* No. 352, ὦ Λῆμνε Χρύσης τ' ἀγχιτέρμονες πάγοι.
[3] Pausan. 8. 33, 4.

default of such testimony it is impossible to speak with confidence on the subject; but the fact that a submergence has taken place, as the result of volcanic action, in the neighbourhood of the island, renders this conjecture the most probable explanation at which in the existing state of our knowledge we can arrive.

Closely connected with this question is the further one of the position of the mountain or promontory called Hermaeum. It has been already mentioned [1] that this is usually identified with the north-east promontory of Lemnos, Cape Plaka, but the direct evidence which can be produced either for or against this view is surprisingly small. The name occurs only in two passages in classical authors—in the description of the fire-beacons in the *Agamemnon*, and in the closing scene of the *Philoctetes* [2]; and neither of these, if taken by itself, can be said to determine anything. As regards the former—we should certainly expect that the site chosen for a beacon would be a lofty point, and this is the case with all the other stations which Aeschylus enumerates; whereas both Cape Plaka itself and the ground in its neighbourhood are insignificant in elevation. From this point of view Mount Skopia, the conspicuous summit that rises behind Cape Murzephlo, has far greater claims to consideration [3]. On the

Mount Hermaeum.

[1] See above, p. 239.
[2] Aesch. *Ag.* 283, Ἑρμαῖον λέπας; Soph. *Phil.* 1459, Ἑρμαῖον ὄρος.
[3] In Smith and Grove's Atlas the Hermaean mountain is placed (with a query) at this point.

other hand, it is in favour of Cape Plaka that it stands in the direct line between Ida and Athos, that it projects far into the sea, and that it is the nearest point in the island to the Troad. With these elements of uncertainty in the subject, when it is considered in connexion with what Aeschylus implies, we may perhaps approach nearer to a solution, if we regard it in relation to the preceding question of the position of the burning mountain. We have seen that Sophocles conceived of Mosychlos as being within sight of Philoctetes' abode, and the same proximity is attributed to Mount Hermaeum, when the hero speaks of it as having re-echoed his groans[1]. Thus, from a comparison of the two passages, we discover that these two mountains were situated at no great distance from one another. This at once destroys the claims of the north-western cape, because there is no ground for believing that a volcano ever existed in its neighbourhood, and we seem forced to fall back on the old view that Cape Plaka is the most suitable locality. Philoctetes' cave, which has become a reality to us through the poet's description, was no doubt a creation of his fancy; but if the supposition given above is true, he must have conceived of it as existing near the promontory among the cliffs of the eastern coast.

[1] πολλὰ δὲ φωνῆς τῆς ἡμετέρας
'Ερμαῖον ὄρος παρέπεμψεν ἐμοὶ
στόνον ἀντίτυπον χειμαζομένῳ. ll. 1458–1460.

CHAPTER XIV.

THASOS.

As the next object which I had in view was to reach Thasos, and that island is hardly more than forty miles distant from the nearest point of Lemnos towards the north-west, it might seem the natural course that I should have engaged a small sailing vessel to convey me thither. Against such a proceeding, however, I was strongly warned both at the Dardanelles and at Kastro, on account of the storminess of the sea in the north of the Aegean at this time of year. Indeed the governor of Lemnos, who, as his administration embraces most of the neighbouring islands, had a good right to speak on this subject, assured me that the season of early spring is worse in this respect than any other, because in winter the winds blow with some regularity, whereas at this time they change suddenly, and frequently do not continue for a whole day in the same quarter. The wildness of these storms is associated with the student's earliest acquaintance with Greek history, for it was owing to them that the fleet of Mardonius was wrecked on the shores of Athos, and that Xerxes, to avoid the recurrence of such a disaster, cut the

The Thracian Sea.

famous canal through the isthmus of that peninsula; and most schoolboys have heard of Thracian blasts, and of 'gales from the Strymon[1].' I determined therefore to avail myself of the facilities offered by steamers; and through these two courses lay open for me—either to return to the Dardanelles by the same vessel in which I had come, and to make a fresh start from that place; or to embark on a coasting steamer of the 'Bell' line, which was expected soon to touch at Kastro on its way to Salonica and Cavalla, the port on the mainland which is opposite Thasos. In either case a long *détour* was unavoidable, but the dislike of retracing my course, together with the desire of once more beholding Mount Olympus, turned the scale in favour of the latter plan. The Hilda, which is the largest boat belonging to the Bell company, arrived towards the middle of the day after my return from the interior, and I at once went on board of her. The captain reported such rough weather on his way from Smyrna, that he had been compelled to put in for the previous night to the small harbour of Petra in the north of Lesbos, and he rather regretted even now that he had quitted it. When we started again, the vessel rolled heavily in the trough of the waves, and continued to do so until we entered the Thermaic gulf; but she made good way, for early the next morning we reached Salonica.

Salonica.   As the islands, and not the coasts, of the Aegean

[1] πνοαὶ ἀπὸ Στρυμόνος μολοῦσαι, Aesch. *Ag.* 192.

are the subject of the present work, it hardly falls within its scope to describe this famous city. It may suffice to say that I spent the day in renewing acquaintance with its antiquities, which are among the most remarkable in the Levant. Three of its churches—St. George, or, as it is commonly called, the Rotunda, with the ancient mosaics in its dome; St. Sophia, which is a reproduction on a smaller scale of the great church at Constantinople; and, finest of all, St. Demetrius, a basilica with a nave and four aisles, not unworthy of comparison with the cathedral of Monreale—are objects of the greatest importance in the history of art; and there are others only second in interest to these. I made my way from one to another of them in a downpour of rain, which caused rivers of muddy water to rush through the steep and ill-paved streets. The upper quarters of Salonica—which is the Genoa of the East in its position, though a great contrast to that noble city in respect of cleanliness and imposing houses—are hardly altered from what they were at the time of my last visit in 1865; but the modern quay, which has been constructed since that time, is truly magnificent, and both in its length and in the noble view over the gulf which it commands may almost rival that of Smyrna. As evening came on, a beautiful effect was produced by the illumination of the minarets, of which this city boasts a great number. It happened to be the commencement of the month preceding the Ramazan, and on that evening, as on every night of the sacred month of fasting, the gallery which runs round each of these aërial structures is hung with a circlet of lamps.

Transport of petroleum. It had been arranged that we should leave Salonica at nightfall, but owing to the large amount of merchandize which had to be taken on board, we did not start until daybreak the next morning. One of the chief items in the cargo was petroleum, large quantities of which have been imported into Turkey from the wells at Baku on the Caspian, ever since that place has been connected by railway with the Black Sea. Considering the way in which this is conveyed, it is surprising that serious accidents are not caused by it. On this occasion the cases which contained it were piled to a great height on the deck on either side of the engine-room, so that if a violent lurch of the vessel had burst the fastenings by which they were secured, they would have come into immediate contact with it: to which it may be added, that some of the cases were so leaky, that whenever we came to anchor in the course of our subsequent voyage, the sea on both sides of us was covered with the oil which exuded. When I called the attention of one of the officers to this, he readily admitted the possibility of danger, but justified the proceeding by asserting that, though it was constantly being done, no evil consequences had as yet arisen. Owing to its abundance the Russian petroleum has for the time the advantage over the American rock-oils in these parts; but it seems to be thought that the latter, owing to their natural superiority, will soon regain their hold on the market.

As we steamed down the gulf we passed opposite Mount Olympus, which was now free from vapour; and as its long succession of peaks, rising above the forests which clothe its lower slopes, had their full complement of winter snows, the aspect of it was magnificent. Southward of this, the conical form of Ossa was conspicuous from its cap of snow, and the depression formed by the vale of Tempe was clearly traceable, but the distant summit of Pelion was concealed by clouds. Gradually the line of islands that run off from the extremity of Magnesia came in view. We now rounded the promontory of Pallene, the westernmost of the three peninsulas which project like a trident from the mainland of Chalcidice; here there were smiling slopes, the ground being either cultivated or covered with wood, and at one point, where there was a small landing-place, a vessel was lying in readiness to carry timber to Salonica. The cape itself rises into conspicuous heights, but the greater part of the peninsula is so low, that, as we looked back in crossing the gulf that intervenes between it and Sithonia, the greater part of it had disappeared below the horizon. As seen from the open sea, the depth of the bays which here penetrate into the land is a striking feature. The central peninsula appeared lofty and finely broken in its outline, and towards its extremity on the western side, the harbour was visible, on which the ancient town of Torone was situated.

Peninsulas of Chalcidice.

We now rounded the bold bluffs in which it terminates, and towards the middle of the afternoon found ourselves approaching Athos.

The Holy Mountain.   It was a pleasing surprise to me to learn that we were to have a nearer view of the Holy Mountain, since the captain had undertaken to land two passengers and some merchandize at the port of Daphne, which is situated towards the middle of the western coast of the peninsula. As we headed for this place, one after another of the monasteries came in view; and it was amusing to find that I involuntarily became the *cicerone* of the party, for no one else on board, except an agent of the Austrian Lloyd's who was now on his way thither, had ever set foot on the Mountain of the Monks. To commence from the north—first appeared Docheiarciu, conspicuous with its lofty tower, and Xenophu, the walls of which are washed by the sea; then the Russian monastery, which has greatly increased in size since I visited it in 1861, and by its vulgar buildings, including a huge erection like a manufactory on the shore, forms a strong contrast to the picturesque Byzantine structures; and on the heights above Daphne stood Xeropotamu, or the 'Torrent,' by the side of which a stream was descending in cataracts through the river-bed from which the monastery takes its name. Then followed Simopetra, the most wonderful of all, perched on a rock at a height of seven hundred feet; and, where the precipices become more and more abrupt towards the southern end, St. Gregory, beneath the cliffs close above the water;

St. Dionysius, the buildings of which are closely packed together within their encircling wall; and finally St. Paul, which is withdrawn from the sea in the recesses of a deep ravine. As we coasted along after discharging our cargo, we passed close to the four last-named monasteries, and at intervals we could descry on the declivities large bushes of cytisus or coronella, which diversified the landscape with their patches of yellow colour. Finally, we rounded the base of the great peak, the cliffs of which have been in all ages the terror of sailors. The sea in this part is very deep, and as there was but little motion on the water, the vessel was able to keep close in to shore. The peak itself was veiled with clouds, but through the openings in these snowy summits from time to time appeared. When we reached the eastern side, shortly before dusk, we caught sight of Lavra, one of the largest and most imposing of all the monasteries, which occupies a commanding position on one of the lower buttresses. On the slopes around it lay its numerous dependencies and retreats (καθίσματα), and below, at the sea-level, stood a round white-washed tower, which guards the 'arsenal,' as the monks call their little port. We now drew away from land, and struck across to Cavalla, which place we reached at 11 o'clock, and cast anchor until morning.

Cavalla, which occupies the site of the ancient Neapolis, the port of Philippi, presents a highly picturesque appearance, as seen from the sea. The peninsula which it occupies rises steeply to a lofty

Cavalla.

summit surrounded by a battlemented castle, and at the northern end, where it joins the mainland, the rocks descend abruptly, but are separated only by a slight interval from the heights behind. The depression thus formed is spanned by a fine Byzantine aqueduct of two, and in some places of three, tiers of arches. The outer walls of the town follow the line of the cliffs at some little distance above the sea, and immediately surmounting them, in the centre of the western side, stand the colonnades and domes of the charitable and educational institution founded by Mehemet Ali of Egypt, who was a native of the place. The remainder of the area within, extending upwards to the castle and as far as the point of the peninsula, is covered by picturesque wooden houses, from among which spiry minarets are seen to rise. The fine bay at the head of which Cavalla stands is environed on the land side by a wide sweep of mountains, while in the opposite direction the view is closed by the long line of Thasos, which forms a barrier to protect it from the open sea.

Thasos. Towards that island we now directed our course (March 30). Though the Hilda was not to stop there, yet in passing through the channel that separates it from the mainland, on her way to the ports that lie further to the east, she would skirt its shores; and consequently the captain agreed for a small extra payment to land me at the port of Limena, which is situated near the narrowest part of the strait. In less than two hours from leaving Cavalla we found ourselves approaching this place, and could descry a tall

mediaeval tower, which is conspicuous enough to
serve for a landmark, rising from among the houses
that skirt the water's edge. The anchorage is little
more than an open roadstead, but is tolerably safe,
being protected towards the east by a small headland; and as it faces the north it is somewhat
sheltered by the neighbouring coast of Roumelia.
There is also a small inner harbour, enclosed by two
piers with a narrow entrance between them, within
which smaller craft can take refuge in unfavourable
weather. The village, though it presents the appearance of a straggling line of dwellings, is notwithstanding this a place of some little importance,
because it is the only landing-place for vessels arriving from Cavalla, from which port come almost
exclusively the goods which are imported into
Thasos. In consequence of this, Limena has now
become the residence of the governor, who until
lately dwelt at the village of Panagia, two hours
distant towards the interior, and at a still earlier
period at Theologo in the centre of the island.

As soon as I had landed, I obtained comfortable *Its beauti-*
accommodation in a newly-built house overlooking *ful scenery*
the sea, and having engaged a youth who was well
acquainted with the neighbourhood to act as guide, I
started to examine the site of the ancient city of
Thasos, within the area of which the modern village
stands. An hour had hardly elapsed from the time
of my arrival, when the weather, which during the
forenoon had been dull and rainy, as it had been
hitherto throughout almost the whole of this journey,

suddenly brightened; and for the rest of the day, and during the three next days, which I devoted to the exploration of this, the most beautiful island in the Aegean, I enjoyed a cloudless sky. The contrast presented by the scenery to what I had been accustomed to in Lemnos was in all respects complete. In the place of grey and somewhat shapeless mountains, here were lofty ranges, sharply cut outlines, and rocks of white marble grain; instead of treeless expanses, extensive tracts of forest land; instead of scanty brooks, full and clear streams; and the whole of this radiant landscape was illuminated by a brilliant sun. The newly fallen snow which remained on the summits added a further element of beauty to the views.

The ancient city.

The ground in the neighbourhood of Limena forms a triangular plain, about two miles in width along the sea-coast, and a mile and a half in length, where it retires among the wooded mountain spurs, which diverge from a conspicuous summit towards the south, and enclose it on either side. The eastern portion of this plain, together with the neighbouring heights, reaching as far as the little promontory, were occupied in ancient times by the city of Thasos, the capital of the island; while the western part, which was far the more extensive of the two, was devoted by the inhabitants to a necropolis, which from its size and the splendour of its monuments must have been almost unrivalled in antiquity. I commenced by following the line of the coast towards the neighbouring headland, and as I passed the mediaeval tower already mentioned, I could see that it was composed of fragments of Hellenic masonry. for in some places portions of triglyphs had been built into it. The closed harbour, which lies in its *Its sea-face.* neighbourhood, in all probability occupies the site of the ancient port, for traces of the old foundations of the piers are still visible. Between this and the promontory the remains of another breakwater, which projects into the sea at right angles, and must have formed an additional protection for shipping, appear below the surface of the water[1]. As we passed along the low heights which overlook this, I noticed a *stele* lying prostrate by the roadside, which bore the figure of a man in bas-relief, now much mutilated, and an inscription recording that it was a votive offering to Nemesis[2]. The person who dedicated it, Euemeros the son of Dionysios, was no doubt a sailor, for several similar inscriptions have been found in the island, either praying for safe-conduct on a voyage, or returning thanks for deliverance from the perils of the deep. They bear witness alike to the stormy nature of the neighbouring seas, and to the superstitious dread with which the traders of that period encountered them. The rocky peninsula at the extremity of the promontory is separated from the ground behind by so deep a depression as to be almost an island. It is called by the natives

---

[1] These seem to be the harbours referred to by Scylax, when he says, Θάσος νῆσος καὶ πόλις, καὶ λιμένες δύο· τούτων ὁ εἷς κλειστός, *Periplus,* 67.

[2] Εὐήμερος Διονυσίου Νεμέσει εὐχήν.

Obriokastro[1] or 'Jews' castle,' a name for ancient sites which is of common occurrence in Greece, and is said to have originated in the permission, which the Frankish conquerors of the country accorded to the Jews, to settle for trading purposes in the suburbs of their towns.

The theatre. From this point we began to mount the ridge of the hill which leads to the acropolis, and before long came upon a considerable fragment of the ancient wall, which followed this direction. Like all the masonry in Thasos, it was composed of white marble, the grain of which was visible wherever the stone was fractured; and the blocks were usually laid in horizontal courses, though in some places they were polygons neatly fitted together. When we had reached the height of perhaps 300 feet, my guide conducted me to the theatre, which is situated in a steep position just within the line of walls, facing Cavalla, and commanding, as so many Greek theatres do, a fine view over the sea. It has been partially excavated, but is in a very ruinous condition. Part of the wall of the *scena* remains, and behind it are the piers of a colonnade, fragments of which—small columns, triglyphs, and other ornaments—are strewn about in the neighbourhood. At the back of the orchestra the slabs of the *podium* which supported the front rows of seats lie on the ground, and most of these bear one or two letters inscribed on them in large Greek characters. Of the seats themselves very few occupy their original

[1] A corruption of Ἑβραιόκαστρο.

position, though in the upper part one or two rows are partially preserved. This building seems to be the one mentioned in the fifth century before Christ by Hippocrates the famous physician, who practised for several years in Thasos, and describes the residence of one of his patients as being 'near the theatre[1].'

We now ascended to the acropolis. The lofty hill on which this stands is divided into three summits, which form a line running from north-east to south-west, and in consequence of this a different system of fortification was required from that which is found in most Hellenic citadels. The north-east height was covered by a rectangular fort, of which only the foundations remain; the site of this is now occupied by the walls of a mediaeval castle, which was constructed out of the ancient material. This building was entered through a massive gateway, the lintel of which, formed of a single block, is still in its original position. Within there is a large cistern, and at the further end rise two square towers, one of which forms a conspicuous object when seen from the port below. The ground at this point is excessively steep, both in front and towards the back, and the pine-trees grow picturesquely among the ruins. The castle is not wholly unknown to fame; for within its walls Ramon Muntaner, the historian and one of the leaders of the Catalan Grand Company in their marauding expeditions in the Byzantine empire in the fourteenth century, was

The acropolis.

---

[1] Hippocr. *Epidemia*, I. 9, vol. ii. p. 660, ed. Littré.

entertained by the Genoese chieftain Ticino Zacharia, who, to use the words of the chronicle, 'put at our disposal the castle and all that it contained, and treated us magnificently.' The depression which intervenes between this and the central height is defended by a wall composed of enormous blocks; indeed, the masonry throughout this part is excessively massive, and elicited expressions of wonder from my young companion, who again and again exclaimed, 'How *did* they get these stones into their place?' The central summit was also occupied in Hellenic times by a rectangular fortress, and one of the blocks of this which I measured was eleven feet in length: at the north-west angle the ground is supported by a wall of twenty parallel courses.

Shrine of Pan.

As we approached the last of the three heights, I saw in front of me a wide but shallow niche, surmounted by a low arch, the whole hewn in the rock, which had been artificially sloped in order to facilitate the approach to it. On the face of the rock at the back of this niche, which might roughly be compared in form to the tympanum in the pediment of a temple, several figures carved in low relief are traceable. Those towards the right of the spectator are almost obliterated; but in the centre Pan is represented with horns on his head, in a sitting posture and playing the *syrinx*, and on the left hand stand three goats, one behind the other, with their faces turned towards him. On the slope of the niche there are other traces of ornament. This little shrine is an interesting sanctuary of the shepherds' divinity, and is all the more impressive at the present day from the solitude in the midst of which it is found. The hill above commands a superb view of the surrounding landscape. Towards the north stretches the coast of Macedonia and Thrace, separated from Thasos by spaces of blue sea, and directly opposite lies the wide alluvial plain formed by the river Nestus, while in the middle of the intervening strait the island of Thasopulo, or 'Baby-Thasos,' forms a conspicuous object. The lofty mountains on the mainland are readily distinguishable by their white summits; especially Pangaeus—the *alta Pangaea* of Virgil—to the west of Cavalla, and further inland the still higher Orbelus, which displays a grand snowy mass. On the other hand appear the wooded heights and graceful bays of the eastern coast of Thasos, with Samothrace in the distance. The ancient city, which occupied the interval between the acropolis and the shore, and the western wall of which is traceable from this point almost throughout its whole length, must have been a radiant sight with its white marble buildings; and still more striking must have been the effect of the necropolis, the monuments of which extended in long lines across the neighbouring plain. Owing to the cool northern breezes which the town enjoyed, it was no doubt a delightful and salubrious abode in summer.

The view.

As the knoll on which we were standing is the most elevated of the three summits, it is surprising that there are no traces of fortifications upon it, or

Staircase in the rock.

of any wall connecting it with the central height. Still, it is impossible to suppose that a point which must have been the key of the whole position could have been left undefended, especially as the line of the city walls recommences at the foot of its western precipices. The descent of those precipices is accomplished by means of a staircase in the rock, the like of which I do not remember to have seen in any other Hellenic citadel. The steps of which this is composed, to the number of twenty-three, are carried in zigzags down the face of the cliff, and are for the most part cut in the rock, but the lowest flight is supported by a wall of six courses of masonry. The stone staircase by which the acropolis of Orchomenus in Boeotia is reached, is a greater work than this, since it is composed of ninety-four steps; but it does not wind in this remarkable manner. From the foot of the cliffs we followed the fortifications downwards, until I was arrested by the sight of an extraordinary object—the figure of an enormous nose and eyes, with the eyebrows, but without any other feature, engraved on the face of a large recumbent block of stone. This weird-looking emblem was probably one of those symbols, which were used by the Greeks for the purpose of averting the evil eye and other sinister influences. Just below this the wall makes a sharp turn, and at the angle is a gateway covered in by a prodigious stone, but the upright blocks which form its sides are now deeply buried in the earth.

The city wall.

Following through the plain the outward face of the walls, which is curiously diversified by a band of black stone being carried along between the lower courses, we pass a second, and afterwards a third gate. The last-named of these, as it occupies a central position between the city and the necropolis, is thought to have been that through which the dead were carried; and this is rendered probable by the funeral monuments which are found in its neighbourhood. Here stands a tall *stele*, in the middle of which is represented a man seated, with a woman standing in front of him, while under the seat a smaller figure is sketched in low relief. Again, just beyond, there is a large sarcophagus, the covering of which is formed by a mass of stone of enormous weight. It is almost devoid of ornament, and an inscription on one side tells that it commemorated Poliades the son of Sosion. It has been broken open, no doubt with the object of carrying off the valuables which it contained. Within the circuit of the walls, and at no great distance behind the modern village, are the remains of a Roman arch, which have been recently excavated by Mr. Bent. The foundations of this remain *in situ*, but the rest is a heap of ruins, for the huge blocks of which it was composed lie against one another at various angles, as they fell. It was erected in honour of the emperor Caracalla, and the dedicatory inscription, which formed two long lines, is perfectly legible, though it is broken into three pieces. When the arch was perfect, it must have been a magnificent object.

Sepulchral monuments.

The necropolis.

Early the next morning I was again on foot in the company of the same guide, in order to explore the necropolis. Following the line of the shore almost to the point where the hills descend to the sea at the western extremity of the plain, I reached a mausoleum, our knowledge of which is also due to Mr. Bent[1]. This consisted of a large marble chamber, erected on a platform which is reached by four rows of steps; and it would appear that this chamber was originally surmounted by another storey, for triglyphs and drums of Doric columns, which must have belonged to it, lie about in its vicinity. An inscription shows that the person in whose honour it was erected was called Philophron, and the sarcophagus which remains underneath the building was no doubt his tomb. The vault in which it was placed can be approached through an opening, now nearly filled up, on the eastern side of the platform. Several of the objects which surrounded the building, including some inscriptions, have been removed since Mr. Bent's visit, but a portion of the body of a marble lion still remains. In the immediate neighbourhood of the mausoleum stands another sarcophagus, resembling in shape that of Poliades, but smaller, and supported on a lofty pedestal; it was the tomb of a lady, Aelia Macedonia, and commemorates her honours and the offices which she held. Having inspected these, I struck across toward the head of the plain through extensive olive-gardens and amid brushwood and undergrowth, in hopes of

[1] See his description in the *Classical Review*, vol. i. pp. 210, 211.

finding the monument of the brothers Eurymenides and Antiphon, which Conze has described. Shortly after arriving at the first hills I discovered the broken fragments of a mausoleum, such as he mentions, and among them a bas-relief representing a man in a sitting posture; but the inscriptions in elegiac verse and other interesting objects had disappeared. This time I returned to Limena with a sense of disappointment, arising from the insignificance of the remains of what was once a collection of splendid monuments. The work of destruction has proceeded during long ages, and especially in the present century, for Baron von Prokesch-Osten, who visited Thasos in 1828, speaks of seeing more than fifty of these sepulchres [1]. Many fine tombs, no doubt, still remain beneath the surface of the ground, and may be brought to light by excavation; but these will hardly suffice to recall the former glories of the place.

[1] Quoted by Conze, *Reise*, p. 18.

CHAPTER XV.

THASOS (*continued*).

Thasos under the Khedive.

BEFORE starting for the interior of Thasos I paid my respects to the Bey, who is the representative of the Khedive of Egypt. It seems strange at first sight that a district which forms an integral part of the dominions of the Porte should be practically in the possession of a vassal potentate; but the arrangement dates from the time of Mehemet Ali, and arose from his connexion with this part of Turkey, for, as I have already stated, he was a native of Cavalla. Among the inhabitants it is reported that he began life as a sailor in this island; but, whether this is true or not, it is certain that he cherished a strong affection for it: and when he rose to power, he obtained it as a gift from the Sultan. The same privilege has ever since been continued to his successors. In consequence of this the natives enjoy a considerable amount of independence, for, with the exception of the retinue of the Bey and a few soldiers, there are no Mahometans resident among them. They are also lightly taxed; for there is no capitation tax, nor are they burdened by duties on live stock and other products, like the inhabitants of other parts of Turkey: in fact, the customs duties, which go to the Sultan, are the only impost. Hence, though the island is poor owing to its natural resources not being developed, the people are well contented with the government.

Another arrangement which is peculiar to Thasos, and which it is well for the traveller to be acquainted with before visiting the interior, is the system of local currency. Strange as it may seem, every village has its own peculiar coins, and these do not pass current outside the area of that village, except at Limena, which forms a general emporium for the island. In this respect the inhabitants have outdone even the ancient Greeks, among whom, though every city had its special coinage, the money that came from elsewhere was freely received. The pieces that are used are the copper, or rather brass, coins, which were current in Turkey until about ten years ago, when they were called in by the government; on these each village imprints its private stamp before they can be put in circulation. The stamp in every case consists of four letters, placed within the limbs of a cross, two of which denote the name of the commune, the other two the dedication of the village church. Thus—to take one specimen out of several which I possess—the coins of the village of Vulgaro are marked with the letters Ε Β Κ Θ, i.e. ' District of Vulgaro: Repose of the Virgin ' (Ἐφορία Βουλγάρου, Κοίμησις Θεοτόκου). This exclusive system

Peculiar local currency.

is believed to be of ancient date. The disadvantages of it are apparent to every one; what its advantages may be, I leave to political economists to determine.

Interior of the island. Having hired three mules, which were accompanied by a young muleteer called Petro, I started at 11 A.M., in the enjoyment of brilliant sunshine and fresh invigorating air. Our course lay due south, in the direction of the pyramidal summit, which I have already mentioned as being conspicuous from Limena, and when we had reached the head of the plain, we entered a lovely valley filled with pine-trees. It was not long before I discovered what are the principal products of the island, for first there met us a mule laden with two large pigskins full of oil, on its way to the port, and shortly afterwards we passed a long row of beehives, which were ranged by the side of the road in a solitary place, where no dwelling seemed near. The hives were cylindrical baskets of wickerwork, with a covering of earth, and a large stone on the top of each. In addition to timber, oil and honey are largely exported from Thasos. At the head of the valley there followed a long ascent toward the shoulder of the mountain behind; and when this was reached, a beautiful view broke upon us of a bay of the eastern coast, flanked by wooded heights, with a wide plain in front covered with olive-trees. On the western side rise the loftiest summits of the island, culminating in the central peak of Hagios Elias, which reaches a height of more than 3000 feet;

and all along the face of these the rocks descend, first in steep precipices, and then in gentler slopes, towards the plain. The path now wound gradually downwards, and at the end of two hours from Limena we reached the village of Panagia, which was formerly the residence of the Bey. The four hundred houses of which it is composed are clustered irregularly within a theatre-formed valley, in the midst of scenery truly Alpine in its grandeur. The traveller has no need to enquire into the employment of the inhabitants, for the whole place reeks of oil, and the numerous clear streams that rush through the streets are doubtless utilized in the service of the oil-mills. An hour's further descent brought us to another village, Potamia, where we rested for our mid-day meal.

At this point a pass commences, which leads over the flank of Hagios Elias into the interior of the island. To reach the summit three hours are required, and during the latter part of the way the ascent is so steep that our baggage mule required frequently to rest. Altogether it is a remarkable mountain route, and the material of which the road is composed is everywhere white marble, though the rocks frequently appeared black from weathering. All about the lower slopes numerous violets were in flower, but after a time the only blossoms that remained were the blue squills, and owing to the elevation and the steepness of the ground, the pine-trees became very sparse along the declivities. Behind us in the distance the great plain of the Nestus and

High pass.

the mountains of Thrace were very imposing, but in the opposite direction a far more beautiful sight awaited me. When we had crossed the ridge, which must be more than two thousand feet above the sea, there opened out a wide view over the southern part of Thasos and the open Aegean beyond : this was divided in two by a lofty mountain immediately facing us, and the spaces of blue water enclosed between this and the nearer heights on either hand presented to the eye two exquisite vignettes, in one of which the conspicuous object was the colossal peak of Athos, in the other the massive Samothrace, whose snow-capt summits rose above the mist that obscured its base.

Theologo. From the ridge a long descent leads to Theologo, which is the chief place in the centre of the island, and was at one time its capital. It is hard to say why the site which it occupies should have been chosen for a village, for the valley in which it lies is a 'marble wilderness,' the slopes on either hand being covered with nothing but bare blocks of stone. The houses are roofed with slabs of this material in place of tiles. Perhaps the position may have been selected because it is intermediate between two spaces of arable ground in the upper and lower parts of the valley, bordering on the stream which intersects it. The inhabitants appeared poor, but, notwithstanding this, there is a large school of recent construction. I was conducted to the *Konak* or official residence, a crazy building of unpromising exterior, in which, however, a clean room, which formed the bureau of the Subashi, was placed at my disposal. That officer, who was a Mussulman from Crete, was most polite in his attentions. Not the least acceptable of these was, that he provided me with a *mangal* or Turkish brazier for charcoal, for notwithstanding the warmth of the sun by day, the nights were cold owing to the elevation at which the village stands.

The following day (April 1) I devoted to a visit to the quarries at Alke, from which in ancient times the Thasian marble was obtained. This place is situated on the southern coast; and as our muleteer Petro was unacquainted with the road, I engaged a native of Theologo as guide for the day. We were accompanied also by a guard, whom the Bey at Limena had pressed upon me with so much polite insistence that I could not well decline to accept his company, though aware that he was intended to watch my proceedings, and to prevent excavation or the removal of antiquities. I have often found that Turkish guards, though they may not be wanted for defence, are willing to make themselves useful in helping one's travelling servant, and doing various little services; but my present attendant was wholly indisposed towards any such offices. He was an Albanian from Monastir in western Macedonia, and possessed most of the faults which are found in his race. Lazy and overbearing, he endeavoured to make every one else act as his servant. As the baggage mule was not required for my use this day, he took it for himself to ride; but in the steeper parts of

An Albanian guard.

the road, where he dismounted, he expected another of the company to lead it. When he wanted water, he despatched one of the country people to fetch it for him. He walked delicately in his mocassins in true Albanian fashion, and was too proud to enquire his way for fear of betraying his ignorance. Petro designated him as 'ballast' (σαβούρα, Lat. *saburra*), that is to say, 'good-for-nothing stuff,' and this was a fair description of his character.

The southern mountains. Leaving Theologo, we crossed the stream, in the neighbourhood of which grow enormous plane-trees, and ascended the opposite mountain-side. This was so stony that there was practically no track along it, and a way had to be extemporised over the rocks. At the head of this desolate region we reached the pine-forest, and for a long time continued to wind in and out of most beautiful dells at a great height above the sea. The scenery of this part is not inferior to that in the north of the island, for behind this enchanting foreground the peak of Athos, here thirty miles distant, rises from the Aegean to the height of 6400 feet, white with snow on its northern face; and from its foot the peninsula of the Holy Mountain, and the neighbouring coast as far as the mouth of the Strymon, extend along the horizon. In the western part of Thasos, which from this point we overlook, the most striking object is the wooded summit of Hagios Matz, the name of which is a corruption of Asomatos, i.e. the Archangel. This district I did not propose to visit, because it contains no objects of interest. At the end of an hour and a half's riding we crossed the ridge, and came in sight of a vast expanse of the open sea, with the islands of Lemnos, Imbros and Samothrace. The turf beneath our feet was here sprinkled with the delicate blue flowers of dwarf forget-me-nots. A break-neck descent now commenced over steep broken rocks, where riding was impossible; and when the foot of these was reached, for two hours more the way led over gentler declivities, until at last the strange peninsula of Alke[1] came in sight beneath us. It resembles a long and narrow island, lying parallel to the coast and close to it, but is joined to the mainland by an isthmus near its eastern extremity. The little bay thus formed, which is conspicuous from above with its clear green water, provides a commodious harbour for ships which come hither to fetch timber for exportation. At the time of my visit a vessel of some size was lying moored to the shore.

The principal remains of antiquity in this neighbourhood are found on the nearly level isthmus. Here was apparently the residence of those employed in the quarries, for in various parts the outlines of dwellings and fragments of walls are visible on the surface of the ground. Near the centre stands a large sarcophagus, resembling in most respects those at Limena, though partly buried in the earth, and much broken at the sides. On the slab which faces west is engraved a long and graceful inscription in elegiac verse, of which ten lines were visible at the

Remains at Alke.

---

[1] The name is Alke, not Alike, as Conze gives it.

time when it was copied by Conze, but now the four last of these are concealed by rubbish: the four first have long been so much obliterated as to be unintelligible. The subject is a lament for the untimely death of an unwedded girl, whose bones the sarcophagus contained. The most important ruins are those of a temple, which have recently been brought to light by the indefatigable spade of Mr. Bent. These are situated close to the sea on the eastern side of the isthmus, just where it abuts against the peninsula. The steep slope which intervenes between the platform on which the temple stood and the water's edge is in a ruinous state, but it is evident that the building was approached on this side by a number of steps, composed of massive blocks of stone. One of these I measured, and found it to be twelve feet in length. Two chambers belonging to the temple have been excavated, and a wall of large rectangular blocks has been laid bare on its south side; but here, as at Limena, many of the objects that have lately been discovered have been removed. Two interesting inscriptions, however, remain. One of these records a votive offering to Athena and Heracles for safe conduct on a voyage, dedicated by a member of a guild of merchants. The other, which is a list of public officers, contains certain titles of magistrates which are otherwise unusual[1]. At the time of Conze's visit, no source of water was known to exist

---

[1] See Mr. Hicks's remarks on Inscriptions from Thasos, Nos. 1 and 14, in the *Journal of Hellenic Studies*, vol. viii. pp. 410, 415; also Mr. Bent's account of their discovery, *ibid.* pp. 434, 435.

in this neighbourhood; but within the last two years a well has been brought to light on the isthmus, the water of which is fresh, notwithstanding its proximity to the sea.

The peninsula which is connected by this isthmus with the mainland, is about half a mile in length, and rises to a height of perhaps 150 feet. Its surface presents an extraordinary sight, for from end to end it has the appearance of being wrecked, owing to the irregularity with which the work of quarrying was carried on. In some places pits, in others vast depressions, are seen, and great faces of rock remain, marking the limit of the excavations in a certain direction. At one point a narrow wall of marble stands up to a great height, forming the line of demarcation between two quarries. The dreariness of this scene of ruin is modified by the softening effect of the undergrowth which has overspread it, and by the pine-trees which grow, though sparsely, among the rocks. But the greatest wonder of the place remains still to be told; for the whole of the western end of the peninsula for a distance of several hundred yards has been cut down to the sea-level from side to side in the process of quarrying, and though a sort of breakwater has been left towards the open sea, the greater part of the area is covered with stagnant water. The appearance of this from a distance is almost that of a marsh, but a nearer inspection shows that the surface is made up of innumerable artificial beds of marble, resembling large shallow troughs. Some of these are matted with

The marble quarries.

seaweed, and the stone, wherever the water reaches it, has assumed a dark hue; but elsewhere it is dazzlingly white, and the places from which the huge blocks were taken are visible, with the marks of the workman's instruments at the sides, forming lines of drilled holes and groovings. At one point a drum of a Doric column, which was being wrought into shape on the spot before removal, remains rooted in the stone.

Forest rights. The route which I followed in returning to Theologo lay southward of that by which I had come, and traversed somewhat less rocky ground. At no great distance from Alke, near the shore, I stopped to examine the remains of a square Hellenic tower constructed of massive masonry, five or six courses of which remain in places; and further on another, circular in form, was visible on a lofty knoll. There are said to be many of these at intervals along the coast, so that the island in ancient times must almost have been defended by a chain of forts. After leaving the sea, for a considerable distance we were once more traversing the forests; and here at intervals we found felled trees lying by the path, in readiness to be transported to the nearest point on the shore. After having been squared, each trunk, we were told, is dragged by two oxen along the mountain paths until it reaches its destination, and considering how narrow and winding these are, the process can be no easy one. The forest land is partitioned between the neighbouring villages; but whereas formerly the inhabitants possessed the right of cutting timber where they liked, at present the privilege is restricted, and while they are allowed to carry off as much as they need for building purposes, the government requires that a payment should be made for felling large trees for exportation. I nowhere saw traces of forest fires, such as frequently are caused in Greece by the recklessness of the natives, who by this means either more easily extract the resin from the trunks, or else improve the next year's crop of grass, which springs up abundantly where a conflagration has taken place. This may perhaps be explained by the employment of forest-rangers (δασοφύλακες), who are appointed by the different communes to guard their rights against encroachment. This institution exists also in Greece, but there the guards are apt to wink at the destruction that is committed.

The eastern coast.

I had planned my return journey to Limena so as to include a visit to the eastern coast of the island, because according to Herodotus the gold mines, which were an important source of the wealth of the Thasians, were situated in that district, or, as the historian himself expresses it, facing Samothrace[1]. For this portion of the way, which is rarely travelled even by the inhabitants, a fresh guide was required. Taking leave of the friendly Subashi, I ascended the valley behind Theologo for some distance in the neighbourhood of the stream, and then struck off eastwards in the direction of the ridge, which here, as above Alke, breaks into steep faces of rock where the descent towards the sea commences. The line

---

[1] Herod. 6. 47.

of these gaunt precipices appearing above and in the midst of the forests, especially when seen from the sea, amply justifies Archilochus' description of Thasos as 'an ass's backbone, covered with wild wood [1].' We now looked down on a bay, in the recesses of which lies a small plain hemmed in by the mountains, while in front it is partly sheltered by an island. Descending on foot, I reached the forest, and followed the path that winds downward through it in the midst of most enjoyable surroundings. The calls of the goatherds to their flocks, the tinkling of the goat-bells, the curling wreaths of smoke from the charcoal burners' fires, and, as an accompaniment to these, the whispering pines, the running streams, and the expanse of blue sea, formed the perfection of rural life and scenery. The plain is covered with olive-trees, the extraordinary age of which is shown by the size of their gnarled and twisted trunks; and the turf beneath them was starred with pink anemones and the blue heads of the grape hyacinth.

Kinira, the ancient Coenyra. The name of this district (for there is no village) and of the neighbouring island is Kinira, and in this we find a clue to the position of the mines, for Herodotus says that they were situated between Aenyra (Αἴνυρα) and Coenyra (Κοίνυρα), and the difference between the latter of these and the modern name disappears in pronunciation. The name of Aenyra has perished, and together with it all trace

---

[1] ἥδε δ' ὥστ' ὄνου ῥάχις
ἕστηκεν ὕλης ἀγρίης ἐπιστεφής.
Archil. *Fragm.* 18, in Bergk's *Poetae Lyrici Graeci*.

of the site, but it must have been situated on the coast either to the north or the south of Kinira, and therefore it is in one of those two directions that we might expect to find the 'great mountain turned upside down in the search for ore,' of which the historian speaks. I enquired of my guide, who was well acquainted with the localities, concerning the tract of country which intervenes between this bay and Alke. He replied that the ground in that direction is very precipitous, so that, though it is traversed by a foot-track, no mules go that way, and when any goods pass from the one place to the other they are transported by sea. Of anything like minerals or traces of mining in those parts he had never heard. My route later in the day lay through the country to the northward of Kinira, and there also the signs of former workings are wholly wanting. The question, therefore, of the position of these mines must be regarded, for the present at all events, as an unsolved mystery.

When we had reached the shore and turned northwards along the coast, we entered on a route, which at once for difficulty and picturesqueness can only be compared to those on Athos, and on the sea-slopes of Olympus, Ossa and Pelion. The path overlooks the sea, sometimes at a higher, sometimes at a lower elevation, but always commanding lovely views of the coast ; and, at the same time, the rocks over which it passes are so broken and slippery, and the way is so tangled with arbutus, heather, myrtle, cistus and other aromatic shrubs, that it is

Exquisite woodlands.

a wonder how the mules can force a passage through them. In the middle of this expanse of undergrowth we reached a small clearing on the mountain side, which bears the name of Palaeochori from a village which is now deserted. I enquired for ancient ruins, but none were known to exist there. At last we emerged from our delightful wilderness into the forest, where we found more level tracks. I had been astonished at the precision—resembling a form of intuition—with which our guide had found his way through this difficult district, notwithstanding the perplexity of diverging paths; but the mystery was solved when he explained that at one time of his life he had been employed in these parts as a forest-ranger. The neighbourhood of the pine-trees is said to be good for the production of honey, and in one place I saw as many as fifty wicker beehives. The old man who guarded them—an ideal Theocritean shepherd with a tall crook—said that he had in all a hundred of these in various parts of the forest. The valley of Panagia now opened out once more before me with a white beach fringing the coast; and in a glen leading down to it I halted for a while under a plane-tree from which gushed a limpid stream.

Return to Limena. Shortly before arriving at this point I had dismissed my guide, since we had reached a part of the country with which Petro the muleteer was acquainted, having come thither on former occasions for wood. The Subashi's dog had followed us thus far on our way, and I supposed that he would return with the guide, but to my surprise I discovered that he had remained with our party, and he continued to accompany us for the remainder of the day. I afterwards learnt that he was an *habitué* of the island, and that he often made the journey from Theologo to Limena and back on his own account. We now descended to the sea near the *scala* or landing-place of Potamia, where there was a small pier and a newly-built warehouse, and then crossed the plain by circuitous ways, in order to avoid the freshly irrigated maize fields. In the stagnant water the frogs were singing *brekekekex koax koax* as clearly as in the days of Aristophanes, the two notes being quite distinct from one another. The view of Hagios Elias from the shore is very fine, for the entire face of its precipices is visible, reaching down to the two villages of Potamia and Panagia which nestle beneath them. Leaving the plain, we ascended to the latter of those places, where we rejoined our former route; and before evening, after an agreeable ride of eight hours, I was once more at Limena.

CHAPTER XVI.

SAMOTHRACE.

Wild weather.

DURING my wanderings in Thasos I had enjoyed such halcyon weather that it seemed impossible that a change could suddenly take place; and accordingly, on my return from the interior, I arranged with the captain of a small merchant vessel that he should convey me across to Cavalla the following day. During the night, however, a strong south wind arose, and in the morning I was informed that it was useless to attempt the passage, because, though we might get across, it would be impossible to land owing to the unprotected character of the roadstead. When I asked in some surprise what happened to the trading steamers under such circumstances, the answer was, that they are then unable to land the goods and passengers that are booked for Cavalla, and are obliged to pass that place without stopping, and sometimes to take refuge in the harbour of Limena, which is sheltered from the south wind. The insecurity of the ports in Turkey, the result of centuries of neglect, involving as it does continual uncertainty as to the possibility of reaching one's destination, is a serious inconvenience to the traveller. I have already referred to this in connexion with Khanea and Rhodes, and the same thing is true of several places on the coast of Thrace: fortunately the most important maritime cities in the Aegean, Smyrna and Salonica, are sufficiently protected by their natural position. On the present occasion it was well that we had not started, for towards midday the wind increased to a furious gale, accompanied by torrents of rain, which continued with unabated violence all the afternoon. So little trust can be placed in a smiling sky on these coasts during the spring-time!

During the night the sky cleared, but in the morning the wind had gone round to the west, and rendered it impossible to reach Cavalla; so, finding that a vessel laden with pigskins full of oil was preparing to start for Port Lagos (in Turkish, Karagatch), which lies to the north-east of Thasos, I changed my plans, and made an agreement to be conveyed to that place. The crew consisted of four men, of whom the captain and one sailor were Greeks, the other two Bulgarians. As we receded from the shore, we left behind us the pyramidal heights of Thasos, and were soon coasting the mainland, where a wide alluvial tract has been formed by the Nestus, the brown and turbid waters of which river are borne far into the sea. As the wind was in our favour, in four hours we reached Lagos, a collection of scattered houses which lie at the entrance of the large salt-lake called in ancient times Bistonis. It would be difficult to find a drearier spot, for it is situated in a dead flat and is sur-

Voyage to Lagos.

rounded by marshes. Great care is here required even for small craft in reaching the shore, since there is only one narrow passage through the shallows; larger vessels are forced to remain in the offing. I was well satisfied not to be doomed to a long sojourn in this scene of desolation. On the following day a Turkish steamer arrived, and in her I proceeded to Dede-agatch, which is the nearest point on the coast to Samothrace.

A raid on guide-books.

On landing at this place I renewed the experience which I had had in Crete fifteen years before. All my books—sixteen in number—were taken from me by the custom-house officers, on suspicion of their containing passages hostile to the Ottoman government. After the lapse of some hours my dragoman was able to recover most of these, but the three guidebooks—Murray, Joanne, and Baedeker—were retained, Murray being regarded as especially objectionable, on the ground that it spoke in unfavourable terms (which it does not) of the Turkish administration of Crete. Even the next morning these officials were still obdurate, so nothing remained for me but to require that the books should be taken to the governor of the place, in order that he might pass judgment upon them. To him accordingly I went, in company with the British Vice-consul, Mr. Misser, who obligingly undertook to arrange the matter for me. The governor was an educated man, who spoke French fluently, and after a brief inspection of the condemned works he restored them to me without further difficulty.

Dede-agatch is a place which sooner or later may rise to importance as an *entrepôt* for the trade of the interior, since it is connected by a branch railway with the main line from Belgrade to Constantinople. This branch diverges from a point near Adrianople, and follows the valley of the Maritza (Hebrus) for the greater part of the distance to the sea. At present the amount of communication is limited, for only one train runs each way every two days. The village of Dede-agatch is entirely a creation of the railway, for until the spot was chosen for a terminus not a single house existed there, and it partakes of the uninteresting character of all such places of sudden growth. At the back a plain of about three miles in width reaches to the foot of the mountains, which are an offshoot from the Despoto Dagh or Rhodope, the principal chain in the interior. The cultivators of this plain are Bulgarian peasants, but the waste ground is occupied by the flocks of Wallach and Bulgarian shepherds, who remain there during the winter months, but in the warmer season migrate to the higher regions. On the outskirts of the village numerous camels, destined to convey merchandise to the inland districts where the railway does not penetrate, might be seen squatted on the ground.

During the two days that followed my arrival no hope presented itself of my reaching Samothrace. The sky was clear, but the wind blew strongly from the south-west, and it was exactly in that quarter that the island, here twenty miles distant, rose from the water, like a sea-girt castle frowning defiance.

There were numerous large *caiques* on the spot, well fitted for such a voyage; but these were now wind-bound, and lay closely wedged together in the tiny port. At last my servant came to inform me that an English steamer of the Joly-Victora Company, the Semiramis, had arrived; and as I was aware that these vessels will sometimes for a consideration deviate from their regular course, I made enquiries of their agent whether they would accommodate me on this occasion, and at what charge. The first demand was eighteen pounds, but by judicious negotiation this was ultimately reduced to five—a not unreasonable sum, seeing that the steamer, which was bound direct for Smyrna, would have to make a considerable *détour*. On these terms the bargain was struck, and I embarked without delay. To my surprise I found that my involuntary detention in Dede-agatch had won for me an honourable reputation. It was currently reported in the place that I was going to discover a gold mine, or at the least a coal mine, in Samothrace; and one of the inhabitants requested permission to accompany me, in order that he might have some share in the profits.

The voyage thither. As soon as we were under way I conferred with the captain, a burly good-humoured Greek, as to the place where I should be landed. He had not himself visited Samothrace, and was unacquainted with its coast—in fact, no steamers ever touch there, and during the winter very few sailing vessels: so the English Admiralty chart was produced, and we proceeded to discuss the possibilities. He was in favour of a spot on the northern coast marked Palaeopolis, where he had heard that there were buildings. It was well that I did not accede to this proposal, for by subsequent inspection I discovered that the only accommodation there was the hollow trunk of a plane-tree. I for my part suggested Kamariotissa, a place in the neighbourhood of the western promontory, to which I was told at Dede-agatch that vessels sometimes went; and this view ultimately prevailed. During the early part of this day the island had not been visible, for the weather had become gloomy, and its position could only be traced by a dark cloud which shrouded it. As we approached nearer the veil withdrew itself, and turning outward its silver lining covered the summits with a fleecy mass, but revealed the steep precipices below, which were generally bare, or rifted with snow, though in some places forests were visible. Leaving these on our left hand, we made for the more level part of the island towards its western extremity. After sunset a strong head-wind got up, and raised such waves, that it became an exciting question whether landing would be possible, or whether I should have to accept the other alternative of being carried on to Smyrna. Night had fallen when we approached the coast, and careful sounding was necessary to avoid running aground. The engine hooted, but no response was elicited: we had evidently miscalculated the position. The vessel drew off again, and made for a point a little

Finding a landing-place.

further on, just where a spit of sand, which is in reality the extreme point of the island, formed a shelter from the waves. This time our signal was more successful, for shortly afterwards by the 'muffled moonlight' we could see a small boat, rather larger than a coracle, approaching, rowed by two boys. Into this myself, my servant, and my baggage were stowed, not without difficulty; and we rowed away to the shore, while the steamer disappeared into the darkness. I landed on the beach, and at last was able to congratulate myself on having set foot in Samothrace.

First impressions. The next question was where to find a lodging for the night. There was no pier by the shore, to suggest that it was a frequented place; and first the contents of the boat, and then the boat itself, required to be dragged over a high bank of shingle, which has been thrown up by the waves. When this was surmounted, we found a dozen *caiques* of various sizes drawn up out of reach of the sea, and behind these, at the distance of a few stones' throws, was a row of one-storeyed houses, consisting of one room apiece. As it was Sunday, the occupants of these had betaken themselves to the village, which is an hour and a half distant, to enjoy their holiday, and had locked up their dwellings. One room, however, which formed the bar and general *rendez-vous* of the place, was open; and in this we found a number of the sailors to whom the *caiques* belonged, sitting round a stove. From them we learnt that the bakehouse, which stood at the end of the row, was vacant, and that the fire was not lighted. It was a somewhat grimy abode, and somewhat airy, owing to the numerous apertures through which the wind could enter; but we were soon established there. In default of other fastenings the door was closed by an iron crowbar which we found within.

The next morning opened bright and clear. We could now see that we were within a curve of the level shore, close to the promontory of Acroteri; and this spot, though it is exposed to the full force of the northerly and north-westerly gales, is the safest landing-place in Samothrace. There can be little doubt that it is the harbour of Demetrium, which is mentioned both by Livy and Plutarch in connexion with the story of the fate of Perseus, the last king of Macedon. After the ruin of his cause at Pydna, that sovereign betook himself with a large amount of treasure to Samothrace, in hopes of finding an asylum in the sanctuary there; but when the Roman fleet under Cn. Octavius took up its station in front of the city, and Perseus discovered that he was about to be expelled as a sacrilegious person on account of a murder which he had committed, he arranged with Oroandes, a merchant of Crete, that he should take him on board his ship, and convey him to the coast of Thrace. Oroandes, however, 'behaved like a Cretan[1],' and when the treasure was safely embarked, made off to his native island, leaving the king lamenting on the shore. The place where this vessel lay, and at which the king hoped to have

Ancient harbour of Demetrium.

---

[1] Κρητισμῷ χρησάμενος, Plut. *Aemil. Paul.* cap. 26.

embarked after stealing out by night from the neighbouring city, is described as 'Demetrium, a harbour by a promontory in Samothrace[1].' The fact that so open a roadstead is the best available shelter for shipping, justifies the remark of Pliny, that Samothrace is 'the most harbourless of all the Greek islands[2].'

Village of Chora.

The only means of transport that could be found were two ponies. On one of these the baggage was fastened, and as George, my dragoman, was not a good walker, I mounted him on the other, and went on foot myself until we approached our destination, the village of Chora, when I took his place and entered in state. The ground over which we passed was rough and stony, and in its look and colour recalled rather the soil of Lemnos than that of Thasos: as the village, which is the only inhabited place in the island, stands at a height of several hundred feet above the sea, the ascent to it, though gradual, is long. Its appearance, when it suddenly comes in view close at hand, is very striking. It occupies a curve in the steep mountain-slope, which forms a complete horseshoe, lying at the foot of two conspicuous peaks of red and grey granite, while on one side stands forth a mass of ochre-coloured rock, crowned by the broken towers of a Genoese castle. The choice of such a site is amply justified by its sheltered situation at the head of the cultivated ground,

---

[1] Demetrium est portus in promontorio quodam Samothracae; Liv. 45. 6.

[2] Vel importuosissima omnium; Plin. *Hist. Nat* 4. 12. 23.

and by its remoteness from the sea, which rendered it safe from the attacks of pirates. The view over it from above, with the castle-rock standing out against the sloping ground below and the blue expanse of sea, is especially fine; but, for all that, the village, like everything else in Samothrace, has a dreary aspect, for there is no vegetation among the bare stone buildings, and even the castle walls are destitute of shrubs to soften the harshness of their ruin. The houses of recent construction are covered in with tiles, but the great majority are flat-roofed and overlaid with clay; and on each of these a round marble cylinder may be seen lying, for use as a roller, though not provided with any handle. These cylinders are in every case the remains of some Hellenic building, for there are no marble quarries in the island, and wherever that material is found it has been imported. As I zigzagged up the excessively steep streets. I enquired for a lodging, and was offered the choice between the *konak* and the school-house. I gave the preference to the latter of these, which was situated at the very top of the village, behind a large newly-built church, and not far beneath the ridge which joins the two peaks already mentioned. In this place I found an unoccupied room, which became my home for the next six days.

As the best part of the day still remained, shortly after my arrival I started for the ruins of the ancient city, or Palaeopoli, as they are now called, which are situated on the coast an hour's ride to the north

Ruins at Palaeopoli.

of Chora. The schoolmaster, M. Christos N. Rhegopulos, proposed to accompany me and explain the position of the buildings; and I gladly accepted his offer, for, like many of his class, he was a well-educated and intelligent man. He was born at Dimitzana in north-western Arcadia, and had resided for some time in Smyrna; but on receiving the offer of a permanent post in this island, he migrated thither, and, having been in weak health before, had derived great benefit from the bracing air of Samothrace. He was thoroughly conversant with the excavations that had been made, since he was on the spot at the time, and was personally acquainted with those who took part in them. Moreover he, or rather the school, possesses a copy of the great work which gives the result of those excavations, the *Archäologische Untersuchungen auf Samothrake* of Prof. Conze. This was a present from the professor himself, and is a great boon to the traveller, because the book contains the only correct account of the Hellenic buildings, and at the same time is too bulky to be carried on a voyage. Conze is remembered by most of the inhabitants, and is generally spoken of by his Christian name, Alexander (ὁ Ἀλέξανδρος). I subsequently made the acquaintance of the Greek who acted as his foreman in superintending the excavations.

The ancient city. As I devoted more than one visit to the examination of this place, it may give the reader a clearer idea of the remains if I describe them without reference to the order in which I saw them.

They consist of two parts, the city and the sanctuary, for the latter was not included within the walls. The city, which was of triangular form and covered a very extensive area, had a northern aspect, and occupied a steep position between a jutting spur of the mountains and the sea. At the summit, which is a mass of rocks, there is no definite acropolis; indeed, the nature of the ground formed of itself a sufficient defence: but at one point a deep depression between the cliffs, which might have been reached by escalade, has been closed by a high cyclopean wall. On the eastern side, from the summit to the sea, the precipices are so steep that no fortifications were required; but here also, just at the commencement of the final ascent, a similar gap is occupied by a wall with a well-built postern, which is covered by three enormous stones, laid across parallel to one another. Towards the west the hillside slopes more gradually, and here a low but well-marked ridge is followed by a continuous line of wall. This is the wonder of the place, and the massiveness of its primitive masonry is hardly surpassed by that of Tiryns. Like that fortress, it is composed of enormous stones piled irregularly together, and no rubble is used to fill the interstices between them. Four gateways remain on this side; in the lowest of them, which led from the city to the sanctuary, the walls on either hand are preserved to the height of fifteen feet; in another, which occupies a return of the wall, the courses of masonry approach one another at the top, and the lintel is formed by one huge unhewn stone. About half-way down there is

Extraordinary walls.

a tower, the regular horizontal courses of which contrast with the other work, and seem to belong to a more recent period, though their solidity shows that they are still primitive. These fortifications of the city of Samothrace are referred to by a Latin author, in connexion with the rites which were celebrated in their neighbourhood, as 'the ancient walls of the Corybantes[1].' At the present day the whole area is most desolate, its only occupants being goats, which find a scanty pasturage on the stony soil.

Genoese towers. Near the foot of the eastern ridge, just where it begins to fall precipitously to the sea, stand three towers of Genoese construction. The uppermost of these, which is also the tallest, gives evidence of having been built of Hellenic materials by the fragments of friezes and fluted columns of white marble which are embedded in it. Here also, until a few years ago, were several inscriptions relating to the pilgrims who visited the neighbouring shrine. It would be foolish to lament the removal of such monuments to the museums of Europe; and in the present instance, though there was no fear of injury from the hands of the inhabitants, yet the votive tablets were not in their original position, and could therefore be carried off without scruple. Still, the traveller may be allowed to regret that he cannot inspect on the spot the lists of 'pious initiated' (μύσται εὐσεβεῖς), and still more the representations (now in the Louvre) of rows of dancing figures, linked hand in hand, which reveal to us something

---

[1] Moenia antiqua Corybantum; Priscian, *Periegesis*, 546.

of the character of the sacred ceremonies[1]. All these slabs have been picked out of the walls; the only inscription that has been spared is in corrupt mediaeval Greek, and relates to the erection of the building. On the western side of these towers there is a steep descent into a wooded glen, in the lowest part of which a copious spring rises under the shade of a spreading plane-tree. In front of this a wide shingly beach reaches to the sea.

A few hundred yards from this point may be seen the broken remains of an ancient mole just appearing above the water's edge. This, as far as we know, was the only defence for shipping that the city possessed in ancient times. The island was not entirely unprovided with a navy, for in the story of the Battle of Salamis we are told that an Athenian ship was sunk by a Samothracian ship, serving on the Persian side[2]: for these vessels, therefore, and also for those which brought the numerous worshippers to the shrine, some shelter must have been required. It is highly probable that the extensive beach which I

The mole.

---

[1] The position of these tablets in the wall of the tower had something of the dignity of historical association, as may be seen from the following passage of Cyriacus of Ancona, who visited Samothrace in 1444, when it was in the possession of the Gatilusi. 'Postquam ad novam a Palamede [Gatilusio] principe conditam arcem venimus, ad turrim ipsam pleraque vetusta arte elaborata marmora videntur composita, ubi plerasque Nympharum choreas conscriptas inspeximus, et alia complura hinc inde vetustatis tantae urbis eximia monumenta comperimus, et nobilia atque veterrima Graecis ac etiam nostratum literis epigrammata :' quoted by Conze, *Untersuchungen*, vol. i. p. 1, from the Vatican MS. of Cyriacus' unpublished narrative. [2] Herod. 8. 90.

have mentioned did not exist in antiquity, and thus the space within which ships could lie would have been greater than at the present day; but even so, as there was nothing like a natural harbour, the accommodation must have been extremely limited. This appears the more strange, when we take into account the violence of the storms which agitate these seas.

<small>Sanctuary of the Cabeiri.</small> We may now proceed to the sanctuary, which was situated westward of the city, outside the walls. But before investigating the buildings which it contained, a word should be said with regard to the worship of which it was the home. There is no need for us to discuss the various theories which have been held on the subject of the Samothracian gods: so much I may say, that to me it seems most probable that they were pre-Hellenic divinities, which passed under the influence of the Phoenicians, and were finally adopted and assimilated by the Greeks. This view agrees with the statement of Herodotus that these mysteries were introduced by the Pelasgi[1], and with the fact of their wide diffusion, for they were found not only in the neighbouring islands of Lemnos and Imbros, and in the Troad, but also in Phrygia. Again, that this cult was affected by Phoenician beliefs and forms of worship is proved by the name Cabeiri, which is evidently derived from the Semitic *kabir*, 'great'—a title applied by the Phoenicians to their leading divinities—for the Cabeiri were known to the Greeks as the Great

---

[1] Herod. 2. 51.

Gods (μεγάλοι θεοί). The existence of this influence does not seem improbable, when we consider that the name Samos (for Samothrace is the 'Thracian Samos,' and is so called in Homer¹) is of Phoenician origin, and that other settlements of that race existed close by, in Thasos and on the Hellespont. The rites thus framed, and the corresponding tenets, would easily be adapted by the Greeks, though even in ancient times great differences of opinion existed as to which of the Hellenic deities corresponded to the Great Gods of Samothrace. This ambiguity would naturally be fostered by the mysterious character of the worship, the secrets of which were only communicated to the initiated; and this secrecy, in turn, was more easily maintained from the island which was its centre being so difficult of access. It was due also in part to its position on the confines of Europe and Asia, that it became the meeting-point of Western and Eastern forms of religion.

The influence exercised by this place as a devotional centre was extraordinary. After Delos, it numbered more votaries than any other spot in the Aegean. As a place of pilgrimage it occupied in ancient times somewhat the same position as the neighbouring Athos does at the present day. How great its repute must have been we discover from the numerous votive inscriptions which have been found there, and which imply the existence of a much larger number in antiquity. The majority of these

Its importance.

¹ *Il.* 13. 12.

proceeded from cities in Asia Minor, but some were set up by states on the European coast of the Aegean[1]. Philip of Macedon and his wife Olympias are known to have been among the initiated[2]. Germanicus was only prevented by unfavourable weather from visiting the shrine[3]. It is interesting also to reflect that, when St. Paul touched at this place on his way from Troas to Neapolis during his second missionary journey, this form of worship existed in full vigour.

History of the excavations. The first excavations on this site were made in 1863 by a French explorer, M. Champoiseau; and his labours were rewarded by the discovery of the statue of Nike, which is now one of the glories of the Louvre. Three years later much more extensive investigations were undertaken by MM. Deville and Coquart, of the French School of Athens; and the results of these were published in the *Archives des Missions* for 1867. But the great work of all, by means of which the whole of the ruins were laid bare, and the character of the various buildings was finally determined, was carried out under the auspices of the Austrian government by Professor Conze and his colleagues, MM. Hauser, Niemann and Benndorf, in the course of two expeditions in 1873 and 1875. The history of their discoveries, and a full discussion of all the points connected with them, will be found in the two magnificent volumes of *Untersuchungen auf Samothrake* already men-

---

[1] See the inscriptions in Conze, *Reise*, pp. 63-71.
[2] Plutarch, *Alex.* 2.
[3] Tac. *Ann.* 2. 54.

tioned. The photographs, plans and drawings, which accompany this work, leave nothing for the reader to desire.

The area which is occupied by the sacred build- *The sacred*
ings, though it is lower than the greater part of the *area.*
city, is still at some elevation above the sea. Its dimensions may roughly be described as 600 feet in either direction: not that it presents a definite shape,

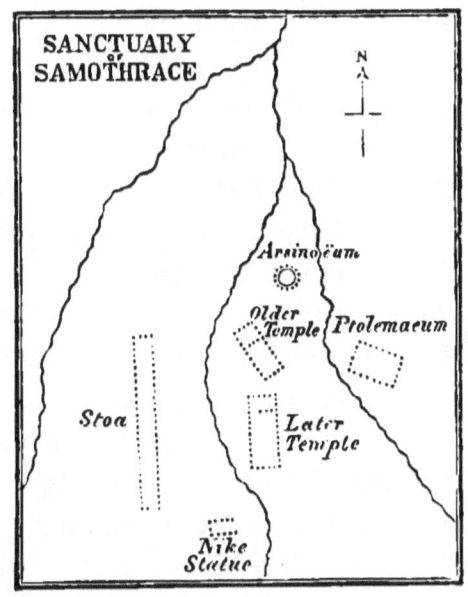

or that there is any clearly traced enclosure; nor has the position of the buildings within it been determined otherwise than by the configuration of the ground, which is peculiarly irregular. At this point three torrents, descending from the mountain side behind, run for the time almost parallel to one another, and then join their waters at the northern extremity of the area. Insignificant though they are, yet their waters have carved out very deep channels, which are flanked by steep banks on either side. These banks are supported here and there by walls and steps, which served to secure the foundations of the edifices that surmounted them. The spaces that intervene between these channels, forming, as they do, irregular levels—and in part also the neighbouring slope towards the east—were chosen as the sites for the buildings, which in this manner were enclosed within natural boundaries. Being outside the walls, they must have trusted for protection to their sacredness.

Temples of the Cabeiri. The most important portion of this area is that which intervenes between the middle and the eastern torrent-bed, for though the ground here is lower than elsewhere, yet it is the most central in its position. In the southern portion of this stood a large Doric temple, which, to judge from the fragments that remain, must have been a very handsome edifice. The material of which it was constructed was white marble, though the foundations, like those of all the buildings in this sanctuary, are of the rough stone of the country. Its architecture shows that it was erected in the early period of the Ptolemies, who were the greatest benefactors of this shrine. This was the later temple of the Cabeiri. To the north of this, and standing at a considerable angle to it, was the older temple of those deities, which was smaller than the other, and, though very little of the superstructure remains from which to judge, must have been much ruder. At its further end, where the ground is lower, it was supported by a wall of polygonal stones. It was to this building that the bas-reliefs of dancing figures, already mentioned, originally belonged, for corresponding ones were found in its area during the excavations. It is not improbable that this temple continued to be in use after the handsomer building had been erected. That they were dedicated to the Cabeiri is shown, partly by their being the only temples in this sanctuary, and partly by a remarkable feature which was discovered in both of them. This was an opening in the floor, communicating with the earth below, which is known from the analogy of other temples in which this peculiarity occurs, to have been used for offerings to the deities of the nether world, among whom the Cabeiri were reckoned. In the larger temple this was found in the pavement of a sort of apse at its southern end, and is semi-circular in form. In the smaller temple there are two such towards the middle of the cella, one semi-circular, the other nearly rectangular. Unfortunately for the traveller, these are now once more concealed under mounds of earth.

Northward again from the older temple are the ruins of a circular building, the foundations of which are visible throughout half their circuit, thirteen courses remaining on the western side. The original shape, which is clearly seen in these, is traceable also in the curved outline of some of the marble blocks that lie in ruin above. Other stones are ornamented with figures of bulls' heads, and on one

The Arsinoëum.

is a fragmentary inscription, from which we learn that the edifice was dedicated to the Great Gods by a daughter of one of the Ptolemies. It was originally suggested by M. Deville, and his view is now generally accepted, that this lady was Arsinoë, the daughter of Ptolemy Soter, who took refuge in Samothrace from the violence of Ptolemy Keraunos, the murderer of her sons. Hence the building is now known as the Arsinoëum. What use it was intended to serve is not clear, but, though it was dedicated to the Cabeiri, it does not seem to have been a temple.

The Stoa and Ptolemaeum. In a parallel line with these three buildings lay others on the higher level between the central and the western stream. Towards the south, in a corresponding position to the two temples, is the basement of an extensive structure, very long in proportion to its breadth, which appears to have been a Stoa ; and northward of this, opposite to the Arsinoëum, there is a large square area, composed of rough blocks, but almost devoid of any trace of the edifice which it supported. The Nike of the Louvre occupied a commanding site to the southeast of the Stoa. Besides these, one building remains to be noticed, which is situated on the further side of the eastern stream. The numerous fragments which here cover the ground show that it was richly ornamented, and the channellings of the white marble columns prove that it was of the Ionic order. The inscription on the frieze, which still remains, though broken into several pieces, tells us that it was dedicated by Ptolemy II Philadelphus to the Great Gods[1]: it belongs therefore to the same period as the later temple and the Arsinoëum, the first half of the third century before Christ. This 'Ptolemaeum' consisted of two halls, and its position between the city and the temples suggests that it may have served as an entrance to the sacred places, somewhat in the style of the Propylaea at Athens. It was raised high above the neighbouring stream by an artificial platform of stone, through the lower part of which there runs in a diagonal line a remarkable tunnel with a rounded vault. It has been conjectured that the object of this tunnel was to carry off the waters of the stream, in which case they must formerly have taken a different course from what they do at present; and this view is corroborated by the peculiar angle at which the tunnel runs. But the most interesting point about it is *Hellenic* that, as this construction could not have been of *arch.* later date than the building above, it affords one of the very rare instances—the bridge of Xerokampo in the valley of Sparta is another—of the use of the arch in Hellenic architecture. There is here a genuine arch with a definite keystone, and, which is still more curious, in consequence of its position it is a slightly skew arch. This tunnel is called by the people of the country Phylake, or the Prison; and the reason given to me for the name was, that before the place was excavated the upper end was closed,

---

[1] Βασιλεὺς Πτολεμαῖος Πτολεμαίου καὶ Βερενίκης Σωτήρων Θεοῖς Μεγάλοις.

and the shepherds used to shelter their sheep within it. On such occasions, undoubtedly, it must have greatly resembled a dungeon.

The effect of this entire group of buildings, when they were standing, must have been very imposing; but it is difficult to reconstruct them in imagination on the spot, since not a single column occupies its original position. Still harder is it, in the midst of the present desolation. to repeople the place with the crowds of worshippers who must once have frequented it.

CHAPTER XVII.

SAMOTHRACE (*continued*).

Depopulation of Samothrace.

THE inhabitants of Samothrace number at the present day about two thousand souls, and with the exception of the shepherds who roam over the mountains, all these are concentrated in the one village of Chora. The scantiness of the population is, however, a thing of comparatively recent date. At the time of the first conquest of the island by the Turks, indeed, in 1457, the island must have been almost denuded of its people, for we are told that the wealthy inhabitants were taken to Constantinople, the youngest and healthiest were sold as slaves, and only the poorest remained behind to till the soil[1]: but in the course of time other settlers seem to have arrived, for at the beginning of this century it is supposed that the number amounted to ten thousand, though this is probably an exaggerated estimate. But it was at the commencement of the Greek War of Independence, in 1821, that the greatest disaster fell upon the place. On that occasion the people of Samothrace declared themselves free from the

[1] Finlay, *History of Greece*, vol. v. p. 59.

Turkish rule, and for a time they remained in fancied security; but after the lapse of four months, on September 1 of that year, a Turkish force landed on their shores, and after defeating the insurgents massacred all the adults who did not escape to the mountains or by sea, and carried the children as slaves to Constantinople. Subsequently, it is computed, three hundred of those who fled by sea returned, and a hundred more from the mountains, but the island has never recovered from this catastrophe. I had the opportunity of inspecting a register, made for purposes of taxation, of the Greek inhabitants of the island in the year 1835, with their properties; the number of families was then 315, but this represented only about 500 persons, since many houses had but one or two occupants. The Turkish residents have also declined in numbers; only three or four families of that race now remain, and they have neither a mosque nor a school. In former times they sent their children to the Greek school, but latterly they have withdrawn them. When this Mahometan colony is extinct, which before long it probably will be, a memorial of it will remain in a little cemetery, with simple headstones of white and grey marble, just above the village. One result of this depopulation is, that the majority of the present inhabitants are of recent introduction, and speak ordinary Modern Greek; while the language of the shepherds, who probably date back to a very considerable antiquity, is the most remarkable of all the Modern Greek dialects, and retains some Hellenic words which

Samothrace.

have been lost elsewhere. By a curious coincidence, something like this took place in classical times, for Diodorus tells us that the aborigines of Samothrace spoke a peculiar dialect, many traces of which were preserved in the language of the sacrificial rites [1].

Of the condition of the people I received somewhat conflicting accounts. I was assured that there was no pauperism among them, for the products suffice for their consumption, and oil is grown in sufficient quantities to be exported. This might well be the case, for there is a considerable area of cultivated land in the west of the island, and a diminished population have always the advantage of an increased amount of property relatively to their numbers. On the other hand, the inhabitants generally had a poverty-stricken appearance, and the medical man of Chora assured me

Condition of the inhabitants.

---

[1] Diodor. Sic. 5. 47. The information which I obtained with regard to the dialect of the Samothracian shepherds is as follows. Its most remarkable feature is the omission of ρ in the middle of words, which leaves behind a drawling pronunciation of the neighbouring vowel: thus for Πέτρος they say Πέτ(y)ος, for κρασί 'wine' κaασί, for σήμερα ἔβρεξε 'it rained to-day' σήμι(y)a ἔβε(h')ξε. Γ is often prefixed to initial vowels, as γήκουσα for ἤκουσα; and is inserted between vowels, as θιγός for θεός; and takes the place of initial δ, as γιά for διά: but these peculiarities are found elsewhere. Some other changes which Conze has mentioned (*Reise*, p. 54), such as the omission of δ and λ, and the change of θ into ψ in the middle of words, my informants would not admit. A striking instance of the preservation of an ancient word is φαυλίζω for the familiar κακολογῶ 'to abuse:' λαλῶ is also used for ὁμιλῶ 'to speak,' but this, though generally obsolete, is regularly employed in Lemnos also. A verb παφλουκιάζω is used in the sense of 'to be scalding hot,' of liquids. For 'entrails' they employ the curious word τὰ ζκιόλα.

that few of them reach old age, owing to the severity of the winter, the exposure they suffer at that season, and the want of fuel. The island is administered by a Mudir, who is subject to the governor of Lemnos. They have little to complain of in this respect, except that the taxes are oppressive. When first I reached Samothrace the office of Mudir was vacant, but before I left a governor arrived, and he was a Christian. Ecclesiastically, the island is subject to the bishop of Maroneia on the opposite coast of Thrace. There are usually 130 children in the school, but at the time of my visit only half that number attended, owing to the prevalence of a bad infectious cough, which in the course of a few months had caused as many as a hundred deaths. From my room in the school-house I used to watch the scholars, mostly bare-footed, assembling to their lessons at the sound of an iron gong or *semantron*. In Lemnos the people of Samothrace have the reputation of being rough and boorish, but for my own part I experienced nothing but civility from all classes.

Paper money. The money that is in use in Samothrace is hardly less curious than that of Thasos. In default of small Turkish money, a paper currency has been established, consisting of small squares of thin cardboard, on which are printed the name of the island with that of the principal church, and the value of the piece. Some of these notes, or tickets, have been sent from Constantinople, but others are made in Chora itself. The smallest, which are about an inch square, are equivalent to ten *paras*, or a half-penny. I doubt whether the Austrian Tyrol in its most advanced days of paper currency ever quite equalled this. Another curiosity, besides some specimens of these, *Ibexes.* which I brought away with me, is a native stool formed of a rough slab of wood, 18 in. long by 8 in. wide, which has been placed on the arch of a pair of ibex horns, so that the whole thing forms a tripod, supported by the root and the extremities of the horns. The seat is fastened on by strong iron nails, which have been ruthlessly driven through the wood into the curving horns. The horns measure three feet in length, and are capable of supporting a great weight. The ibexes are found in the desolate mountains in the eastern part of Samothrace, and are perhaps of the same kind as those which exist in the Taurus in Asia Minor. The kids are sometimes captured by the natives, and are carried to Constantinople as pets by the Turkish governors when they quit the island; but I am not aware that they have attracted the attention of any naturalist. Not having seen the animal myself, I am unable to say whether it resembles the Cretan ibex.

It was a surprise in a remote island like Samothrace to meet with a man as learned as M. Phardys, *A learned physician.* the physician of Chora. He is a native of the place, but at ten years of age he went abroad, and only a few years ago returned to his family. He speaks French fluently, having lived for some time in Marseilles; and he also passed two years in Corsica, as manager of a school for the Greek colony which for two centuries has been established in that island.

z

The history of that interesting colony which he has lately published is by far the most authentic account of it that has yet appeared; and as I had myself visited the Corsican Greeks, we had in them a topic of common interest. One day he produced for my inspection what proved to be a post-card from Mr. Gladstone. It appeared that M. Phardys had sent a copy of a former work of his (on Greek accentuation, I think) to the English statesman, and received this acknowledgement of it. Since, however, he was unacquainted with English, he had never deciphered its contents; and as the signature, to say the truth, was somewhat hieroglyphical, he had not quite certified himself whether it was what he believed it to be. Great, therefore, was his satisfaction and his gratitude, when I identified the hand-writing, and translated the communication for him. Many years ago a monk in a monastery on Mount Olympus astonished me by saying that he was aware that the late Lord Derby had translated Homer; but to meet with a post-card from Mr. Gladstone on Samothrace appeared to me more wonderful still.

Castle of the Gatilusi. The mediaeval castle, which forms so conspicuous an object in Chora, was erected by the Gatilusi, whom we have already heard of in the other islands of the northern sea; and on its walls are inscriptions, which, like that in the fortress at Lemnos, contain the emblem of the Palaeologi, with whom they were connected by marriage. The family of the Gatilusi are a typical specimen of the stout-hearted, hard-handed merchant-princes of the West, whose influence prevailed in these seas for two centuries and a half after the capture of Constantinople by the Latins. The founder of their fortunes, Francesco Gatilusio, was cruizing about the Aegean with two war-ships on the look-out for some lucrative enterprise, when John V. Palaeologus engaged his services. By his assistance that emperor gained his throne, which had been usurped by Cantacuzene, and he rewarded him in 1355 with the hand of his sister Maria, and with the principality of Lesbos as her dowry. He was subsequently instrumental in delivering John from the hands of the Bulgarians, by whom he had been taken prisoner. In the course of time the islands of Lemnos, Thasos and Samothrace, and the town of Enos on the coast of Thrace, were added to the dominions of the Gatilusi. They ultimately became tributary to the Turks, but retained their possessions until they were deprived of them by Mahomet II.

My next expedition was to the Therma Loutra, or warm baths, which are situated on the north coast of the island three hours distant from Chora. The first part of the route was the same as that to Palaeopoli, and traversed a stony tract, in which the melancholy juniper and stunted prickly shrubs only added to the dreariness. When we reached the sea, at the point where the spring of fresh water rises below the ruins, the way followed the shore, and for the most part lay over the shingle; but here the mules which we had hired in the village found a track, since they were accustomed to make the journey during the summer months, when the baths

The northern coast.

are much frequented. The scenery of this part is the most agreeable which the island has to show. The mountains gradually recede from the water's edge, and form a plain half-a-mile in width, which is covered with an aromatic undergrowth of arbutus, myrtle and tree-heather, while the shore is fringed by agnus castus bushes: beneath this shrubbery the brake-fern was now putting forth its fronds, and the courses of the brooks were marked by numerous plane-trees. At the back the ground is clothed with oak-scrub, and rises with increasing steepness to the foot of the precipices, above which tower the highest peaks. The pines, which form so conspicuous a feature in Thasos, are here entirely wanting. In the glades and clearings numerous ponies had been turned loose, and were feeding in a half wild state. On our return journey the two lively boys who accompanied our mules set to work to catch one of these—a hopeless task, as it seemed at first sight; but the boys were more knowing than the ponies, and they soon secured their prize, which they mounted, and rode until we left the shore.

The Therma Loutra. At the further extremity of this level district, just where the hills once more approach the sea, the Baths are situated, on one side of a clear stream of some size. Between this river and the sea numerous fruit-trees give evidence of human cultivation, and among them stands a two-storeyed house, and hard by it a sort of shanty with four chambers: these are the only permanent provision for visitors, and the majority of the bathers live either in tents or in booths constructed from the branches of trees. A little way off a waterfall, which had been swollen by the late rains, was plunging down the steep cliffs. The place was now completely deserted, but during the summer, which is the bathing season, it is resorted to by numerous patients—among them by M. Misser, the consul at Dede-agatch, who comes hither with his family. Favoured as it is by the cool northerly breezes, it must be a delightful resort for a *vie champêtre*. Just before I entered the house in order to rest for a while, a sight unexpected at this time of year presented itself—a snake three feet long lying close by the door. It was in a half torpid state, and was easily dispatched. The name which the natives give to this kind of serpent is *saita*, the Modern Greek word for 'arrow' (σαϊτα, *sagitta*). Within the house were numerous wooden beehives, which are formed of sections of trunks of trees hollowed out. I had seen similar ones in the north-west of Spain, in which country also Southey noticed them, and he has introduced them as a local feature of the Asturias in his *Roderick*. In Samothrace they are the only sort of hive in use, and form a marked contrast to those of the neighbouring island of Thasos, which are universally of wicker. In the ancient world both kinds were employed, as we know from the poets and from writers on husbandry[1].

[1] See Varro, *De Re Rustica*, 9. 6; Columella, 3. 16. 15: and compare Virg. *Georg.* 2. 453, 'vitiosaeque ilicis alveo,' and 4. 34, 'alvearia vimine texta.'

Mineral springs.

The mineral springs are situated on the further side of the stream, at the foot of the rising ground, and the whole of this locality is pervaded by a strong odour of sulphur. Here I found a source too hot for the hand, and the water was very salt to the taste. An open channel communicates between this source and a building, now ruined, which from its mixed courses of brick and stone looks as if it dated from Byzantine times: within this there is a deep tank, about thirty feet long by twenty wide, full of green water, which has become tepid by exposure to the air. It is said that within the tank itself there are additional springs. This place, such as it is, affords the chief accommodation for bathers. The surplus water from the spring is discharged over a sloping face of rock, which it has thickly encrusted with a coating of sediment, in some parts of a rich brown, in others of a green hue. At one point this crust overhangs, leaving a hollow space behind.

Position of Zerynthos.

The greatest puzzle in the topography of Samothrace is the position of a town called Zerynthos, with a famous cavern sacred to Hecate[1]. This seems to have been situated on the northern coast of the island, but no place has as yet been discovered which can be identified with it. It has recently been suggested[2] that the neighbourhood of these baths is

---

[1] See the reff. in Baumeister's note to the Homeric Hymn to Demeter, l. 25, and in Owen's note to Ovid's *Tristia*, book i (smaller edition), p. 91.

[2] By Mr. Stuart-Glennie in the *Contemp. Rev.* vol. xli. p. 842.

the most probable site, and there is much to be said in favour of this conjecture. As hot springs were thought by the Greeks to indicate a connexion with the nether world, no place could be better suited for the worship of Hecate. The difficulty is to advance beyond conjecture, for no traces of an ancient site seem to have been found, nor could any one of whom I enquired tell me of a cave as existing there —or indeed in any part of the island. It is conceivable that there may have been such a cavern near the springs, and that this may have been either removed to make room for the bath-house, or otherwise ruined or destroyed. This, however, is only speculation; the most that we can say is, that this is the most probable spot that has yet been discovered.

My return was signalised by a tempest of rain and wind, bearing down from the summits of the island, which at times it was difficult to face on muleback. Wild weather of this description prevailed during a great part of my stay, and after such experiences it is easy to understand why Samothrace is shunned by seamen. The neighbourhood of the Hellespont is the meeting-point for the storms that sweep downward from the Balkan and the Euxine, and upward from the Greek seas, and these are naturally attracted by the lofty and solitary island. To the inhabitants these visitations are often disastrous from the destruction which they cause to the crops. *Stormy character of Samothrace.*

It was a long-cherished desire of mine to ascend to the highest point of Samothrace, because I

Ascent of Mount Phengari.

believed that from its position it must command one of the finest panoramas in the Aegean; but such an expedition can only be made under favourable conditions. At last, on the fourth day of my stay (April 11) an opportunity presented itself, for the wind had fallen and the sky was cloudless. I had engaged as guides two men of about thirty years of age, who proved to be capital companions and excellent mountaineers. They were clad in blue jackets, baggy trousers reaching to the knee, brown stockings, and mocassins of hide, fastened over the instep by innumerable straps; the advantage of these last over my Alpine boots in crossing slippery rocks was an unfailing topic with them during the day. One of them, who was excessively dark in complexion, was called Maniates, because his grandfather had come from Maina (the Taenarian peninsula in the south of the Peloponnese), and had married and settled here. Starting at 6.30 A.M., we passed the crest of the hill which lies directly behind the highest houses of the village, and ascended gradually in a southerly direction, overlooking the fertile ground towards the Acroteri, in the neighbourhood of which the bright surfaces of three salt-lakes were seen. After a time we rounded a mountain-spur at a point where a deep gorge lay below us, and turning eastwards, entered a vast semicircular basin, which is surrounded by the highest summits. Opposite to us was our destination, Mount Phengari, or the 'Moon¹,' which in ancient times bore the name of Saos or Saoce; and

[1] Φεγγάρι is the only word for 'moon' in Modern Greek.

to the right, on the further side of the gorge, rose the lower, but still elevated, peak of Hagios Elias, beneath which a spot was pointed out to me, which marked the position of the famous fountain of Sphidami, the only one in the upper part of the range. But the most striking feature was the wild, bare, forbidding wall of grey precipices, broken along their upper ridge into rude battlements, which surrounded the whole area. With these we were destined to become intimately acquainted, for we ultimately made almost the complete circuit of them. At the end of an hour from our departure we reached the last spring which was to be met with on this side, and rested to drink. Here began a steep ascent through groves of oaks not yet in leaf—the remains, we may suppose, of those forests, which caused Homer to designate Samothrace by the epithet 'wooded[1].' Up to this point we had followed the tracks of the wood-cutters, but as we emerged from among the highest trees these came to an end, and we found ourselves on the open mountain side. At first the oaks were replaced by juniper bushes, but before long these also ceased. A few friendly flowers still relieved the barrenness—blue squills, brilliant yellow crowfoots, and above all golden crocuses, such as I had formerly found on Parnassus and on the mountains of the Peloponnese. At 9.30 we reached the first patch of snow.

I could now see clearly that my guides were not acquainted with any definite route; but they knew *Crest of the island.*

[1] Σάμου ὑληέσσης Θρηϊκίης, *Il.* 13. 12.

the point in the ridge which they ought to make for, and towards this they directed their course. Winding in and out of small gorges, and at last ascending very steeply, at 10.30 we reached the crest, and looked down on the northern part of the island, where the Baths, or rather the houses in their neighbourhood, lay immediately below us. The amount of snow on this side was much greater than on that by which we ascended, where it was found only in the rifts; here there were large sheets of it, wherever the slope was sufficiently gentle to allow of its resting. I now began to realise that the expedition, which before starting I had expected to find an easy one—for though Samothrace attains the greatest elevation of all the Aegean islands after Crete, the height of Phengari is only 5248 feet—would give me a really hard day's work. At Chora no one had any idea of the time it would occupy, but all agreed that it was necessary to start very early (πρωί, πρωί); and as in the distant views of the island which I had obtained both from Lemnos towards the south, and from Dede-agatch towards the north, I had been struck with the steepness of the upper precipices, I might have concluded that the crest must be very

Its ruggedness. narrow, and would present some difficulty. In order to reach the summit, it was necessary to follow the ridge, now on one side and now on the other, according as the ground allowed, climbing up and down with hands and feet, and passing in and out through the broken jagged masses, which at times were composed of rotten stone, untrustworthy to the hand.

After twenty minutes of this work we came upon what looked like a cairn, but proved to be an erection of stones hollow inside: this was in reality a tiny chapel, dedicated, like one of the neighbouring peaks, to Hagia Sophia, and within it were one or two small objects which had been left there as votive offerings. Continuing along the crest for another hour, shortly before midday we reached the summit, which is but little elevated above the rest of the ridge, and lies somewhat on the southern side of it. We had come at an excellent pace the whole way, with few halts; and latterly our steps had been quickened by the appearance of envious little clouds, which gathered near, and moved around and above the peaks, for Samothrace is more persistently cloud-capped than any other mountain in the Aegean, Athos not excepted. We now partook of a dry breakfast, for there was nothing but snow wherewith to quench our thirst.

Let me next attempt to describe the view. During the three-quarters of an hour that we remained there, it was at no time perfectly clear; but as the clouds never rested on the peak where we were seated, and were constantly shifting their position, it was possible, part by part, to see the whole panorama; and one or two points, where other summits of the island interposed, I can supplement from what I observed either in ascending or descending. Let me begin with those islands which I had recently visited. Lemnos, low-lying and encircled by the sea, was visible in every detail. All the mountains, harbours

View from the summit.

Western portion.

and promontories, which had become so familiar to me, were most delicately traced; and the white salt-lake on the eastern coast was especially conspicuous, with the bay of Mudros penetrating far into the land, and the tiny headlands which project into it. Behind and above Lemnos Aï Strati appeared, and beyond that again in the same line was the form of another and larger island. When first I noticed this in the course of the ascent I fancied that my eyes were deceived; but now it was quite clear, and the object was unmistakeably Scyros, the island of the great Achilles. To the right of these were two of the islands which run off from Mount Pelion, and the coast of Thessaly was seen in faint outline. Here the pyramid of Athos interposed, looking comparatively near, though in reality sixty miles distant; and stretching into the sea beyond it was the extremity of Sithonia. To the northward of these a long line was formed by the peninsula of the Holy Mountain, and above it appeared in the extreme distance—no cloud, assuredly, but the sharply-cut outline of a white mountain. It seemed incredible, considering that the whole width of the Aegean intervenes—but it was nothing else than the long snowy Olympus ($\mu\alpha\kappa\rho\grave{o}\varsigma\ \dot{\alpha}\gamma\acute{a}\nu\nu\iota\phi o\varsigma\ ^{"}O\lambda\nu\mu\pi o\varsigma$). Next followed the pyramidal heights of Thasos, and on the mainland the summits of Pangaeus and Orbelus. All along towards the north stretched the coast of Thrace, backed by the chain of Rhodope, as far as the valley of the Hebrus, which here is close at hand, and seemed to be extensively flooded. The mouth of the river recalled the story of Orpheus' death, which Virgil and Milton have celebrated in undying verse :—

> When by the rout that made the hideous roar
> His gory visage down the stream was sent,
> Down the swift Hebrus to the Lesbian shore.

As we look from our present point of view, where Imbros and Samothrace are seen to intervene between the mouth of the Hebrus and Lesbos, it seems strange that the Lesbian shore should be mentioned. Milton, however, was not in error, for he was following the ancient tradition, which related that the head and lyre of Orpheus were carried to Lesbos; a story which simply embodied in a poetical form the fact, that Terpander, the founder of Greek music, was born in that island.

Towards the east the view was far less clear. The long gulf of Saros (Melas Sinus), which forms the innermost angle of the north-east of the Aegean, was close at hand, but no part of the sea of Marmora was visible, nor the Dardanelles—though that narrow piece of water is probably concealed at all times. The plain of Troy and the mountains in its neighbourhood were dimly seen, but the long range of Ida appeared behind, though its highest point, Gargarus, was shrouded in cloud. Off the coast lay Tenedos, and behind it the heights of Lesbos projected far into the Aegean. Imbros was at our feet, and a most graceful island it appeared, with its winding shores and rolling hills, which, though not low in themselves, seemed insignificant as seen from this elevation. The beauty of these island views was

Eastern portion.

greatly heightened by the tranquil sea of purest blue in which they were set. As to Samothrace itself, I can only describe it as a huge boulder planted in the sea. The fertile ground at its western end, indeed, has a smiling appearance, and towards the south, where the landing-place of Ammos, the only one on that side of the island, is marked by its white shingle, there is a small plain green with olives : but for the rest, I have rarely seen such a bare stony wilderness as that which met the eye at every turn.

Mythological associations. The view which we have now been surveying is associated in many points with the early mythological stories of the Greeks. Diodorus has preserved for us the legend, that Samothrace was visited by the great flood which occurred when the waters of the Euxine overflowed their limits, and forced their way first through the Bosphorus, and afterwards through the Hellespont, into the Aegean. By this inundation the lower part of the island was submerged, and the evidence of this was found in later times, with a felicitous anachronism, in the capitals of columns which fishermen used to bring up in their nets. So high did the waters rise, that the inhabitants fled for security to the mountain tops, and it was only through their prayers to the Gods that the progress of the deluge was stayed. Hence the Samothracians enjoyed the right of calling themselves antediluvian[1]. But it is in the *The Homeric deities.* Iliad especially that we find the neighbouring islands and seas connected with the movements of

---

[1] Diodor. Sic. 5. 47.

the divinities. When Hera passed from Olympus across the Aegean to meet Zeus on Gargarus, the poet describes her as visiting the Thracian mountains and Athos, whence she took her flight by way of Lemnos and Imbros to Ida[1]. The spaces of sea that extend on either side of Imbros were the haunts of the marine deities. When Poseidon prepares to visit the Trojan plain, he leaves his horses in a cave beneath the sea between Tenedos and Imbros[2]. When Iris is sent from Olympus to bear a message to Thetis, she plunges into the deep 'between Samothrace and rocky Imbros,' and there finds the goddess with her attendant sea-nymphs[3]. Finally, the peak which we occupy was the station of Poseidon, from which he regarded the combats of the Greeks and Trojans. There, we are told, 'the mighty Earthshaker held no blind watch, who sat and marvelled on the war and strife, high on the topmost crest of wooded Samothrace, for thence all Ida was plain to see; and plain to see were the city of Priam, and the ships of the Achaeans[4].' This quotation cannot fail to recall to our minds the passage in *Eothen*, where the traveller, whose mind has been perplexed, when studying the map, by finding Imbros interposed between these two points, is relieved from his doubts by discovering that the peak of Samothrace is visible from the Trojan plain, towering above the intervening island.

At 12.30 we commenced the descent, following *The descent.*

[1] *Il.* 14. 225-30, 281.   [2] *Il.* 13. 33.
[3] *Il.* 24. 77-84.   [4] *Il.* 13. 10-14.

a different route, which led southwards towards Hagios Elias, along a ridge that runs transversely to the main chain. This was far more difficult than anything we had yet experienced, and the mountaineering skill of my guides was put to the test. We made our way down deep gullies, and along steep faces of rock, in passing which they showed admirable judgment in determining what places were practicable. It was three o'clock when, after scrambling down the flank of Hagios Elias by a rough screes, we reached the fountain of Sphidami (τὸ Σφιδάμι), which, as I have already said, is situated on the opposite side of the *cirque* of mountains to that by which we had approached it. This spring is famed for its salubrious qualities, but the water had no mineral taste, and was deliciously fresh. It has also the reputation—not unknown in the case of some other sources[1]—of becoming colder as the heat of the sun increases, so that in the middle of the day it is icy-cold. Just below this we re-entered the oak-forest, and were glad to find wood-cutters' tracks and easier walking. Here we were joined by three charcoal-burners, all of whom carried tall shepherds' crooks, as also did one of my guides. Those who are engaged in this occupation start from the village every morning, and return every evening, notwithstanding the distance. Descending at last into the gorge above which we had passed in the morning, we found a clear stream overhung with plane-trees, in the bed of which were large stepping-

Famous fountain.

---

[1] See Herod. 4. 181.

stones. The place is called the Ford—a statement which I insert in compliance with the injunctions of one of my companions, who, having seen me jotting down notes in the course of the day, said peremptorily, 'Put it down, put it down, the Ford' (γράψε το, γράψε το, Γιάβαθρο: *i. e.* Διάβαθρον). After a steep ascent on the further side, we pursued our course by a level track along the sloping ground; and thus about sunset (6 P.M.) I returned to Chora, the pastoral staffs following in procession in single file.

The next morning the wild weather had reasserted itself, and for forty-eight hours the wind increased in violence, battering the house which I occupied, and almost banishing sleep. At last it moderated its force, and the sun once more shone; so, finding in the village a Turk, who owned a good *caique* and had the reputation of being an experienced sailor, I agreed with him to convey me across to the main land. The schoolmaster and the physician, together with the newly arrived governor and others among the inhabitants, kindly escorted me to the outskirts of the village, where I took leave of them, and rode down to the landing-place of Kamariotissa. An hour and a half were spent in preliminaries, while the little vessel was being ballasted with shingle and launched; but at midday we were under way, carrying with us the mails of Samothrace, which are, as might be supposed, 'occasional.' The wind was in our favour, and five hours' sailing over a rather tossing sea brought me once more to Dede-agatch. There

Return to Dede-agatch.

I found the barques tightly wedged together in the port, just as I had left them a week before; and I learnt, moreover, that in the interval two *caiques*, which were trying to reach the place, had gone down with their crews in the sight of the people on the shore. Without the help of the Semiramis I should never have reached Samothrace.

Two days more elapsed before I had any opportunity of leaving Dede-agatch. On the third day a well-appointed Austrian Lloyds steamer arrived, the accommodation of which appeared magnificent after my recent experiences. On board of her I once more passed the Dardanelles, and was finally landed at Constantinople.

INDEX.

A.

Acroteri, promontory, in Crete, 25; in Santorin, 105; in Samothrace, 317.
'Acts of St. John,' 183.
Adramyttium, bay of, 128.
Adria, use of the term, 1.
Aeschylus, on Agamemnon's fire-beacons, 239, 373; on the Lemnian fire, 270.
Aethaleia, ancient name of Lemnos, 270.
Agiasso, 124.
Aï Strati, island, 248.
Alexius Comnenus, bull of, on Patmos, 188, 192.
Alke, peninsula of, 301.
Amorgos, 108.
Anaphe, 85.
Anemones, 48.
Antiparos, Grotto of, 111.
Apocalypse, monastery of, in Patmos, 181.
Apodulo, 58.
Apollonius Rhodius, on the origin of Thera, 109; on the shadow of Athos, 248.
Aptera, ruins and inscriptions at, 41; legend of, 42.
Arch, question of the use of by the Greeks, 213, 331.
Archangelos, 229.
Archilochus, on Thasos, 306.
Archipelago, duchy of the, 81.
Architecture in the Islands, Italian, 17.
Ariadne, fountain of, 80.
Aristophanes, 9, 77, 85, 270, 309.
Aristotle on the fishes of the Euripus Pyrrhaeus, 133.

Arkadi, monastery, 52; siege of, 53.
Arsinoĕum, at Samothrace, 329.
Artamis, Doric form of Artemis, 220.
Artamiti, monastery of, 219; origin of the name, 220.
Asomatos, monastery, 56; mountain, 300.
Atabyrion or Atabyron, Mount, 219; ascent of, 220; mentioned by Pindar, 221; origin of the name, 221.
Athos, 240, 257, 280, 298, 300; its shadow, 248; farms belonging to it in Lemnos, 253; monasteries of, 280.
Ayasolouk (Ephesus), 157.

B.

Ballad of the Sphakiotes, 62.
Bee-hives, cased in stone, 223; of wickerwork, 296, 308; wooden, 341.
Bell line of steamers, 139, 276.
Belon, on the Lemnian earth, 260.
Bent, Mr., 165, 177, 291, 292, 302.
Bernardakis, the brothers, 129, 131.
Biliotti, Mr. A., his exploration of Cameiros, 216.
Budrum, castle of, 198.
Bull of Alexius Comnenus on Patmos, 188, 192.

C.

Cabeiri, origin of the name, 324; worship of in Samothrace, 324;

sanctuary of, 324; temples of, 328.
Callimachus. on Delos, 7, 9.
Calymnos, 197.
Cameiros, site of, 218; Homeric epithet of, 218.
Canaris, his fire-ship, 153.
Candia, origin of the name, 72; siege of, 72.
Captain. title in Crete, 64.
Caracalla, arch dedicated to, 291.
Catalans, 101, 287.
Cavalla, 281.
Cave of the Apocalypse, 182.
Chalcidice, 279.
Champoiseau, M., 326.
Chanak-kalesi, 233.
Cheshmeh, 153.
Chesios, river, 177.
Chios, 140 foll.; earthquake in, 141; massacre in, 142; town of, 144; channel of, 152.
Choiseul-Gouffier, on Lemnos, 271.
Chora, town of, in Samos, 175; in Samothrace, 318.
Christodoulos, St., 183, 188; relics of, 193; his garden, 194.
Chryse, island of, near Lemnos, 272.
Church of St. John in Rhodes, destroyed, 203.
Cicero, studied in Rhodes, 202.
Circular lake, in Delos, 12.
Cnossus, coins of, representing the Labyrinth, 68; site of, 72.
Cocks with horns, 269.
Coenyra, 306.
Cold in the spring in Greece, 2, 28, 55, 120, 255.
Colossus of Rhodes. 205.
Concealed Christians in Crete, 36.
Conze, on the Lemnian earth, 265; on the site of Hephaestia, 267; on Thasos, 293, 302; on Samothrace, 320, 326.
Cos, 197.
Cretan, dialect of Modern Greek, 50.

Crete, general features of, 31; oranges of, 32; Greek universally spoken in, 33; disastrous condition of, 48; population of, 74; their character. 75; appearance and dress, 76.
Crucifix of Chrysopegi, 37.
Cultivation, of the vine in Tenos, 16; in Santorin, 98; in Samos, 162; of the orange in Crete, 32; of the olive in Lesbos, 122; in Thasos, 296; of mastic in Chios, 144.
Currency, local, in Thasos, 295; in Samothrace, 336.
Cyclades, the islands round Delos, 9.
Cyclopean walls, of Myrina, 246; of Samothrace, 321.
Cycnias, Mount, in Tenos, 16, 20.
Cydonia, site of, 36.
Cynthus, Mount, ruins on, 8, 9; its conspicuous character. 9.
Cypress, used for building in Crete, 42.
Cyriacus of Ancona, on Samothrace, 323.
Cyril, discoverer of the tunnel in Samos, 168.

D.

Dardanelles, town of, 233; the strait, 234; current of, 236.
Daubeny, Dr., on the Lemnian earth, 266.
D'Aubusson, Cardinal, 209.
Dede-agatch, 312, 353.
Delos, a granite island, 6; origin of its greatness, 6; attached by Phoebus to Gyaros and Myconos, 10.
Demetrium, harbour of, 317.
Demogerontia in Crete, 60.
Dialect, of Crete, 50; of Sphakia, 62; of Samothrace, 335.
Didymae, islands, 4.
Diodorus, on the city of Mytilene, 137; on the aborigines of Samothrace, 335; on the flood, 350.

Index. 357

Dionysius of Agrapha, Guide to Painting of, 186.
Dionysus, associated with Naxos, 80.
Dioscorides, on the dittany, 46; on the Lemnian earth, 257, 259.
Dittany, the, 46.
Dorian hexapolis, 198.
Duchy of the Archipelago, 81.

E.

Earthenware, of Rhodes, 225; of the Dardanelles, 233.
Earthquake, in Crete, 27; in Melos, 90; in Santorin, 100; in Chios, 141; rare in Lemnos, 271.
Egypt, insular Greeks in, 196, 243.
Elias, Mount, in Santorin, 98; in Lesbos, 125, 128; in Patmos, 179; in Rhodes, 219; in Lemnos, 252; in Thasos, 296; in Samothrace, 345; extensive use of the name, 126; similarity to Helios, 127.
Embroidery, of Rhodes, 226.
Emery, exported from Naxos, 84.
English chapel in Rhodes, 209.
Erotocritos, poem, sung in Crete, 73.
Euripus Pyrrhaeus, 130, 133.
Euroclydon, or Euraquilo, the wind, 2.
Evil eye, emblems intended to avert, 290.
Exoburgo, in Tenos, 18.

F.

Fabricius, M., on the Idaean cave, 70; on the tunnel in Samos, 169.
Fair Havens, site of, 58.
Finlay, on the massacre in Chios, 142; on the Maona of the Giustiniani, 145; on Canaris' fire-ship, 153.
Flowers—mandrake, 11; narcissus, 14; asphodel, 15; anemone, 48, 123; *Iris tuberosa*, 61; *Iris sisyrinchium*, 90; *Scilla bifolia*, 125, 297, 345; *Gagea lutea*, 125; *Orchis saccata*, 133; *Serapias cordigera*, 162; cistus, 219; cyclamen, 219; peony, 219; forget-me-not, 301; crowfoot, 345; *crocus aureus*, 345.
Forest-rangers, 305, 308.
Forests—pine, 130, 219, 223, 284, 300, 304; oak, 345.
Fountain, becoming cooler as the sun becomes hotter, 352.
Frogs, note of, 309.

G.

Galen, on the Cretan boots, 77; on the Lemnian earth, 257-9.
Gatilusio, family of, in Lesbos, 135; in Lemnos, 247; in Samothrace, 338; history of, 339.
Gaudos, island, 61.
Genoese, in Chios, 145; in Thasos, 288; in Samothrace, 318, 322.
Geranos, cape of Patmos, 179.
Giustiniani, in Chios, 145.
Goats, *see* Ibexes.
Gold mines of Thasos, 305, 307.
Gortyna, ruins of, 64.
Gothic architecture in Rhodes, 206, 209, 224.
Great Gods, of Samothrace, 325.
Grotto of Antiparos, 111.
Guérin, M., 167, 204.
Gyaros, 5.

H.

Hagios Thomas, tombs at, 69.
Hagius Deka, 63.
Halicarnassus, 198.
Hebrus, river, 313, 348; Milton on, 349.
Hecate, island of, 6.
Hellespont, current of, 236.
Hephaestia, 258, 261, 267.
Hephaestus, his connexion with Lemnos, 270.
Heraeum, in Samos, 175.

Hermaeum, Mount, in Lemnos, 273, 274.
Hermupolis, capital of Syra, 3; its origin, 4.
Herodotus, on the lake in Delos, 12; on the islands of the Aegean, 83; on Naxos, 84; on Phoenicians in Thera, 108; on the antiquities of Samos, 164, 167; on the gold mines of Thasos, 305.
Heroum, in Santorin, 107.
Hiera, volcanic island near Lemnos, 272.
High places, fondness of the Greeks for, 93.
Hippocrates, on the theatre in Thasos, 287.
Historic family names in the islands, 82.
Homer, his burial-place in Ios, 87; on the palm-tree in Delos, 12; on the heroes crossing the Aegean, 120; on Lemnos, 241; on Samothrace, 345; on the islands of the Thracian sea, 351.
Honey, exported from Thasos, 296.
Horned cocks in Lemnos, 269.
Hot springs, in Lesbos, 123; in Lemnos, 251; in Samothrace, 342.
Houses, flat-roofed, 21, 179, 319; excavated in tufa, 96; of Rhodian peasants, 217.
Hunt, Dr., on the volcanic character of Lemnos, 271.

I.

Ialysos, site of, 215.
Ibexes, in Crete, 28; in Samothrace, 337.
Ida, Mount, in Crete, 62; in the Troad, 125, 128, 349.
Iero, bay of, 122.
Imbrasos, river, 177.
Imbros, 235, 349; associated with Athens, 237.
Inopus, river in Delos, its legendary connexion with the Nile, 7.
Insurrection in Crete, 48, 67, 75.
Ios, 86.
Islands of the Aegean, their appearance, 5; absence of Byzantine influence in, 17; their size, 21, 86.
Iuktas, Mount, 70.

J.

Jews, in Rhodes, 200, 207.
Joly-Victora line of steamers, 139, 314.

K.

Kalavarda, 216.
Kallone, inlet of, 127, 129.
Kamariotissa, 315.
Kastro, capital of Lemnos, 240, 246.
Katakhanas, Cretan name for the Vampire, 43.
Kaumene islands, 98, 101.
Kedros, Mount, 61.
Khanea, 26, 74.
Kinira, 306.
Knights of St. John, in Rhodes, 202, 224; their fortress, 202; street of, 208; their fortifications at Lindos, 228.
Kotchino, castle of, 256; defended by Constantine Palaeologus, 256; place of the 'Lemnian earth,' 257.
Kynops the magician, in Patmos, 184.

L.

'Labyrinth' near Hagius Deka, 66; not the original one, 68.
Lagos, 311.
Latin Church, influence of in Tenos, 22; in Naxos, 83.
Lemnian earth, 257 foll.; an antidote to poison, 264.
Lemnos, 235, 347; associated with Athens, 237; its peculiar geography, 252; absence of trees in, 253; its modern connexion with Egypt, 243; a place of banishment, 244; its volcanic character in antiquity, 269.

Index. 359

Lenten fast, 15, 91, 133, 159.
Lepers, 72.
Leros, 195; connexion with Egypt, 196; satires on, 196, 197.
Lesbos, 121; narrow inlets in, 121, 127.
Lethaeus, river, 63.
Library on Patmos, 190.
Limena, in Thasos, 282.
Lindos, 224; its classical antiquities, 226; its castle, 227; earthenware of, 225.
Livy, on Demetrium, 318.
Lyell, on Santorin, 98, 100.

M.

Malea, promontory of, its dangerous character, 2.
Mandrakes, 11.
Manuscripts, on Patmos, 190–192.
Maona of Chios, 145.
Marble, of Naxos, 79; of Paros, 116; of Thasos, 284, 297, 303.
Maritza, river, 313.
Marpessa, Mount, 84, 114.
Massacres, at Arkadi, 54; at Venerato, 71; in Psara, 128; in Chios, 142; in Samothrace, 334.
Mastic, 144.
Mausolea, on Thasos, 292, 293.
Megalo-castron, 71, 73.
Mehemet Ali, in Crete, 34; born at Cavalla, 282; received Thasos from the Sultan, 294.
Melos, 85, 90.
Messara, plain of, 62.
Miltiades, his conquest of Lemnos, 236.
Milton, on the death of Orpheus, 349.
Mimas, headland of, 128, 140, 152.
Minarets, illumination of, 277.
Monasteries — Evangelistria in Tenos, 17; Arkadi in Crete, 52; Asomatos in Crete, 56; Nea Mone in Chios, 148; of the Apocalypse in Patmos, 181; of St. John in Patmos, 187; of Artamiti in Rhodes, 219, 222; of Athos, 280, 281.
Mosaics, 151, 277.
Mosychlos, Mount, 271, 272.
Mountains, of Crete, 32, 61, 68, 106; of Naxos, 79; of Lesbos, 125, 128; of Samos, 179; of Rhodes, 219; of Lycia, 221; of Thrace, 289, 348; of Thasos, 296.
Mudros, bay of, 252, 256.
Müller, W., his poem on Canaris, 154.
Muntaner, on the castle in Thasos, 287.
Murnies, treachery at, 34.
Mycale, strait of, 163, 166.
Myconos, 15.
Myrina, 241, 246, 258.
Mythonaes shoal, 239, 271.
Mytilene, town of, 120, 121, 134; the ancient city, 136.
Myzethra, 46.

N.

Naussa, harbour of, 78.
Nautical terms in Modern Greek from the Italian, 85.
Naxos, island, 79 foll., 83; town of, 80; duchy of, 81.
Nea Mone, in Chios, 148.
Neapolis, 281.
Necropolis of Thasos, 284, 289, 292.
Nemesis, votive offering to, 285.
Nestus, river, 289, 311.
Nida, 68, 70.
Nike of the Louvre, 330.
Nubians in Crete, 26, 33.
Nunnery, a Greek, 22.

O.

Obriocastro, origin of the name, 286.
Ochyroma, 215.
Octopus, eaten in the islands, 90, 133.
Olive, cultivation of, in Lesbos, 122; in Thasos, 296.
Olympus, Mount, in Lesbos, 125; in Thessaly, 279, 348; extensive use of the name, 126.

Orange, cultivation of, in Crete, 32.
Orbelus, Mount, 289.
Orpheus, his head and lyre carried to Lesbos, 349.
Ossa, Mount, 279.

P.

Palaeopoli, in Lemnos, 266, 267; in Samothrace, 319.
Palati, island of, 79.
Pallene, peninsula of, 279.
Palm-trees in the Cyclades, 87.
Pan, shrine of, in Thasos, 288.
Pangaeus, Mount, 289.
Panoramas — from Tenos, 20; from Naxos, 83; from Olympus in Lesbos, 127; from Patmos, 188; from Atabyron in Rhodes, 221; from the acropolis of Thasos, 289; from the south of Thasos, 298; from the summit of Samothrace, 347.
Paper money, used on Samothrace, 336.
Paroekia, 114.
Paros, 5, 84, 114; quarries of, 115.
Pasch van Krienen, Count, 87.
Patmos, 179–181; scenery of, suited to the Apocalypse, 189; acropolis of, 194.
Pausanias, on the connexion between Delos and the Nile, 7; on Mytilene, 138; on the birth of Hera in Samos, 177; on the disappearance of the island of Chryse, 272.
Perseus, King, on Samothrace, 317.
Petroleum, transport of, 278.
Phardys, M., 337.
Phengari, Mount, ascent of, 344; view from, 347.
Phileremo, site of Ialysos, 215.
Philoctetes, site of his cave on Lemnos, 239, 274; supposed to have been cured by 'Lemnian earth,' 258.
Philip of Macedon, initiated at Samothrace, 326.

Phocylides, his epigram on Leros, 196.
Phoenicians, in Crete, 77; in Thera, 108; in Samos, 157; in Samothrace, 325.
Pilgrimage to Tenos, 18, 139.
Pindar, on the temple on Atabyrium, 221; on Diagoras of Rhodes, 227.
Plaka, cape in Lemnos, 238, 273.
Pliny, on the dittany, 47; on the Lemnian earth, 257; on Samothrace, 318.
Poliades, monument of, 291.
Polycrates, 6, 163, 166.
Pool of Siloam, conduit of, 171.
Poseidon on Samothrace, 351.
Pozzolana, exported from Santorin, 103.
Prehistoric dwellings in Santorin and Therasia, 103, 105.
Primitive art in the Aegean, 104.
Prince of Samos, 161.
Priories of the Knights of Rhodes, 209.
Priscian, on the walls of Samothrace, 322.
Prochorus, legends relating to, 183, 185.
Psara, 128.
Psilorites (the Cretan Ida), 62.
Ptolemaeum, at Samothrace, 331.
Ptolemies, so-called tomb of, 212; their buildings at Samothrace, 328–331.
Purgatorial suffering, story of, 109.
Purnia, bay of, 255.
Pyrrha, 130, 132.

Q.

Quarantine in Greece, 15.
Quarries, in Paros, 115; in Thasos, 303.

R.

Rattle, use of, 82.
Resurrection, the, how represented in Greek art, 151.
Retimo, 45.
Rhencia, necropolis of, 14.

Index. 361

Rhodes, island of, its pleasant climate, 200.
Rhodes, city of, 201; population of, 200; its ancient grandeur, 202.
Rhodian peasant's house, description of, 217.
Rhodian ware, 217, 225; embroidery, 226.
Rithymna, 45.
Rock oils, introduction of, 132.
Ross, on Pasch van Krienen, 88.
Russians in the Aegean, 87, 92, 187, 247, 280.

S.

Sailors, Greek, 84, 159; their nautical terms, 85.
Saint John, legends concerning, in Patmos, 184 foll.
Saint Paul, expelled wild beasts from Crete, 57; touched at Samothrace, 326.
Salonica, 276; its churches, 277.
Salzmann, M., his exploration of Cameiros, 216, 219.
Samos, origin of the name, 157; constitution of, 161; wine of, 162; ancient city of, 165.
Samothrace, 235; difficulty of reaching it, 313; its harbourless character, 318; city of, 320; sanctuary of, 324 foll.; a centre of storms, 343; its barrenness, 350.
Santorin, 94 foll.; absence of wells in, 96; description of, 97; eruptions of, 99; prehistoric dwellings in, 105; names and myths of, 108.
Sanudo, in Naxos, 81.
Saoce, Mount, 344.
Sarcophagi, 291, 292, 301.
Scala Nova, 158.
'School of Homer,' 156.
Schools, Greek, 60, 124, 243, 255, 298, 319, 336.
Scio, *see* Chios.
Scirocco wind, 117, 233.
Scylax, on the harbours of Thasos, 285.

Scyros, seen from Samothrace, 348.
'Sealed earth,' 258 foll.
Semantron, 188, 336.
Sepulchre of Zeus, 70.
Shrine of Pan, 288.
Sikinos, 90; temple in, 92.
Simbulli, antiquities near, 211.
Sithonia, peninsula of, 279.
Skopia, Mount, 273.
Sommaripa, family of, 82.
Sophocles, on the shadow of Athos, 248; on the Lemnian fire, 270; on the island of Chryse, 272; on the Hermaean Mount, 273.
Spanish language, spoken in Rhodes, 200.
Spanish names in the islands, 101.
Sphakia, mountains of, 32; dialect of, 62.
Sphidami, fountain, 345, 352.
Sponge fishery in the Sporades, 181.
Sporades, 86.
Staircase cut in the rock, in Thasos, 290.
Stanley, Dean, on Patmos, 189.
Stelae, 285, 291.
Strabo, on Pyrrha, 133; on Mytilene, 136, 138; on the meaning of *samos*, 157; on the wine of Samos, 163; on the city of Samos, 167; on Leros, 196; on the grandeur of the city of Rhodes, 202.
Street of the Knights in Rhodes, 208.
Suda, bay of, 40.
Suspicion in Turkey, 26, 147, 210, 247, 256, 312.
Syra, 3.

T.

Temples— of Apollo in Delos, 13; of Apollo in Sikinos, 91; of the Goddess Queen in Santorin, 107; of Hera in Samos, 175; of Zeus on Atabyrium, 221; of Athena at Lindos, 227; at

Alke, 302; of the Cabeiri at Samothrace, 328.
Tenos, 16 foll.; a place of pilgrimage, 18; numerous Roman Catholics in, 22.
Terra Sigillata, 260.
Thasos, 282; beautiful scenery of, 284; city of, 284 foll.; subject to the Khedive, 295; gold mines of, 305.
Theatres—in Delos, 8; at Aptera, 42; at Samos, 166; at Lindos, 226; at Thasos, 286.
Theologo, 298.
Theophrastus, on the dittany, 47.
Thera, town of, 95.
Therasia, 102; prehistoric dwellings in, 103.
Therma Loutra, in Lemnos, 251; in Samothrace, 340.
Thracian sea, stormy character of, 232, 275, 285, 353.
Tigani, 164, 268.
Timber, exported from Thasos, 301, 304.
Titus, patron saint of Crete, 65; church of, 65.
Tmolus, Mount, 159.
Tombs, on Rheneia, 14; at Hagios Thomas. 69; near the city of Rhodes, 211; at Lindos, 226; near Hephaestia in Lemnos, 267.
'Tongues' of the Order of St. John in Rhodes. 203, 207.
Tour de Naillac in Rhodes, destroyed, 203.
Tournefort, the traveller, 11, 109, 176.
Touzla, salt lake, 266.
Triopian headland, 198.
Troy, plain of, 234; seen from Samothrace, 349.

Tuesday, superstition about, 43.
Tunnel, of Eupalinus in Samos, 167 foll.; in Samothrace, 331.
Turkish ports, neglected condition of, 25, 135. 199, 310.

V.

Vampire superstition, 11, 43 109.
Vathy, 160.
Venerato, massacre at. 71.
Venetians, in Tenos, 19; in Crete. 26, 56, 72; their policy in the Aegean, 81.
Villa Nova, in Rhodes, 216.
Vine, cultivation of, in Tenos, 16; in Santorin, 98; in Samos, 162.
Virgil, on Delos. 10; on the Cretan dittany, 46; on beehives. 341.
Volcano, of Santorin, 28, 97; anciently in Lemnos, 269.
Volcanic soil of Patmos, 181.

W.

White Mountains in Crete, 32, 62, 68, 74.
Winds—Kaikias or Euraquilo, 2, 120; Eurus or scirocco, 117, 233; of the Thracian sea, 275, 311, 343, 353.
Wine in the islands not resined, 57; Malmsey wine in Tenos, 16; wine of Dionysus in Naxos, 80; wine of Santorin, 98; of Samos, 162.
Wood imported, in Santorin, 96; in Lemnos, 253.

Z.

Zerynthos. 342.
Zeus, birthplace and sepulchre of in Crete, 70.

THE END.

www.ingramcontent.com/pod-product-compliance
Lightning Source LLC
Chambersburg PA
CBHW032043220426
43664CB00008B/842